# MARY ME

## One Woman's Incredible Adventure with God

### ELIZABETH B. BRISTOL

*Cover photo: Deborah McCracken*
*Author photo: Lisa Gillit*

Printed in the United States of America

*With love to Dad*

# ACKNOWLEDGMENTS

How often have we heard that it takes a village to raise a baby?

I had no clue how much help I'd need in order to release this baby into the world. I don't even want to try to name names because I'd forget someone. Basically, everyone who has been in my life for the past ten years has sown something into this book.

It begins with my family, the first ones to get exposed—whether they like it or not. I'm sorry and I love you.

And I'm grateful to all the others who play a role in the tough parts I wasn't going to tell. I pray that our stories keep people from making the same mistakes or find healing after they have.

Thank you to each member of the Burgess writing group, to my greatest contender as well as my biggest cheerleader who never wavered in her support and encouragement.

Thank you to the Hoffman Center, the MacGregor Literary Agency, and everyone who edited, proofread, and prayed. I appreciate all the help and lessons along the way.

I'm grateful I had the chance to discuss theological differences and hear from others who had visions of the book in final form. Thank you to everyone who lent me their beach house to write in, drove me to the airport, watched my dog, and swam with me.

I'm grateful for every single one of my incredible and crazy friends who have lived this with me, believed in me and loved me well, thank you.

You all rock and we did it!

Most importantly, I'm grateful to my Lord and Savior Jesus Christ. Talk about "can't do it without" someone, I can't imagine my life without Him and I'm ever-so-glad I'll never have to go back to that!

# YUP, SHE'S RIGHT!

"Thinking about God scares me, makes me feel . . . dirty? Wrong? Slightly evil?" My friend sipped her espresso as we sat across from each other at the Manzanita News coffee shop. "I hope I'm *good enough*."

"Loved?" I raised an eyebrow, a bagel paused halfway to my mouth.

"Exactly," she nodded.

"That this God who supposedly made me," I leaned in, "actually likes me?"

"Bingo!" She toasted me with her cup.

I kept stumbling into these God conversations, which would force me to put my own experience into words. How did I get from "*God? No thank you!*" to chats like this, with people turning to me for insight?

I grew up in a family with high expectations, skilled at control and manipulation. Eventually, I moved out but ended up with more of the same in the form of roommates and boyfriends because it felt *normal*. Needless to say, I didn't thrive in those environments. Who does? After busting my butt to please everybody else, I quit trying and decided to focus on what made me happy. But I was still circling through codependent relationships as if stuck on the spin cycle; I turned to one thing after another to take the edge off—like drugs, alcohol, a new man, or another adventure.

At twenty-six, I had peered inside a smoking volcano, then patted a silverback gorilla in the jungle. I danced. I sang. I slept under the African skies contemplating incredible beauty.

Nothing quenched my soul. So, I added a spiritual component to my quest, which was weird because I grew up in church but didn't really like it. I never felt like I fit in. I always felt like a misfit, and not just in church. That's okay. I'm good with it now. Truth be told, I'm not your average bear. I didn't go back to the church for spiritual direction—I studied chakras, walked labyrinths, and searched for a sweat lodge. I made pilgrimages to Jim Morrison's grave, Loch Ness, and the Shrine of the Blessed Virgin Mary. For what? I could not figure that out . . .

Instead of the norm, a family and profession, I had friends and stories. I'd work multiple jobs for a season and run off again. Something was missing, I didn't know what. Okay, I sort of did. Maybe it was the things my parents wanted for me, like a husband, kids, and a *real* job? I struggled with anxiety and loneliness, even in a crowded room. I never felt like I was enough. I ate Tums like candy. And I know this sounds all beauty-contestant-answerish, but I just wanted inner peace, a place to come in out of the rain.

I needed, well, God, really, but you couldn't have told me that then, not until the crap hit the fan. You know, those no-one-can-save-you-but-God things? An actual life or death experience. I'm not kidding, I didn't think I was going to live, but instinctively I cried out and BAM! There God was, not judgmental and mean, but the ultimate friend. He came through in a big way!

I'll be honest with you, I flippin' drank the Kool-Aid.

I didn't set out to look for God, but He didn't trick me either. He's not like that. So much about God is not like I thought. He's way cooler than anyone said. And I *did* need Him, just not in the way others tried to package Him. This One, who's capable of bringing us out the other side of whatever we've been through, is gentle, never hurried, and always present, even when He's silent.

And not to glorify the stray, but it was only at the end of myself that I got desperate enough to give God a chance. Terrified I was about to die, I promised if He'd save me, I'd do whatever He wanted.

He upheld His end of the deal. I decided to keep my side of the bargain since, you know, I was still breathing. Suddenly, unexpectedly, my entire life changed. Instead of the massive let-down I'd always felt I'd been to my parents, I felt encouraged to be *me* like never before. I felt led, even, on a journey to fulfill *my* deepest desires, not someone else's.

I never expected this ride to include God, but His radical love and acceptance blew me away. Nothing else mattered, like who I was or what I'd done. He saw it all and still, He loved me.

"How the heck did you get here?" my old friends ask.

"Right?" I shrug my shoulders.

And I know, as we stand in the checkout line at the grocery store reading the latest scandal sheet, our culture tells us we can boil everything down to ten steps. But when it comes to a thing with God, I can't do that. I think He's got a unique adventure for each of us. For those who want it.

"You like telling your stories," said my friend in that coffee shop, "because you're secure enough in your current self, the self that's firmly established in a godly life, that you can laugh at your mistakes, even the dark moments, while pointing to the light you stand in right now and say, 'See? if I made it, so can you.' "

I think my friend was right. So, how did I get here? Let me tell you . . .

# MY NEW LIFELINE

## Jomo Kenyatta International Airport, Nairobi, Kenya, 1990

Africa, the untamed lion of the continents, never pretends to be a harmless cub. She's born free all right but is just as wild as the king of the jungle himself. Her native drum beats. Columbus monkeys leap through her trees, and a woman in the distance emits a primal scream, "Lee-lee-lee-lee-leeeeeeeee."

No wonder her people can't keep from dancing.

I limped reluctantly across the hot tarmac. The plane back to Boston waited in the twilight as I moved toward it, one painful step after another. Several skin shades darker than when I'd left home four months ago and with cornrows in my hair, I winced as I shouldered my pack, my arm in a sling. I didn't yet know my back was broken. No wonder it hurt, but not as much as my hand.

That felt like a giant machete had sliced it open. Seventeen stitches etched a jagged new "lifeline" across my palm. No one else would call it that, but the symbolism wasn't wasted on me.

Well aware I could have died four days ago in the accident outside Nairobi, I stopped to shift my load. The velvety blue sky exposed the first stars of night and bent down to kiss the tangerine horizon. The African firmament's final performance was a parting gift.

Kathy's familiar whistle caused me to turn toward the gate. There she was. My Canadian tent mate wincing at the pain from her broken pelvis as she leaned on her crutches, piercing the hush between us. I bit my lower lip and smiled at my three hooting, hollering friends next to her, all wearing the same ragged clothes they had worn for months. They were here to see me off.

Clive, our leader, dropped his tie-dyed pants to shine me one final moon. The "1.5" we'd shaved into the remaining strip of hair on the back of his bald head reminded me again of the average number of women he had slept with on each of his trips, a fact we'd learned playing Truth or Dare around the campfire one night.

Graeme ignored Clive and offered an earnest, heartfelt wave goodbye. Graeme and I never did hook up, but he'd saved me from certain death.

Then I thought about the missing one, the one who didn't survive . . .

And a piece of my heart broke off and fell to the ground. Should we have expected that possibility in our adventure travel? Probably.

While overlanding, which was a cheap way to access remote locations, I focused on the journey rather than the destination. But it was a risky way to travel. Each traveler purchased a segment of the ongoing trip and joined the group for six weeks or six months, exploring the countryside from England through the Middle East and on into Africa.

Primitive, but with guides, we camped in small, flimsy tents, shopped for food in local markets, and took turns cooking for the group. They were complete strangers four months ago, but now maybe we knew each other even better than those we had left back home.

Leaving these friends behind was going to be even more excruciating than the pain in my body. I wiped the tear that slid from the corner of my eye and handed a boarding pass to the flight attendant at the top of the steps before turning one last time, waving, and then ducking into the plane.

Going home to family, I raised a glass in my mind and made an imaginary toast as I tried to pull myself together. *To American medical care,* I thought, limping down the crowded aisle.

My thoughts returned to my friends on the runway and I pursed my lips, emotional. *Am I doing the right thing by leaving?*

*Why do I always have such a hard time making up my mind?*

I climbed into my window seat, glanced outside, and finally let the tears fall.

"Oh, Sweetie," an older lady said as she settled in next to me. I let her fold me into her ample bosom. "Whatever it is, it's going to be okay." She comforted me like the mother gorilla I'd seen in the jungle, soothing her baby.

What was this, mommy number seventeen? I'd been collecting mothers, probably because of the tense relationship I had with my own. This one, with her gray hair and spectacles, a little more grandmotherly than the others, all huggy and loving, seemed like a perfect seatmate for the long ride ahead.

"I'm coming back here," I sobbed. "I'll go home, see the doctors . . ."

She peered at me with warm eyes magnified by her glasses and wondered aloud, "What is it you're looking for?"

*Great question.* "Adventure, healing, and freedom, for sure! And I wouldn't mind a knight in shining armor," I grinned as I wiped my nose on the back of my hand. "To save me from the screwed-up situations I keep getting into. But mostly, I just want to be happy! Know where I can find all that?"

"Who else could handle that tall order but God?" she laughed.

"I am *not* looking for God." I stiffened as I raised my voice, definitely not.

"Okay, okay," she dug through her purse and pulled out a bag of M&M's, real ones, not some international knock-off. My new best friend filled my hand with chocolate.

As I popped one in my mouth, I remembered, *I'm going to see Dad in a few hours!* A smile came then left just as quickly. I stared out the window and chewed. Noticing the relapse in my demeanor, the lady took hold of my hand and leaned down to make eye contact, "You okay?"

"Yeah," I looked down at my lap as I swallowed the last of the chocolate. "It's just, when I stopped in Nairobi a couple of weeks ago, I got a message from Dad."

I picked up my black leather bag, the one I got at the bazaar in Istanbul, and foraged through, finding a crumpled pile of letters rubber-banded together. I pulled one out.

She studied the well-worn page covered with crude computer graphics. "A woman pushing a carriage. A bride. A car salesman or a cruise director? Are these life choices your dad wants you to pick from?"

"Yeah," I tried to laugh, but my voice caught. "Then he wrote, 'my advice to people having kids these days: Shoot 'em while you have a chance!' " I wiped my eyes again.

"Oh, Honey." She reached into her pocket for a tissue. "He's joking. And you know you get your own choice of what you do with your life, right?"

"You don't understand." I shook my head. "This is my second time returning home, alone and without a job. Strike two, he's not going to be happy and gonna want to know my plan."

# THE LIES WE BELIEVE

True or not, our beliefs get embedded in our psyches and guide our actions like the rudder of a ship. For a long time, I didn't get that. I didn't recognize the thoughts that propelled me through life. I just took a step at a time.

All too often, I reacted to the thing in my head screaming the loudest, like: *You're doing it wrong!* Where do these one-liners come from? Our experiences, right?

Looking back, I see connections, like how my deepest desire began in a pre-memory. You know, those things you kind of remember, but they happened when you were so young, you don't have exact context? I picture it like this . . .

In a small town outside Boston, a brisk wind blew. Red, orange, and yellow leaves swirled like flames—the kaleidoscopic dance of autumn. My rubber boots on, I strode through the foliage strewn across the lawn, *rustle, crackle, swoos-sh-shh.* The yummy scent of their decay took root in my nose as the jack-o-lantern on the porch of our home smiled with benevolence. I jumped in a puddle and squealed. Then I gazed up at big, tall Daddy, longing for his approval.

What was Dad doing?

I don't ever remember him doing anything as normal as raking, and this was before we had the flying lawn mower or the Cocker Spaniel whose warts Dad covered with Compound W. But I do remember his instruction, "You want to make a difference in this world, Elizabeth, leave a mark." His expectation clear, he left the method a mystery.

With my brown eyes open wide, I twirled a finger in my pixie haircut and imprinted on him like a baby swan. *But how, how can I make a difference so Daddy will love me?*

Growing up, we lived on a dead-end street next to train tracks. When the train whistle blew, the dishes rattled in the cupboard, and I ran to the end of the street to wave at the conductor until Mom said, "What're you doing?"

"Looking for Daddy."

"Oh, Honey, he's not a conductor. He's a different kind of engineer."

"If you don't drive trains," I asked him at the dinner table that night, "what do you do?"

"I've got patents on inventions that measure flow." He shoveled a forkful of green beans into his mouth and washed it down with a gulp of milk. Wiping his lips on the back of his wrist, he stood and headed to the living room to watch Walter Cronkite on the evening news.

Even though I've asked many times, I'm always left feeling as if I should understand his over-my-head explanations. To this day, I can't describe his work any better.

"Work hard. Pay your way and save. And whatever you do, *DON'T WASTE!*" I think Dad believed we were more likely to do what he said if he screamed, like when he noticed the flames of the gas stove licking the sides of the pan as I boiled water. "Dammit! You're doing it wrong."

Tensing, I'd cringe. Quivery bits inside shrieked, *"RUN!"*

Cripes, I was only eight. Why didn't he just say, "Honey, let me show you how?"

Nope, in our house, there was a right way and a wrong way to do everything. And I was always *doing it wrong*. My desperate attempts to please never helped. I was always *"WASTING GAS!"* or heat, or electricity, or plastic bags too nasty to rinse clean.

At the time, I'd never heard of Asperger's Syndrome or "the spectrum" in reference to autism, but I believe that if Dad was going through the school system now, he'd have been diagnosed—even though he disagrees.

My sisters and I knew Dad's weird ways of picking up food off the floor to eat it or wearing his nametag on his forehead at formal events, well, that was *just Dad*. We'd smile privately amongst ourselves, roll our eyes, or call him out.

He's smart, went to MIT, and became recognized in his field of process control. Sometimes people kowtowed to him, kissed his ass even. Never impressed, Dad looked at a person and said, "Yeah, whatever."

And that's tame. You never knew what was going to come out of his mouth.

While others flipped him off or called him rude, my sisters and I cut him slack, understood him somehow. And even with all his anger and frustration, we knew the "Luv, Dad" on the bottom of his emails was real. His love pats subtle, we valued them because that's what we got, what we understood he was able to give.

But I'm not saying being on the other side of him wasn't ouch-y. I hated getting into trouble, going to the back hall, the room off the kitchen leading up the steps, where I was to serve my sentence after being punished. Dark and cool and, for the longest time, the only place you could smell the dead squirrel that got stuck in the flue of the fireplace.

Sitting there, on my own, I despised the isolation.

So, I stuffed my pain and quit crying, trying not to draw attention to myself. I gave up crying as if that was something I should do. Instead, I'd climb into Daddy's chair, the brown rocker in the corner of the living room, and escape to a fantasy world of my own creation, a new reality that brought comfort to the chaos inside. I learned to need less and figure out life on my own.

A chameleon with many colors, I blended into any room and took responsibility for everyone else's feelings, so my own greatest fear, that of being unloved, wouldn't become reality.

And then, at fourteen, I smoked my first joint on the railroad tracks behind the house. I took a hit off the hand-rolled *cigarette*, like my friend showed me, then coughed out the smoke. I hadn't expected the burning in the back of my throat.

"Hold it in as long as you can, like this," she urged as she took her turn. "You'll get higher."

An odd smell lingered in the air like smoldering trash crossed with skunk cabbage. I looked over my shoulder, half-expecting to see Mom peering out the bathroom window with a pair of binoculars. Laughing nervously, I passed the joint back to my friend until, finally, the giggles got the best of me. "So, this is what getting high's about!"

Drugs offered an appealing alternative to all the striving for accomplishment and perfection. One thing led to another: pot and hash, then LSD, cocaine, and Quaaludes. In the midst of all my angst, acid was the only thing I knew that made me laugh until my body ached.

When you don't want to feel the way you do, that's gold.

I loved the rambling, relaxed conversations, the wild topics, and seemingly creative solutions I had when high. That's when I came into agreement with the lie: Doing drugs, that's how I can do it all. Tune out my parents with this *OFF* button, block the noise, and dull the emotional pain.

On the outside, my family looked like upstanding pillars of the community, but our actions shrieked for help. Mom lay on her bed in depression. Like Dad, I spewed my anger into curse words until the street drugs did their *thang*. Victoria, my younger sister, kicked her aggression into a soccer ball all the way to state championships. And Catherine, the youngest, struggled with thoughts of suicide. She didn't want to die, just longed to escape the emotional pain, and saw no other way. I got that.

In our Victorian house on Maple Place, I would spend my nights rocking in bed, trying to get rid of the ball of angst in my stomach. The whistle of the train called out night after night. Chugging past, it taunted: "You're never enough, never enough, never enough."

I imagined myself on it going far, far away until I drifted off to sleep with those threads of belief tangling knots in my thinking—that I was never enough, and doing life wrong, and needed to make a mark on this world.

"You okay?" The lady on the plane startled me as she reached over and rubbed my back.

"Yeah," I smiled weakly.

"Why don't you tell me what happened? Maybe together we can come up with a plan your dad will like."

*Cool, someone to talk to,* I thought. She was someone who might not dismiss me at twenty-six, like other people had, as if my ideas and dreams were just silly fantasies. But what would she think of my stories? I hesitated because I liked her acceptance, didn't want to scare her away, then figured, *What the heck?* "Got a couple of hours to kill?"

"As a matter of fact, I do." She extended her hand. "Hi, my name's Truth."

Seriously? I gave her a skeptical look. "Where do I start?"

"How about," she winked, "when the trouble began?"

I snickered. "That'd take way more time than we have."

Smoothing my sarong, I took a deep breath, unsure of what I wanted to share and what I wanted to keep to myself, but desperate for answers and grateful for a distraction.

# A WHOLE NEW WORLD

How shall I relay the start of my troubles? I went on the safari. That was not the start, but it was a catalyst.

The first night, I sat in the bar on a ferry crossing the English Channel. I instantly liked Clive, one of our tour guides from London, though he was a little quirky. A tall, thin, bald man of thirty, he pushed his John Lennon glasses up his nose as he took a swig of beer, one of many on our trip.

He always had a smile and a story, or three, and he viewed the world of travel with wonder. Like a child seeing it for the first time, even though he'd seen more of the globe than anyone I knew.

As the ferry rocked below us, Clive was on a roll, "I lay in the middle of the tracks as a train zoomed overhead, inches from me head." *On purpose,* I thought, *is he flippin' nuts?*

"Then there was the company's first trip." He barely took a breath that night, stories spilling out of him. "The guide stood on top of the caravan chucking the tents down when lightning struck. Bzzzzt! He dropped to his death right there. The others put him in the storage bin and carried him to the nearest city."

I choked. "Might not be the best story to tell newcomers on their first night."

Nope, this was not going to be like the safaris I'd seen in movies, with everyone sitting inside white tents drinking Champagne. For sure, there'd be alcohol. Moonshine that tasted more like gasoline, no doubt. I don't know why, but it didn't hit me that these stories just might be a sample of things to come. I guess I was just trying to figure out the dynamics of the new group. Where did I fit in? Who'd be my bestie, and did I like any of the guys?

Graeme, Clive's co-leader, had potential, definitely. I totally ignored him, though. That's what I did when I liked a guy.

That next morning our group—Clive, Graeme, Kathy, Shane, Jan, Fiona, Julie, and I—hit the ground running, venturing off the ferry in our fortress-on-wheels pieced together with Mercedes parts, an enclosed vehicle that thankfully had windows. There would be no canvas-covered vehicle for us. Her name was Hot Doris and she was a tank. She held twenty-eight seats, twenty-four faced front, and four looked back on two square tables in the middle.

Salzburg, Thessaloniki, Cappadocia, Pamukkale, exotic destinations became real as we pitched our tents and explored. After Europe, we travelled through Turkey then Syria. In Palmyra, we'd pulled up amongst ruins. Kathy and Clive tugged our packs out of the back locker and got our tents down while the rest of us hopped up onto columns, or pieces of them, and posed like our version of Egyptians.

After dinner, Clive offered us a bottle of brown liquid, saying, "We're going to get to know each other tonight. Here's the deal: you answer a personal question or take a shot."

We played that game a lot. It helped us to bond.

A few weeks later, in Aqaba, Jordan, we met up with the rest of our group who'd come from Kathmandu on another truck. They'd trekked together from India but hailed from Holland, Australia, New Zealand, and England. Just as we'd connected, so had they.

Initially, we had an us-versus-them thing going. In an attempt at merging into a cohesive team, Kathy and I set out with Andrea, who was from the other team. We stocked up on bags of rice, dried fava beans, and creamer for coffee.

"Onions and carrots will keep," Sue, the other driver's girlfriend, taught us. "Tomatoes won't. Besides, you can buy them everywhere. Sometimes there isn't much local produce. That's why the guys brought dehydrated food from England."

"I wish you were coming with us," I said as I wrote down her advice. "Let's keep in touch."

Then the twenty-four of us who'd signed up to continue south on Hot Doris said our good-byes to those who hadn't and ventured into the first six countries of northeast Africa: Egypt, Sudan, Zaire, Central Africa Republic, Uganda, and Kenya.

Along the way, we each had jobs. Not only did I shop for bulk food in major cities, but I coordinated activities to keep everyone entertained, like in Syria. Gathered around the fire one night, Clive said, "I know of an empty castle where we can camp tomorrow night!"

"Perfect for a murder mystery," I said as I leapt out of my folding campstool, already brainstorming personas for each group member. "For dinner, we'll have an American BBQ. We can even make French fries out of the potatoes we got at the market today."

"Awesome, to-o-otally awesome!" One of the internationals tried their best to impersonate or make fun of me. I wasn't quite sure which.

On long travel days, like the three weeks it took us to get through the Sudanese desert, we congregated around the tables inside the tank. We made friendship bracelets or played mean games of poker, except when we'd get stuck in the sand. Then we'd coax and prod Hot Doris by placing sand mats—strips of metal sheeting—in front of her tires, running alongside her to keep from bogging down. One day, it took twelve hours to go two miles.

On a bathroom stop, I walked by the skeleton of a camel glinting in the sand. *That could be you.* "Nope!" I averted my gaze as I wandered from the truck to pee. With miles of sand in every direction, no matter how far I went, everyone could see. I pulled my pants down and *ah, my period.* "Shane," I called out to the redheaded New Zealander, who'd become like a brother or surrogate husband when necessary, as he passed by. "Bring me a tampon?"

He nodded. As you can imagine, we got pretty close.

After the desert, the lush jungle of Zaire and its many waterways had us bathing like Africans in the first water we'd seen in weeks.

In an attempt to gain privacy, the girls raced upstream while the boys stayed down. However, that was where the ever-present crowd of locals first appeared. Fifty, or sometimes five hundred, Africans hunkered down and watched everything we did. Naked, I tried keeping my back to the mob. With an eye on my towel and clothes, it was not an easy feat!

Back on the truck, Clive said, "This is our new normal. Watch each other's backs. As the crowd grows, it can get wild."

Just then, we drove by a horse lying in the same river we'd bathed in, stiff legs pointing skyward. People alongside it were swimming.

Clive said, "And get tested for parasites when you go home. Millions of people die here annually from poor sanitation."

"Leave it to Clive," I whispered to Kathy, "to point out the things you wouldn't put in a brochure." We chuckled as he parked alongside a local market so the day's cooking team could shop.

"Get some beef!" someone yelled. It became a chorus. After all that time in the desert, protein sounded good.

When the crew hadn't returned in over two hours, Kathy joked, "What are they doing, butchering a cow?" Sure enough, Shane boarded the bus with a banana leaf full of raw red meat, still quivering, fresh from the kill. *Ugh!*

*Quack! Quack!* Scared ducks and angry geese flapped out of my way when it was my turn to shop as if they knew they were fighting for their lives. We chased them till we caught one and weighed it in our hands. We searched for the bird with the most meat on its bones before proclaiming a death sentence.

Sometimes we got off easy and the Africans cut their heads off for us. Other times we had to do it ourselves. I'd turn away as the executioner set the headless fowl on the ground and let its frenzy wind down before I plucked the feathers out. This was nothing like scanning the yellow Styrofoam containers in the grocery store back home.

For water, we pulled up at a local watering hole to fill our tanks, and that's when I caught sight of them, the women at the well who were just like the ones they'd told us about growing up in Sunday school. Here they were, real ones. Dark, skinny women dressed in brightly colored sarongs made of material like we'd seen in the markets. Their head coverings matched the sashes they used to tie their babies on their backs. Their muscles glistened with sweat as they heaved jugs filled with three, maybe even four gallons, onto their heads.

I'll bet they needed a massage when they got home.

With eyes wide, I climbed out of the truck, grabbed a black, plastic container, and ran to join them. The women took a collective step back and drew their kids close. Realizing their discomfort, I stopped. Slowly, I knelt and smiled at a little girl. She hid behind her mother's legs, but an older one bravely offered me a shy grin. I beamed.

I reached inside Shane's pail full of water to fill my Army-green bottle, lifted it to my lips for a long swallow, then choked involuntarily on the grit and taste of dirt. Before realizing what I was doing, I spit the water to the ground. The liquid in the bucket was cloudy, gray.

*Where's my raspberry flavoring?* I wondered.

When I looked up, my new friend had turned away, our brief connection broken.

*Wait!* What was that I saw on her face? This culture's body language was so different from my own. Did I offend her? I didn't mean to insult her.

Then it occurred to me, she and I would drink from the same well, but I added purifying pills to make it *safe*. I'd rinse my vegetables in water colored purple by a chemical called permanganate, for the same reason. I'd wash my hands in Dettol, with its stringent smell of gasoline, before I touched my food.

I bet she didn't use tablets or chemicals or flavoring.

As an entitled twenty-six-year-old American, I'd never considered inequality or my own privilege before now. I cared, sort of, so I wrestled with my guilt, looked for a scapegoat. Speaking of Sunday school, where was God? Shouldn't He help? At the very least, He could get the dead horse out of their bath water and maybe provide plumbing.

Then I mentally put on the blinders my Mom used at home and joined her in the *art* of denial. I looked the other way, stopped myself from thinking about it.

Later that day, we pulled up to a river with no bridge!

The path continued on the other side, but we had no way to get across, so Clive parked the truck. "We'll stop here, camp for the night, and build a bridge."

"With what?" I asked Kathy as we fought to get our tent closest to the truck. We didn't want to be last in line in case another vehicle drove up behind us in the dark and was caught unaware.

We needed a bridge, all right. The physical connection from one riverbank to the other was imperative if we wanted to keep going. But even more than that, it seemed like we needed bridges, or links, to the people.

I guess that woman at the well got under my skin.

# THE DESPAIR IN DISPARITY

Believe it or not, the next morning, our team built a flippin' bridge. How cool is that? We build it with logs and palm fronds, got to the other side, motored into Goma, and set out on a five-hour trek up Mount Nyiragongo.

Sweat trickled down my face as stray thoughts vied for attention. I know this sounds horrible, but all the inequality I kept seeing was getting in the way of my quest for happiness. But seriously, what could I do to help?

I stopped climbing and tugged my water bottle out for a sip, just as the bottom dropped out of the sky. Kathy and I glanced at each other and howled with laughter while digging through our packs for rain gear.

As usual, she looked like a model for a camping store, and my cheap, flimsy rain jacket stuck awkwardly to me, the material not doing a single thing to earn its name.

The slog up the now-slippery path kept my mind busy until we stood shivering near the top at sundown. We stepped inside a tin hut, passed around a small bottle of whiskey while shoveling the bits of food we'd brought with us into our mouths, then settled in to sleep. In an attempt to keep warm, we spooned.

At sunrise, we climbed the last half hour to the tippy, and I mean tippy, top. I peered inside at lava simmering and bubbling below, like the porridge I'd wished we'd had for breakfast. Instead of eating, we raced back down the mountain, high on adrenaline and re-provisioned for a hike to see gorillas.

Clive's English accent always made everything sound so *la te da* until I tuned in to what he was saying, "Gorillas live in the lowlands and have exceptionally small penises in comparison to the rest of their bodies." Well okay, then.

In single file, we followed Graeme into the jungle past the occasional grass hut where we'd surprise a family of Africans as they went about their daily lives.

"Look at these!" I squatted beside two women sorting beans of many shapes and colors spread out in a round wicker basket and took a picture.

Graeme pulled gently on my elbow. When I looked up, he pointed, "Check out the kids' toys." One played with a *truck* made of an empty water bottle while another two chased tires, pushing them along with a stick.

*Hm.* Some are happy with simple things.

Several hours later, we reached a wooden cabin. *Nice! Our home for the night*, I thought. Inside we sat at a table and oohhed and aahhed over a catered dinner. "Yummy!" I said, "What is it?"

"Haven't you learned not to ask?" Kathy poked me. "Just enjoy it!"

How much had we paid for this excursion, twenty bucks? The visit with gorillas was definitely worth that, but all this, too? It was super inexpensive to us, but more than an annual salary for most of the people we'd meet.

"Did you peek inside the bedroom?" Kathy asked.

"No, why?" I ached after spooning on top of the volcano the night before.

"Real beds," she said. "With sheets! I can hardly wait to go to sleep."

Had it only been a couple of months since I'd slept on sheets? It was heaven till that woman at the well came back to mind. I tossed and turned as I wondered, *Had she ever slept on sheets?*

*Tap-tap-tap.* One of our African guides rapped on the door with a machete early the next morning. Graeme called out, "Ready? Let's go!"

I knocked back a cup of black coffee and put my daypack on as we headed out. Always prepared, Kathy sprayed bug goop on the back of my legs, and I fell in step with my cohorts, one behind the other as the guide tracked oily, fly-covered splats of poop the size of dinner plates.

Then again, just like the day before, after a magical hour of hiking, we burst in on an African gorilla family of a different kind, a momma, a baby, two sub-adults, and a silverback!

The guide held us back with his knife and put his finger to his lips. Very slowly, we lowered ourselves amongst them. The baby made a beeline for Andrea, picked flies off of her and ate them, then rolled on her. I could tell by the look on Andrea's face, this baby was heavier than it looked.

The guard grabbed my arm and pushed me toward the big guy. Really? A bucket list item, for sure. I snuggled in next to the silverback as Kathy took my picture, but when I pet his arm, the guide made a sound with his mouth I'm not sure I can replicate. I got the message, though, and buried myself in the middle of our group before anything else happened.

All too soon, the guides made that noise together as they rallied us to head back.

As soon as Clive saw us coming down the path, he called, "Jump on board, everyone, we've got to make time."

My head, still swimming with the recent experiences, I said, "Why the rush?"

"We've got to reach the campsite in Kinshasa near the Congo River," he said. "You'll board a flotilla in the morning and ride all day. I'll pick you up in Kisangani before nightfall."

"A flotilla?" I crooked my neck and looked at him sideways.

"Five barges tied together. It's a floating market. You'll love it."

As we climbed on board the crowded platform the following morning, a woman called our attention to a large cluster of fruit cut fresh from the tree. "Bananas!" *And what was that smell?*

Fish! They were, of course, piled in a slippery heap. Another woman filled an empty can with water and handed it to her friend who bathed her kids. A man tried on a pair of pants from a mound of clothing. Just like we'd do inside a dressing room, he turned this way and that looking into the mirror of the faces around him as he contemplated a purchase. Men danced and chanted to the beat of a drum, always the African drum.

They peddled their wares while transporting them downstream. I recognized the plastic pitchers we'd seen in most outhouses, intended to wash hands after they've been used instead of toilet paper.

Only a few days before, my friend had run to an outhouse after too many mangos. An African man stopped what he was doing and ran, too, filled one of those pitchers, and brought it to me to give her. The look on his face told me he knew how she felt.

Of course, we carried toilet paper. Well, purple crepe paper we had bought in Cairo, but here we were again. I'll bet he didn't have money for things like that.

As I thought about him, another man put a small black monkey with a white beard in my hands and, instantly, I fell in love.

Growing up, I'd told friends, "I'm having monkeys instead of kids."

"Fi' dolla, please?" He held out his hand.

I wanted to, but I couldn't, not until I got permission from Clive. All day, I played with the little guy, but what would I do if I returned to the truck, and Clive said, "No"?

However, that night, he said, "Sure! You want a monkey, get one."

"Woo hoo!" I jumped up and down, but when we drove by a dead one hanging from the roof of a hut, my stomach lurched. Was that to be someone's dinner? Tempted to judge, I recalled a young boy who found out we had shampoo, "You got? Me want!"

Imagine knowing soap that keeps your scalp from itching is available, but you're never able to afford any. And maybe, for someone like him, imagine how delicious the rare monkey tastes when options vary so little and provision is never enough. *Ugh!*

As much as I'd wanted a monkey, what was I thinking? I couldn't take one with me when I left. And good thing I didn't buy one because, the following day, we pulled into a campground in Epulu.

"If we'd found a monkey in your possession," the guide passed around a chimpanzee they'd confiscated, "we'd have charged you a $5,000 fine. Naive tourists purchase animals from locals all the time, which, of course, only encourages the natives to take the babies from their mothers.

"Why? Because it's a way for them to make a living in a poor society. Problem is, when the travelers go, the babies are left on their own."

*Shit!* I cringed, learning another hard lesson.

As we rode off the next day, thoughts simmered in my mind. The disparity was getting harder to ignore. In an attempt to shake it off, I said, "Kathy, when we stop for lunch, let's eat fast and walk ahead of the bus, get some exercise."

"You bet," she said. We leaned down and peered at puddles swelling with hundreds of iridescent butterflies drinking rainwater. "Have you ever seen anything so cool in your life?"

I beamed as I stopped to take it in. But, later, I wasn't smiling when in the market when she pointed at something. "Velvet pictures of African scenes?"

"No," she shook her head. "Look closer."

"Landscapes of . . . no-o-o!" I turned away. It wasn't velvet. The pictures were made out of butterfly wings.

I pictured Africans plucking wings off of butterflies, killing them to make the pictures to sell to tourists, like me, in order to survive.

Again, she pointed. I didn't want to, but I turned to see bracelets like those I'd been collecting. I leaned down to check if they had a new style when I saw the black and white one, like the one I had on my arm, and read the sign next to it: made from real ivory. *No!*

Back in our tent that night, I couldn't sleep. Kathy and I smoked a joint.

"How often do we," I asked, "as Westerners, go to great lengths saving, I don't know, the purple-footed-booby-mantis instead of the people who live amongst them? We get mad at them for making a little bit of money off the animals so they can feed their kids. We care more for a flippin' booby-mantis than a person. Can't we save them both?"

I'd judged the Africans for the way they put food on their tables without having a clue how difficult their lives were. The unfairness pierced me.

Staring out the window the next day, I noticed a pile of neatly cut logs on the side of the road. Clive stopped the bus. "Jump out and grab it for firewood." A couple of the guys did. As we drove away, an old woman came up from the brush waving her hands, screaming.

Instead of stopping, Clive stepped on the gas and left her in the dust.

*That's enough!* I should have screamed so we could give her back her wood or pay for it.

We didn't mean to steal. We weren't like that. Clive just freaked when she came up the hill. He didn't know how to deal with her wrath and followed his instinct to run.

Emotion bubbled inside like the lava in that volcano. I could no longer focus on the woo-hoo-ness of adventure and ignore the injustice. I never understood how blind I was until I saw.

Where was the release Mom's blinders used to offer? I still saw what I pretended not to. What good was that? And now, what would I do with my new understanding? My glimpse-and-look-away morphed into a stare and then a gape. Thoughts dogged me as I struggled to decipher the incongruity, never having enough time to process. I turned to the stars, my friends who followed me everywhere, and I made my nightly wish, or prayer of sorts:

Starlight, star bright,

I wish I may, I wish I might,

Have the wish I wish tonight,

I wish I knew how I could help![1]

*MARY ME*

# TRADE YOUR SKIN WITH ME?

Growing up, I'd spent hours at the dinner table, thinking about starving children around the world until I ate everything on my plate. Now I sat face-to-face with real kids, hungry ones with names. They didn't just need food, but everything I took for granted. I'd never realized three meals a day was a privilege. Now I could no longer deny the disparity.

On this trip, I saw more of the continent than many of the locals ever would, as a rich white tourist. I'd never thought of myself that way, but the eight dollars a day I'd budgeted was more than many Africans made in a year.

In our campground one morning, a guide waited at the edge of the forest to take us on a short hike into a pygmy village, six mud huts huddled in a circle.

Men, dressed in loincloths, smoked pot from a five-foot-long pipe. Women with childlike faces wore swaths of material around their middle, their weathered breasts exposed. Upon our arrival, one glanced up from braiding her child's hair. The others ran to see what we brought.

Clive had prepared us, "When we camp with the pygmies, it's nice to bring a gift. The adults like cigarettes. Last time, we introduced the kids to balloons. I brought some."

As he pulled them from his pack, the kids squealed in recognition, readily joining in a game of volleyball once we blew them up, but the parents barely acknowledged their gifts. Maybe all Westerners who come bring them cigarettes, so they expect them?

*Tch, tch,* the guide made that seemingly universal African sound I still didn't quite understand and waved at us, then pointed toward a group of men heading into the woods. I turned to Clive, my ever-present interpreter of life these days. "What're we doing?"

"The fifteen dollars we each paid includes a hunting trip, for Dik-dik."

"Dik-dik?" I scrunched my forehead and refused the temptation to comment.

"Don't get too excited." He teased. "They're small antelopes."

We followed the men and crouched by a tree (like the guide had pantomimed) while the tribe wrapped a long, low net around it. Then they tied the other end of the mesh a hundred feet away to another tree. As the pygmies hiked back into the forest and attempted to chase an animal into the net, the guide spoke one of few universal words, "Sh-h-h."

We "hunted" there, then in another location. No Dik-dik. So, an hour and a half later, we traipsed back through the forest behind the men to their camp.

"No more hunting?" I asked Clive.

"Apparently, we're too loud. Antelopes run from noisy tourists, go figure."

"Or maybe pygmies don't track when they have guests? They know we brought food because that's part of the deal, right? So, if you were a pygmy, would you waste your few animals on us when you have the option of saving the wildlife for another night when no one brought you dinner?"

"Are you kidding?" Clive drew out a cigarette and offered me one. "I think they're sick of Dik-dik!"

I took one and lit mine, then his, with a lighter. "Rice and vegetables, it is. And chocolate, right? Always chocolate." I looked over at the men who sat down and filled their pipe with more pot. "I like the way these guys think."

As I rolled a joint of my own, the guide came over and herded me toward a hut with his machete. I jumped out of the way. "Hey, watch that thing." He laughed and pointed at what he was trying to show me, inside a hut, an older pygmy nursed a newborn.

"There was no baby before we went hunting," I said, then pointed inside, "Mother?"

"No," he pointed to a young girl who was sitting by the fire taking a hit off the pipe. Across from her stood a young boy, looked about twelve. "Father?" I asked.

He agreed, I think.

I turned back to Clive and confided, "When I was sixteen, I wanted a black baby."

"Well, you know what you've got to do to have one of them."

"I wasn't fantasizing about men. I just wanted a black baby." *But why does this one look white? Does the word pygmy have anything to do with pigmentation?*

"Poor thing," Clive read my mind. "The kid's albino. The others might not accept him. Could ostracize him."

"Exclude him from the tribe?" I groaned at yet another harsh reality. This baby didn't do anything to deserve that. I tried to balance on a chair, or rather a tripod made out of three sticks which had been tied together and strategically twisted to hold the weight of a human being or at least a pygmy. I wanted to hang with them, but they retreated to their own small fires.

Disappointed, I realized, *We're only a job.* But not to the tiny kids. After their mothers fed them, they came back to us. Kathy and I held two or three on our laps at a time and sang, "Old MacDonald had a farm," making animal sounds they recognized. "With an oink, oink here and an oink, oink there."

Though they didn't speak English and had no idea what they were singing, they replicated what they heard and imitated the creatures perfectly. They sang with us, then for us until bedtime.

As I searched my mind for songs from my childhood, another surfaced:

> *Jesus loves the little children,*
> *All the little children of the world,*
> *Red and yellow, black and white,*
> *They are precious in His sight . . .*[2]

What would Jesus do if He were here? Would He play with them, feed them, do the same things we were doing? *Hmm.* Did He have something to do with my desire for a black baby?

The next morning, I zipped up my pack in preparation to follow the guard back to the truck. One of the boys I'd had on my lap the night before came to say good-bye. Standing there in his loincloth with a bulging stomach, he reached up and held out his tiny hand.

A tear slid down my cheek. I choked on the unexpected emotion. With the back of my hand, I wiped my eye and reached for him with the other. I wanted to pick him up, put him in my pack, and take him where, on the road? The responsibility of a child scared me, even though he was the manifestation of a long-held dream.

Overwhelmed, I backed away.

But this moment of connection anchored my heart to that little boy. It's like a piece of his soul attached itself to mine, came with me, and grounded me in a way I can't explain.

Well into the following week, back on Hot Doris, we ventured toward the Central African Republic. As the beauty of Africa slipped past my window, I thought about the small boy's stomach.

Another case of food poisoning attacked my own. Clive had said, "His bloated stomach is a sign of malnutrition." Wasn't there a cure?

After the adult pygmies took our gifts and dismissed us, I'd been frustrated with their wants, but I hadn't thought about their needs till now. Could I have done something to help?

At lunchtime, Clive pulled the truck over to the side of the road. Since I didn't feel well, I stayed inside and watched through the open window as Kathy interacted with locals. While my other friends congregated in a circle on the other side of the truck, she entertained me with yet another crowd of kids.

As if in a silent movie, she gestured while eating her sandwich. They gawked as if they'd never seen anyone like her with her white-blonde hair. They probably hadn't.

She finished her lunch, wiped her hands, and gestured for them to pay attention.

"Hm-m-m." She hummed and raised her hands like a maestro, looked at me, and giggled. We might have been high. The kids examined her expectantly. Then, surprising us, they matched her tune. I sat up, feeling better already as the little choir continued their impromptu concert.

Graeme jumped on the bus. "I've got an idea. Give me a hand."

He threw me a bag of balloons, and I began blowing them up. As the others finished their lunch and piled onboard, Graeme enlisted their help, too. We blew up as many as we could, then tied them to leftover Christmas streamers. We couldn't wait to see the kids' response.

As the truck pulled onto the dirt road, we opened the windows and launched the balloons, catching the kids by surprise.

Before our eyes, the cherubs transformed into banshees and beat each other as they battled for a possession of their own. Big kids pushed little ones to the ground and trampled on them. The balloons popped in the midst of the chaos.

*What just happened?*

In our simple attempt to bring joy, we caused suffering. Our gifts called forth greed. In this tiny village with so little, the possibility of owning something created anarchy. In our naiveté, we invaded culture, ignited materialism, set it on fire, and drove away leaving pandemonium behind.

The beauty of the moment became ugly because of us.

How often did that happen? As if I'd been hit with a cast-iron skillet, the realization struck me. As foreigners, we like to think we swoop in and save the day, but it's just not true. We often hurt more than we help in our attempts to offer relief.

And I'm so influenced by the people I know and love. After the experience with the little pygmy boy, I care more for his tribe. Having his face in mind helped me to realize I needed more friends like him in order to care about more people groups.

While I struggled with communication gaps, I winced when we returned to areas where we spoke the same language. In these places, the clarity of our interactions exposed our selfish intentions, made them obvious, and caused my stomach to churn yet again.

Before, I could hide behind a guise of misunderstanding. But not anymore.

In an open market, mingling with locals, I didn't know what to say when one of the older boys asked, "Will you trade your skin with me?"

I choked on a Coke. *What did he want?*

"I want to be you and you can be me now."

At least, that's what I understood. I wondered how he would explain it. The advertising in the shop behind us was showcasing white models. I pointed to it and said, "African women are beautiful. Why don't they put pictures of them in the ads?"

He shook his head. I'd referred to the surface layer, he, the underlying privilege. The world favors the Caucasian.

He knew that. Why didn't I?

# NO, I DON'T WANT TO DIE

I needed a break from thinking about all the heavy stuff. As we pitched camp near a river with a small set of rapids, the raging water seemed to cry out like a carnival barker, "Free rides, let me show you a good time!"

I stood on the bank in my bathing suit, planning to swim across, walk upstream, dive in, and head back to the other side. Easy peasy, or so it seemed.

*Br-r-r!* The frigid water stole my breath. I swam across quickly, tasting the salt of my sweat as the river rinsed it from my sunburned face. The current dragged at my body. I fought it. On the opposite side of the river, I quivered as I crawled up onto a rock. The swim took more from me than I'd prepared to give. I breathed deeply in an effort to build up strength and confidence for the return. Because of all the things I do, people think I'm brave. I'm not. I don't want to die any more than anyone else does.

As I headed back, I spotted Graeme moving toward me. With his ex-military body and sexy English accent, he was hot. A mutual attraction kept us eyeing one another, but since he'd slept with a few of the others, I played it cool. I didn't want to be a name on his list. But still, with him watching, I wouldn't let my fear show.

I knew he wouldn't let me drown, but why was he running?

I leapt in, swam across, and reached for a rock, but I misjudged the slipperiness and the swiftness of the current. *Crap!* As my hand slid along the bank, the rapids whisked me downstream, faster and faster, deeper and deeper. *Shit!* A foot of water now covered my face, and I couldn't catch hold of a thing. The only reason I didn't lose it is that I could see Graeme's face as he ran alongside the bank, calculating where to jump in so he could save me. He steadied my nerves and kept panic at bay as I reached out again and caught hold of a rock.

In one swift move, he grabbed my arm and snatched me out of the water like a ragdoll. I sat on the bank next to him, shaking, as I caught my breath. Through fragmented thoughts, I heard that carnival barker snigger.

"You okay?" Graeme asked. I nodded, still visibly shaken, but attempted to appear calm.

"Thanks," I said casually. When I could stand, I feigned a saunter over to a picnic table where three of my travel mates looked at pimples on their feet.

"They're from chiggers," Clive said. "Bugs lay eggs inside the blisters. Watch the babies crawl out in the pus when you pop them."

"I wouldn't mind having one of those," I said. "How d'ya get 'em?"

"What, do you have a death wish?" Anna teased.

"Definitely not! I'm just saying if I had to pick one of the crazy things we've seen so far, I'd choose this instead of a scorpion bite or one from a snake hiding in the cool pit of an outhouse." Or dying in a river.

That night, I stepped away from the group. Under the stars, I let my thoughts roam free. I allowed them a voice. *What if I had died today?* I shook my head and shivered again. I have walked through life thinking I have all the time in the world when people of all ages die every day.

*Was there a heaven?* And what did I have to do to get there?

A series of memories surfaced like a dead whale. In first grade, I was shy. I had no idea how to make friends. Recess terrified me until Karen Williams included me. I put her on a pedestal. In third grade, we went to Vacation Bible School at her Baptist church. All I remember is: "God loved the people of this world so much that he gave his only Son, so that everyone who has faith in him will have eternal life and never really die" (John 3:16, CEV).

I liked that, but I didn't like the scary story she told me when she spent the night at my house. "Lucifer—that's what Satan was called when he was the beautiful angel of worship—got jealous of all the attention the angels gave God. So, he rose up in a battle so fierce it divided them. Satan was cast out of heaven and took a third of the angels with him to rule the earth. And if we don't make Jesus Christ Lord of our lives, we end up in hell with Satan for all eternity" (Karen's paraphrase of Isaiah 14:12-14 in the Bible).

"We don't talk about that in my church," I told her, but her words still scared the crap out of me. *What if they're true?* I'd heard about hell, and I didn't want any part of it. I didn't know if I had a ticket to heaven, but I certainly didn't want to go to hell. The weird thing is that her story didn't make me want to pick Jesus either. "Choose me or you wind up in hell." I hated the my-way-or-the-highway stuff I had been taught. I didn't have a death wish, but did I want Jesus? Not if He'd boss me around like everyone else did. I didn't want to do the wrong thing, but I hated control and the way its marionette strings caused me to dance.

I planned to turn to God at the end of my life. I just wanted to have fun first. I would turn to Him at the last minute, but what if, what if, I didn't have time?

As if I were a tightrope walker hovering over an abyss, I leaned down and grabbed hold of the wire. Nope, I did not have a death wish. Death scared the crap out of me. I thought I was headed to heaven, but this close call made me wonder.

Was I?

# IS GOD MAD AT ME?

A couple of months later, as I sat next to that nice lady on the plane headed home, the clank of a breakfast cart woke me.

With the back of one hand, I wiped my mouth while I shook the fear of death from my waking mind. I tried to stand when something caught me. Where was I? I peeked out from under a covering and realized, *Oh, yeah. On an airplane, going home.* I unbuckled the seatbelt, pulled the blanket off my head, and shivered. My grandmotherly seatmate with the odd name stared at me sympathetically. I smiled back, sort of, and pushed my way past, en route to the bathroom.

"Eight and a half hours and I'll be home," I said aloud to myself in the mirror with a smile. *But am I ready to face Dad with his expectations and questions? Of course not!* How could I ever prepare for that? But at that moment, I wished I could answer the question that had been dogging me: "What do I believe about God?"

There, I'd said it. Or part of it. I knew God was real. All my life everyone affirmed that, but it seemed like He wanted to talk to me. I liked His calming presence, but why was He following me around? Was I in trouble?

I considered the conversation I'd been having with my seatmate as I washed my face. Maybe I could talk to her, or would that convince her I was crazy? She mentioned God when we first sat down. And after today, I'd never see her again. Really, she was the perfect person to have this conversation with, the safe stranger. I looked in the mirror and said, "Go for it, baby!"

Back in my seat, Truth handed me the plate of breakfast she'd requested from the flight attendant in my absence. "Thank you," I said, opening the package of utensils. "I gotta tell you something, and you're gonna think I'm nuts."

"No, I won't." Having finished her food, she held out more M&M's. "How 'bout some breakfast dessert?"

Bypassing the sausage and eggs for a minute, I cupped my hands together. "Remember my Dad's letter with the suggestions for my future? Get married. Have a baby or a career." His approval had always mattered to me, probably too much. "But what if," I asked myself as I tested my belief out loud for the first time. "There's a destiny for each of us? A specific reason for our existence? Crazy, huh?"

"No." She smiled as laugh lines crinkled in the corners of her mouth. "It sounds beautiful."

I'd gotten used to people misunderstanding my weirdness, but all of a sudden I was nervous she'd criticize me, so I got a little defensive. Why did I feel so prepared to fight for what I was about to say?

I leaned in closely, quieted my voice, and looked deeply into her eyes, almost daring her to laugh. "We have a purpose. When we find it, our hearts sing. Does *that* sound stupid?"

I watched for her reaction. Without any judgment, she held my gaze. "If you could do anything you wanted, what would it be?"

"I would make a difference in the world," echoing Dad's advice from my pre-memory. Then I blinked and looked away. *Wait, what was her question?* Oh yeah, if *I* could do anything, what would *I* want to do? Is that what I wanted or what Dad wanted?

As if she was reading my mind, she said, "In order to please your father?"

"Probably," I rolled my eyes.

"Then that's not the answer to my question. I'm asking about *your* dream."

"Huh, before I just wanted to have fun, but that's not enough anymore. I want to fall in bed at night, exhausted, with a smile on my face. If I've learned anything on this trip, it's that Dad's right. I need to make a difference, but how?" Suddenly, I hoped she'd know the secret.

She laughed.

Dammit, I was serious!

"Sweetie, if I knew that, I'd be a millionaire." She sipped her orange juice. "But think about what you just said, you and your dad share a desire. That's what you've been looking for, common ground! Just remember, we're all different. The answer to this question is unique for each of us. Mine was family, but maybe yours is something else. You don't need it, but you have my permission to choose your own path."

Dumbstruck, my hands flew to my cheeks. I didn't know what to do with that download; common ground with Dad *and* permission to choose my own way? Cool! But used to seeking his approval, I needed time to think before I explored that topic out loud.

So, like a rat in a maze that had learned to hit a bar for a treat, I pressed my default button of deflection: *Tell a story.* But nothing came to mind. I retraced my steps through the treasure map of recent memories looking for a "start here" sign while longing to process my jumbled thoughts with her about God. I just wasn't sure how to start. I sat quietly until, finally, the words bubbled out, and there I was again, spilling my guts.

"One afternoon, a few months back, Shane and I called dibs on two of the four seats that hovered over the back row of seats in the truck. We opened the windows in the roof and sat with the top halves of our bodies blowing in the wind."

I didn't tell Truth we went up there to get high.

"Shane wore a red-and-white checkered scarf 'round his head like the local Arab men. They held theirs on with a black rope. He didn't have one, so he tied his scarf around his head like an old lady, to protect his freckled skin from sunburn.

Jokingly, he admonished the Africans running alongside, 'Repent, you sinners, repent!' "

I took a hit off the joint and held my breath. *Repent* was a church word, wasn't it? What did it mean? In this case, I was grateful for the communication gap with the locals because I wondered, *What exactly are we saying to these people?*

"I grew up in church," I told Truth on the plane. "I rocked babies in the nursery 'cause, no offense, sermons bored me. I dressed like an elf for the Christmas fair. I didn't go to the movies on Sunday, you know, all that stuff Mom said Christians weren't supposed to do. But on this trip, something happened. It's like I got an invitation to figure out what *I* believed."

Truth pursed her lips, but she didn't say anything, so I kept going. "On Mount Sinai, we laid on the ground *doing a dead ant.*"

"A dead ant?" Truth tilted her face sideways, asking the question with her whole head.

"Out in public, one of the people in our group would scream, 'Dead ant!' And we'd drop to the ground and act like, well, dead ants, lying on our backs with our arms and legs curled. It was funny, but on Mount Sinai we laid in the middle of all these religious people trekking up the mountain as, ah, I don't know, an act of devotion."

My friends had laughed when I told this story, but Truth didn't.

A twinge of guilt stabbed me, as if I'd desecrated a holy site. I saw the pain I felt on Truth's face. We'd been doing dead ants all over the place. No one had said anything or even given us a funny look. I hadn't thought about how I impacted others until now. I felt a little disrespectful maybe.

A few weeks before, I'd stood on Mount Nebo where Moses caught sight of the Promised Land. I'd wrinkled my nose, and shook my head. "It doesn't look very promising to me."

As soon as the joke came out of my mouth, disapproval yanked at my conscience. As I told Truth, something niggled at me again, reminding me of the dead ant thing. Even though the desert did look barren, it didn't feel right to deny God, like I did with Truth when we first met.

"You must be looking for God," she'd said.

I freaked. Why? Because God's not a popular subject with my friends. Not unless we're high. Weirdly enough, then we chat about Him a lot.

So, was I in trouble because I disrespected God? It felt like I should be.

And it seemed like God would have something to say. If I listened, He'd address my observation and teach me why He called it the Promised Land. As I looked for my own version, here I was ragging on God's without even giving Him a chance to tell me His side of the story.

Again, a little afraid of what I might hear, I let my mind wander, circling the target. I was afraid to get too close, but desperately trying to put the pieces together, to understand.

# MAYBE GOD'S
# LOOKING FOR ME

"Truth." I heard a childlike shift in my voice.

"Yes, Sweetie." She opened her eyes.

"You know how I said I wasn't looking for God?"

She smiled.

"Do you think God might be, well, looking for me?" I chewed on the corner of my lower lip.

"Why do you ask?" She opened her purse and pulled out a pack of gum. My eyes lit up as she offered me a piece. I took one. *Mmm.* I savored the taste of American gum after not having had any for a long time. "It seems like I keep running into God everywhere I go."

"What do you mean?" Truth shifted her body once again and gave me her full attention.

"Tell me if this story hits you the same way it did me . . ."

Where were we? Back in the Sudan. The sun beat down and colored us golden brown as we travelled through the southern part of the country, surrounded by sand. In our favorite spot, Shane and I rode in those seats on top of the truck, smoking the African cigarettes forbidden inside, and pointing out the occasional rare bird. Two days before Christmas, we searched for the elusive holiday spirit. We tried singing carols, but *Jingle Bells* wasn't the same with sweat trickling down your back.

I closed my eyes and pictured my family nestled in snow. *How was Dad wrapping his presents this year? Spray-painting each package?*

When I was five, he gave me a wig because Mom wouldn't let me grow my own hair long. I loved the gurgling fish pitcher he bought me at the aquarium. I'd miss his present. Who was I kidding? I missed him. We gave each other a hard time, but maybe that was because we cared.

Growing up, as a family, we attended Bethany Congregational Church. I helped with Sunday school by reading Bible stories to five-year-olds about what a nice guy Jesus was. Somehow, I had missed God in the telling. Wasn't He the father figure who'd step in when discipline was necessary? And the Holy Ghost? Well, the idea of God being a *ghost* freaked me out, so I ignored that part. For me, church included Bible stories and community.

I loved the people of Bethany and the potlucks, the Christmas pageants, and the talent shows, where the minister's good-looking son played with his band.

On Saturday nights, we'd end our time together holding hands, swaying back and forth, and singing those old Christian songs, like Kum Ba Yah. I've heard people make fun of that, but there was a real sweetness in it; that *was* church for me.

Then in junior high, friends became super important. I asked Mom, "Instead of Bethany, can I go to St. Mary's with my friends?"

"No," she said, "we're not Catholic."

"Why does it matter? I don't even know what we even believe. *They* take tests in Sunday school. *We* color pictures."

"What do you want for lunch?" Mom asked, as she inserted the skeleton key into the lock of our front door, ignoring my question like she always did when she didn't have an answer.

It was probably for the best. If she'd given me an answer, I'd have done the opposite. The lack of answers gave me a chance to figure out my own convictions. So, like everything else, religion became a point of contention. "Forget it then, I'm not going to church!"

"Yes, you are." Mom didn't bat an eye. "You live under our roof, you go."

I went to my youth group Halloween party dressed as a hooker.

*Why had I been such a jerk?* I wondered on that truck in Africa, where I promised myself I'd never miss another chance to gather with family for Christmas. Sure, I complained, but I loved them. More than any others in the world. I didn't get the God stuff, but I was trying to figure it out, to distinguish my own beliefs. And now, I couldn't imagine being anywhere else besides Bethany Congregational Church for the Christmas Eve service where Mom would be in the balcony singing her annual solo, *O Holy Night*.

That was home. The homiest home got. What was I doing so far away?

I tilted my head back and faced the noonday sun. The road, easy for a change, allowed us to make time until a man drove up in a jeep and waved us over. En masse, we groaned. Another passport check? In populated areas, we got stopped daily. Police examined our papers *ad nauseum* without caring how long they detained us, just making up excuses to collect a bribe from us.

But this time, the man with the European accent held his arms open wide, "Won't you join me for coffee?"

There, in the middle of the desert, we got an invitation!

"Sure!" We followed him to a compound filled with fifteen empty trailers. He jumped out and welcomed us like old friends.

No handshakes, only hugs. "I am Gionpierre. Please, come in, let me feed you."

Well, okay then, one steaming cup of cappuccino after another accompanied pickled mushrooms, ham and egg pie, artichoke hearts, and Christmas cake, incredible delicacies after all the dehydrated food. We filled our bellies and listened to his story.

"I come from Italy to build roads for the Sudanese people, but the railroad company, they charge outrageous sums to transport supplies. We cannot afford them. We must go."

*Great.* Here was another case of rampant corruption in all levels of government chasing away the people who've come to help.

"Now I guard the place with a small team until we break down," he continued. "Will you come for dinner, be my guests for the night?"

With pleading eyes, we all turned to Clive. I'd never seen him as a father figure before, but he had the final say. And as usual, we ran behind schedule and should probably keep moving. Thank God, Clive lifted his coffee in a toast. "A holiday invitation; we delightfully accept!"

First, though, we drove into the city of Nyala to shop for the next leg of our trip. It was too late as there were no more oranges, pumpkins, or freshly killed animals left in the market.

Clive met with local officials to finalize our plan for Christmas Day. For weeks, he'd been saying, "We'll hike six-kilometers to the top of Jebel Mara and lounge in the hot springs."

But after his meeting, he shook his head, "We can't."

"Why not?" I crossed my arms.

"There's a war. Four neighboring villages are fighting about what to call the place."

"Doesn't it already have a name?" I threw my hands in the air.

"They executed two people yesterday." Clive used a palm branch as a toothpick.

"Ah," I said, "so much for peace on earth." As the sun set, we piled into the truck to head back to Gionpierre's compound. Although it was illegal, the easiest way to get through the sand was to straddle the railroad tracks. Only one train passed through each week. Usually, we rode alongside the tracks, using them as a guide. But when the ground was soft, like then, we overlapped. Occasionally we got stuck anyway. I groaned and rolled my eyes; can't we get in the truck and go, just once?

As if in answer to my question, a train whistled in the distance, "Wo-o-o Wo-o-o."

*Shi-i-it!* We looked at each other. *What-do-we-do?*

*Run?* We couldn't leave Hot Doris. She was our shelter, our transportation. Clive hit the gas, then reversed, back, forth, back, forth.

*Jesus-s-s!* I screamed in my head. Just in time, the truck lurched off the track and *whoosh!* The train whizzed past. "Wo-o-o Wo-o-o."

I pinched myself—still alive. *Whew!* Once again, I'd called out to God while hovering over the edge of disaster, cried, and expected help. Over and over, He came through. Most of the time, I never even thought to say, "Thanks!"

Instead, I complained out loud, "Gionpierre better have something stronger than coffee."

He did. With an apron on, he swung the door wide. "Come! Sit down. How have you been?"

Twinkling lights sparkled around the dim room. *Silent Night* played on cassette. "Mm, what was that smell, pepperoni pizza?" My mouth watered as Gionpierre passed by with a full tray, calling out over his shoulder, "Phone your family if you want! Grab a carton of cigarettes. Each trailer has a double bed and hot showers. Make yourself at home."

"It's like I died and went to heaven," I said to Kathy as I leaned back in my chair. "Maybe that train killed us, and we *are* in heaven. We just don't know we're dead yet. And Gionpierre is an angel."

I took a hit off my beer and toasted him as he rushed by, giving, giving, giving. How could serving make him so happy? It's like he smiled with his heart even after all he'd been through.

When the pink sun rose over the desert the following morning, I didn't want to go. Gionpierre posed for pictures and hugged us. "Thank you for coming!"

*Thank me?* He blessed our socks off, and I'd never even use that word, but nothing else fit. Funny thing is, he seemed blessed, too. *I wonder if loving people would make me that happy?*

I forced myself onto the truck and waved goodbye as I felt my heart grow, just like in the scene from *The Grinch Who Stole Christmas*. In the television special, the mean Dr. Seuss character steals the Christmas decorations, presents, and food from the people of Whoville, but he couldn't steal their thanksgiving. When the Grinch hears the people singing praises in spite of their loss, his tiny heart grows and grows and grows. Their joy is contagious.

Tears of gratitude filled my eyes as we drove away.

Sitting on the plane, picturing Gionpierre and his selflessness made me tear up all over again. Truth rubbed my back as I asked, "Doesn't that seem like God to you?"

She squeezed my hand and returned my question with an enigmatic smile.

# I CALLED GOD FRED

"**A**m I bein' a pest?" I asked Truth. "Mom tells me to leave people alone, but I have whole-plane-ride chats all the time, and I don't think it's always my fault."

"I'll let you know if I need a break." She looked up from her game of solitaire.

Good, I was about to take a chance sharing this next bit, but I'd finally built up the courage to sort of get to the point. Sort of. I stared out the window. "Away from the group one night," I told her, "I sat under a sky full of stars, not the same ones I saw at home, but recognizable friends, nonetheless. Half a world away, I liked a little familiarity and needed thinking time. God had my attention now."

As the native drum kept rhythm with the nighttime symphony of the African bush, the cry of a hyrax (a small, furry animal that sounded a lot scarier than it looked) pierced the night. A hyena howled. A warthog ran through our camp. What was he running from? Sitting in front of my tent, I tried to figure everything out. I wouldn't have called what I did *prayer* but maybe *wonder*.

Night after night, I'd listened to the rush of a river or watched my own personal light show as lightning spider-webbed across the heavens, danced in the distance, and serenaded me with a muffled growl. Until a crash—so loud it seemed to break the sky—caused me to twitch as a shiver ran up my spine.

"You know how it is when you feel someone staring at you from across the room?" I said to Truth. "You turn to meet the gaze. It was like that, but I saw no one. I just felt a comforting presence as we sat together in silence."

"You think it was God?" she asked.

"Yeah, but I called him Fred. Not so overwhelming, more personal."

She smiled but did not look up from her card game as I continued, "It's like a blanket of peace covered not only me, but my problems, my friends here, and my family across the sea. Night after night, this calming force drew me from the tent, kept me company. Until a voice so subtle I thought it was mine spoke to my heart. It knew things I didn't and never told me what to do or gave me a hard time about not having a profession or a family. It never pushed or asked where I'd been, it was just plain there for me. You think I'm crazy?"

"No, Sweetie, I don't." She shook her head as she looked up and into my eyes, "What did the voice tell you?"

"It spoke just a few words at a time, though they held giant consequences, every time. Like the one-liner I heard when we almost leapt off the bridge . . ."

As we pulled into a campground on a river, on our way to Kenya, an overpass hulked in the background, unusual for Africa. We stood at the rail and looked down. After the "carnival barker" stretch of river rapids nearly killed me only a few days before, I should have learned. I didn't.

We made a joint decision to jump. But since darkness was fast approaching, I said, "Let's do it in the morning."

"Before breakfast," Kathy agreed.

After we set up our tents that night, we pored over comments in the guest book. "An exhilarating plunge. THE way to start the day!" Kathy and I looked at each other and smiled. As I slept, though, I sensed an internal alert. A message from Fred? *Don't jump!*

I got up the next morning and ran from tent to tent, saying, "We can't do it. We've gotta pass!"

After a night's sleep, our imminent plan wasn't so pressing anymore. Hungry for breakfast, no one argued. As I lifted a spoonful of eggs to my mouth, I glanced under the bridge and froze. A skinny African man stood bathing in the ankle-deep water. It never occurred to us to check the water level. The pictures in the camp book must have been from a different season.

*I could have died.*

Again, I should have known better. Five years earlier, my sister Catherine and I had stood on the edge of a cliff in North Carolina with a group of guys we'd met at a wedding. She jumped first. I yelled, "You okay?"

"No," her voice cracked.

From up top, I took a step and leapt seventy feet to her side and swam her across the river with one of the guys. We waited for the ambulance.

No one thought to warn her, "Hold your arms across your chest or lift them overhead." Her vertebrae snapped on impact as her elbows hit the water and broke her back.

After that, it would be logical that I'd have reservations about jumping off a bridge, but I didn't. I didn't want to run from fear. Now that I was listening to Fred, though, I *knew* things. I wouldn't have called my response *worship*, but a cry rose up from deep inside. I made a nest with my arms and buried my face in it. So grateful for the inner warning, I sobbed.

Yup, Fred definitely had my attention now.

# FOREVER ALTERED

I heard Fred, a.k.a. God, say things. At least I thought I did. It wasn't my mind playing tricks on me, was it? I didn't think so because the warnings came true.

Communicating with God wasn't the same as with a person. I mean, it could be, but also it could be so much more. Like when this sentence, as if on a teleprompter, marched through my brain:

This truck is going to be in an accident.

*Wha-a-at?* I shifted in my seat. A train of thought is usually connected, but not this time. Since I'd been directing my attention, well, *up there,* I assumed this came from God.

So, what was I supposed to do? The dream urging me not to jump off the bridge held its message, but this wasn't, "Get off the bus." Was that a given? And where should I go?

I was simply told it would happen, and I had to make my own choice.

Today, I've learned. I'd trust my gut, warn everyone, and encourage the leaders to pull off the road for an early day. I'd get off by myself if I had to. Back then, though, I'd assumed these mystical experiences had to do with Fred, so why didn't I ask Him? I guess I was afraid of what might be required. If I didn't ask, I wasn't responsible for what I didn't do, was I?

Rain pelted the windows of the truck—a crap day, by African standards. With half our group on a side excursion, the rest of us weary trekkers, plus two hitchhikers, rode in unusual silence. Months of travel had exacted a toll.

At lunchtime, we parked next to a hut and made our way to a food counter. I ordered a "hamburger" and refused to scrutinize the meat. Instead, I enjoyed the rare opportunity of a real meal in a real restaurant, while tentatively asking the others, "Think we're safe?"

"I wondered about that, too," Kathy said.

*No!* In five and a half months, lots of things freaked us out, but never the possibility of an auto accident. "Maybe we're just not used to the speed after the dirt roads?" Kathy held up a French fry then drenched it with neon "catsup."

After lunch, we dropped Shane off at the base of Mount Kenya. With all my pent-up concern, I don't know why I didn't join him on the trek. Yes, I do. Even with the warning, I found false security in the fortress of our tank.

"Be careful of strangers and wild animals," Kathy and I brooded over him. "Don't make us come looking for you," she continued. "Meet us in Nairobi on Friday."

*If we make it,* I added, but only to myself.

Blowing him kisses, we got back on Hot Doris for our remaining three-hour trip into the city. My internal angst rose to a crescendo, but what the heck? I said nothing. Instead, I lay back across an extra seat and dreamt about our upcoming trip to Ngorongoro Crater . . .

—until screeching brakes jolted me awake.

The truck bounced then rolled down an embankment. It ripped to pieces before emptying us onto the ground. Hot Doris shook us like dice, our futures forever altered.

I'd closed my eyes on a typical afternoon. Now, I opened them to a real-live nightmare. Outside the vehicle, I leaned against the back-right tire. *How did I get here?* The truck rocked back and forth, and a voice screamed, "Get out of the way! It's gonna roll!"

Who was it? A few feet away, Kathy crept in the opposite direction. She must have screamed. She always knew what to do.

With the metallic taste of blood in my mouth, I crawled twenty feet before looking back at my home away from home crushed like a bug. My friends were scattered across the red dirt.

As if on drugs, I felt disconnected from my body as I gazed down. My sarong was gone, but my bikini was still intact. I lifted my head to the sky and acknowledged a drizzle with a shiver that zigzagged down my back. In slow motion, I bent my head toward my throbbing hand. Noticing a deep groove across the base, I peered at the muscles and capillaries inside, like transparent layers of a medical book. One by one, I pulled the seven metal bracelets embedded in my palm out of the sticky, congealing blood and set them on the ground.

Andrea's face filled my field of vision, and I jumped. She assessed my injuries and quickly returned with a sweatshirt, putting it over my head. Then she wrapped my hand with a towel and said, "Don't worry, mate. It's only a scratch," before she ran to nurse another.

"Don't worry," echoed in the same detached voice that had screamed before. It wasn't Kathy's, but my own. "It's only a scratch." I believed Andrea instead of my eyes.

Then Maasai warriors stood before me. They were African supermen dressed in colorful regalia carrying swords. My heart raced when one tipped his head toward me, as if to say, "What's wrong?"

*I had something he wanted to see!*

I beamed, sort of, as I unwrapped the towel. He hovered nearby, concern etching his face. I lifted my hand. It flapped open, and he turned away, squeezing his eyes shut. "Some warrior you are." Tears filled my eyes. "It's only a scratch."

I couldn't yet feel physical pain, but his disapproval stung.

People stopped, causing traffic. Some helped. Others stole. Everyone moved so slowly.

A car pulled over, and Graeme waved for me to come. Wavering back and forth, I stood, then hobbled. He loaded Kathy and me into the back of a stranger's car, a Good Samaritan who sped toward the Aga Khan Hospital in Nairobi. At each jostling curve of the ninety-mile ride, we whined, afraid of what had already happened.

Stop-and-go traffic slowed our pace as we entered the city. Out the windows, we watched as people set fires, broke into storefronts, and threw things. What was going on?

"Riots everywhere," our driver explained. "Someone found the body of the foreign prime minister's daughter."

"Don't stop talking," Kathy begged me, her back wedged up against my side. We didn't yet know her pelvis was broken.

In the backseat of that stranger's car, no words came. So, I eked out a bit of our favorite Eurythmics song, Sweet Dreams. I sang about traveling the world looking for that illusive something that brought what, happiness? At least, that's how I interpreted it. Without seeing it at the time, I'd done exactly what the song said. And there I was, speeding toward a hospital with happiness nowhere in sight.

Ten minutes later, an attendant at the hospital said, "Where are your clothes?" as she took the sheet off the stretcher to cover me. She was more upset by my lack of covering than the gouge in my hand, in Africa, where people wander around naked all the time.

Inside the emergency room, a nurse stitched up my hand and my head, then x-rayed my back and my knee, but refused to give me painkillers. "You might have a concussion," she explained as she wheeled me to a ward and put me to bed.

I whimpered like a puppy, unable to sleep as the shock wore off. The numbness had helped, hidden the pain, and slowed my response time emotionally as well as physically—my kind of defense mechanism. Unbearable pain now replaced it. I rocked back and forth, moaning, unable to lean back because of a gash across my shoulder. Trying to remember, then hoping to forget.

In the morning, my Good Samaritan shook me awake. "She's dead," he said.

"Who?" My voice rose as I tried to sit up.

"Your friend." He backed away as a howl rose from somewhere deep inside me.

"No-o-o!" I screeched, as he disappeared down the hall, never to return.

Hours later, I don't know how many, Clive perched on the edge of my bed and eyed the plate of rice and beans in front of me. "Are you going to eat that?"

"I can't." I shook my head and pushed the tray toward him. "I keep thinking of Kathy. Gone." I started to cry again.

"What do you mean?" He shoveled the food in. "Just saw her. Down the hall."

"What?" I brightened. "Thank You! Thank You! Thank You, God!"

"Never knew you were so religious." Clive wiped his mouth. Breathing deeply, I hugged him. "Kathy didn't die. Anna did."

"Anna?" I drew back and crumpled.

Clive put the fork down and looked at me. "She was crushed by the back locker when the truck rolled. She never regained consciousness. The others heard her flat-line when she passed in the emergency room."

# ANOTHER CHANCE

Long after Clive left, I lay in that hospital ward, the only American among Africans, thinking about Anna. The twenty-four-year-old anesthesiologist from Australia, dead.

Only weeks before, she and I had eaten dinner at a restaurant in Uganda right after I'd had bad news from home. I'd been hearing Mom's voice in my head, another sentence. "I've got sad news to tell you."

In the big city, Anna had waited with me in the usual long line at the crowded phone bank just so I could have a few minutes of scratchy overseas connection. It was never the ideal place to hear bad news, but it was the only opportunity to phone home.

Someone had died. I knew it. My grandmother lay in a nursing home. Surely, it was her.

With everyone pushing and shoving, I heard Mom say the dreaded words. Covering my ear with my left hand, I screamed into the receiver, "Who? Who died?"

"Your cousin Julia. Hit by a truck on the way to work. New Year's Eve." The call dropped. With my questions and emotion, I stood in that crowd of people.

Did she see it coming? Did it hurt? Where was she now?

*God*, I prayed, not The Lord's Prayer or anything official like that. *Thank You, for the nights we had last summer. Be with her.*

Spending the previous summer together on Cape Cod, Julia and I had talked about everything: her drum and bugle corps, the X-rated hypnotist, God, ourselves, and maybe even death.

Anna had comforted me that night in the restaurant after the phone call. Neither of us wanted to think about mortality, or what *the end* meant. So far away. Yet, apparently, so close.

Anna and I had ordered spaghetti and talked about our travels and the losses we'd experienced. Grief wove its way through our conversation like black embroidery thread. Together we stared at the back of the messy cross-stitch it represented.

But now, having flipped it over, I saw the picture on the front. She and I had no way of knowing how soon her turn would come, but our conversation felt connected.

I wanted to know that Julia and Anna were okay, that I'd see them again, but I didn't take my wonderings to Fred. The answers scared me.

Three days later, we had a memorial service for Anna. I don't know who thought to put one together, but there we sat—our ragtag group in the front two pews of the church across the street from the Grosvenor Hotel, staring at the minister like a herd of deer in the headlights of death.

"We all have an appointed time to die," he said. "Are you ready?"

What the hell? Ever so slightly, I rocked, craving an escape from the pain in my shoulder, my knee, and my head. My back flippin' hurt, but not as much as my heart. Surrounding us, a slew of Africans jumped up and down, cheering. *Woo hoo?* Seems they couldn't wait to die.

I didn't get it. In Massachusetts, we lay our dead out in a casket and somberly pass by. Catholics cross themselves. I didn't know what that meant, but that's what we did when someone died. We picked a flower from a bouquet and lay it on the satin pillow next to the deceased. I had no grid for this kind of celebration. *Why were they so happy?*

I considered what I knew. Many suffer in Africa. With bloated stomachs and goiters hanging off their necks, the infirmed line the streets begging for money. Some people eat rice and beans every day. Others don't even have that. If that's how I lived, I could get excited about going to heaven. But I liked my life. I was in no hurry to die.

As I cried for my friend and my cousin, my eyes fell to my arm in the sling and the injury on my hand. The new lifeline etched into it nothing a palm reader would recognize, but it was a gift of time all the same. A second chance. A mark of destiny?

Up until now, I'd taken everything for granted. But I really wanted a life worth living.

Fred had my attention, all right. Heck, we were on a first-name basis. I liked His comforting presence, similar to an anonymous benefactor lurking in the background. Knowing He worked on my behalf felt good, really good. If there was more—and I was pretty sure there was—I wanted it. I just didn't have the nerve to hear what it was yet.

# THREE PROSTITUTES
# AND A U.N. DRIVER

In the whirlwind of the next few days, there weren't any quiet nights to escape and sit under the stars when I needed it most. In Nairobi, at the Grosvenor Hotel, I wondered. *How can I find peace in the midst of this?*

Two days after the accident, Kathy and I left the hospital and joined the rest of our group in the cheap rooms frequented by overlanders and prostitutes. The women stroked us with their henna-dyed hands, caring women who *mommed us*. Unaccustomed to injured tourists, they listened to our stories and sympathized. They knew about tough times.

The phones only worked from room to room. In order to reach my mom, I hobbled three blocks to the Fairview Hotel, the nearest place with public access to the outside world. Mom knew we'd been in an accident because I'd called her from the hospital. In the two days it took me to get back to her, she'd made a plan. "Go get your x-rays and fax them to me."

"Mom, this isn't America," I wailed, lacking the energy and patience to explain. "I can't just go pick up x-rays. I'm wiped. I'm going back to the Grosvenor to lie down."

Sometimes Mom knew exactly the right empathetic sounds to make, but she wasn't making them that day. In the hot pink *Out of it in Africa* shirt I'd designed for the group, I limped back to my room. Two hours later, the receptionist rang, "Your driver's here."

"My what?" I peered out the window and laid eyes on the first man I'd seen in a long time dressed in a suit. Behind him, he'd parked a Volvo with red diplomatic license plates. This man, a representative from the UN, held a note in his hand. After I wobbled out and climbed into his car, I found out it was from my mom. It had the same instructions on it that she'd tried to give me earlier in the day.

As he drove, I held on for dear life. When had life become so dear?

I followed him to Admissions, where he acquired my x-rays. Then we stopped by the UN to fax them to Mom before he deposited me "home."

Lesson learned: Never underestimate the power of your mom.

As I lay back down in bed, Clive ducked into our room, dried blood still stuck to his forehead from the accident. "Think you can get your UN guy to help me organize another vehicle for the rest of the trip?"

"I don't know," I said as he paced.

Even though the accident wasn't our fault, we faced impending delay and legal disturbances. The driver coming from the other way had left us no room on the road.

Mom's voice echoed in my head, "You're coming home."

"I am *not* leaving my friends," I'd told her on the phone. As usual, they'd become super important. She should get that. She's the one who taught me *there's no such thing as a stranger*. She talks to everyone at checkout counters, on planes, and in lines waiting to use ladies' rooms.

This accident glued our team together. I needed to stay.

But my back hurt, and no one knew why. And I wanted to feel my fingers again. So, when I heard her voice in my head repeat, "You're coming home," I thought, *Should I?* Wavering, I stared at Clive. My internal thoughts wouldn't shut up. I agonized as Kathy rolled another joint.

After Clive left, I muttered, "I think I'm going home."

Knowing my ambivalence toward my family, Kathy said, "I don't think you should."

"Why not?"

"Are you going because of your mom?" She looked me in the eye. "Eh?"

"No," I glanced down.

"Your friends?" She didn't waver.

"Nope," I answered not only Kathy but also myself.

Then she nailed it, "Are you going because you want to?"

"Wow, you're good! No, not *want* to, but I am choosing to get the medical help I need. Then I'll come back." Boy, did that feel freeing, making a decision of my own. I took another hit off the joint and laughed again. "Thank you for making up *my* mind!"

I called Mom. "Book me a ticket. Just give me a week to wrap things up."

When I called her back, she said, "Your flight leaves tomorrow night at eight." *Dammit!* But I shifted emotions from anger to relief by the time I woke up the next day.

Kathy sprang out of bed, "Girl, we got some shopping to do."

"The doctor said you should stay off your feet for two weeks with that broken pelvis."

"Not if you're flying out tonight." She escorted me to the market. We traded my remaining possessions for soapstone carvings, wooden spoons, and batik wall hangings, drawing attention from the locals as we waddled back to the hotel—she on crutches and me with my arm in a sling. The Africans with physical ailments begging on the streets did a double take as we passed.

Did they think tourists never got hurt?

When this unique opportunity presented itself, we stopped to compare boo-boos. I felt a bond with those locals which I hadn't with others. And after stewing over all the injustice I noticed along the way, there was something about this that felt just. Gave me a peace about the whole thing.

Back at the room, Clive waited. "Where do you want to go for your last supper?"

"Carnivores." My eyes lit up.

An hour later, Clive, Kathy, and I sat around a table as waiters brought skewers of meat. "Wildebeest?" One asked me, and then sliced a piece with his machete when I agreed. Another hovered near Kathy, "Zebra?" pronouncing the word with a short e like the Brits, rather than a long e like the Americans.

And then it was time. At the airport, the good-byes hurt more than the injuries. Not knowing how to deal with all the emotion, I focused on the five copper bracelets Clive wore. Driving south, I'd collected similar ones, twenty-five cents each. With the intention of reselling his in the UK, he bought them en masse. So, he paid only ten cents apiece because he'd purchased so many. He'd given me a hard time for paying so much for mine. In the accident, his scattered. These were all he had left.

"Pretty expensive trinkets you've got there," I couldn't resist. "What're they, twenty bucks each?" We smiled, looked into each others' eyes, and said more without words than we ever could with them.

"You can stay." Clive reached for my hand. Others may have thought I was part of the "1.5" average-number-of-women he slept with on the trip, but I wasn't. Clive and I were buddies, and I was going to miss him. As my departure drew near, we hugged without any more words but way too many feelings.

# CHEAP TRICK

Seems weird, doesn't it, to have been twenty-six and so stand-offish about including a partner in my life? I wanted one, but without the pain I'd experienced in the past. After my desperate attempts for Dad's approval failed, I sought attention from boys. At fifteen, I'd shared my latest theory with a friend, Sophia, as we stood in front of the mirror in my closet, putting on makeup, "The secret to happiness is finding the right guy."

"Well, that's a no-brainer!" She applied another layer of lipstick and flashed me the smile that got her into the Barbizon School of Modeling. Then we headed to a party. I just wanted to fit in. I was desperate for approval. As I transitioned from living in my parents' home to launching out on my own, I explored with a vengeance. *Who was I?* And with an over-bearing mother and a father who wasn't clued-in, I hungered for male attention.

So, there we were, at what's-his-name's house on New Year's Eve. There were no parents, plenty of alcohol, and a band on their way over after their gig. *Rock stars.* Happy 1979! With a beer in one hand and a joint in the other, Sophia and I sang the song blaring from the stereo.

She got together with the lead guitarist, a white guy with an afro, and Alex and I hooked up. He looked like Steven Tyler and he made me feel pretty important when he started picking me up at school. One afternoon, we took Sophia with us to the mall. Stoned, he bought me everything I admired.

"Wow," Sophia said, "He really loves you!" I smiled.

At one of the band's concerts, Sophia's man showed his "love" by making his guitar talk from the stage, "Hello-o-o, So-phi-a!" We strutted past the other girls throwing themselves at the band and met the guys backstage.

Alex dropped me off that night. Mom looked out her bedroom window and saw us kissing good-bye, but she thought he was a girl with his long hair and slight build. She wasn't much happier to find out he was eighteen and in college. Of course, her uncertainties made him more appealing. Until she started getting along with him.

Like she did with everyone else, she pumped him for information, "How much does a joint cost?" Hearing her question as I came down the stairs to meet him for a date, I backtracked. Grabbing my sister, I said, "Tell him I'm in the car," then I snuck out back.

A month after we met, Alex said, "The band's going to party at a motel this weekend."

I thought about New Year's Eve. Okay, so it would be like that. "Cool!"

The following Friday, I walked into the living room and found him lying across the floor, patting the dog as he talked to my parents. The other guys I'd dated quivered respectfully by the front door, but not Alex, I think his casual style gave my parents the feeling they could trust him.

I guess it lured me in, too. But right away, more was expected sexually than I was used to with boys my own age. I could take care of myself, though. At least, that's what I thought.

When he started pushing my head toward his crotch, I repositioned myself, letting him know *that* was a non-negotiable request. Guess I told him, right? Maybe not strongly enough . . .

I was a virgin and I wanted to keep it that way until I got married.

Why? Well, raised in church, I knew I wasn't supposed to sleep around. Thou shalt not commit adultery (Exodus 20:14, KJV) and all that. And saving myself just appealed to me, but my little world, my society, my culture didn't reinforce my truth. I needed a little rebar.

As Alex and I made our way to the door that night, Mom said, "Where are you going?"

"Out for dinner then to a movie," I lied.

"Have a good time and be home by midnight."

In the car, Alex pointed to a gallon of wine inside a brown bag. "Never seen a bottle that big," I said. "Guess we *are* gonna party tonight." He pulled down a back road and parked, opened the jug, and rolled a big, fat joint. An hour later, I staggered into the motel room, hanging on his arm. I slurred, "H-h-hey! Where iz evry-one?"

A half-naked couple got off the bed, grabbed their clothes, and disappeared. Without any other furniture, I flung myself on that bed. The light shone from the vanity around the corner. I watched Alex circle and climb on the opposite side. He pulled me close, kissed me. I felt his hands all over me. Dizzy, I felt something inside. *His finger?* He'd done that before. I reached down to check and—*no-o-o!* Vomit came out of the depth of my being. Retching, I sat as the couple emerged from the bathroom. Was it their turn on the bed?

"Ew," the girl said, "There's puke everywhere!"

Alex laughed nervously as he dragged me behind him, mumbling, "Sorry."

I don't remember the trip from the bed to the toilet, but something happened. I didn't drink anything else, but the intoxication intensified to alcohol-poisoning.

In the bathroom, Alex said, "I can't believe how drunk you are!"

I reached for the shower curtain thinking it was a wall and fell into the tub. Sitting on the toilet, he snickered. Trying to steady myself, I leaned on the toilet paper holder. It ripped from the wall and fell to the ground. Again, he snickered, my catalyst of shame. I shivered and looked down. *Where were my clothes?* I didn't remember taking them off. Then he pulled me up and over himself so that I straddled him on the toilet. Up then down. Up then down. Since he'd already penetrated me on the bed, resisting seemed pointless.

Inside, I crawled to the far end of a dark tunnel, curled up, and that's the last thing I remember . . .

Until the next day.

Gagging, I leaned over the side of the bed and grabbed hold of the wastebasket, but only experienced the dry heaves. Wiping my lips with the back of my hand, I looked at my clothes strewn across the floor of my bedroom. *How did I get here?*

Then I felt an ache inside, *down there,* and remembered what happened.

An inner voice accused, "You're not a virgin anymore. What if you got pregnant?"

*Shit!* I thought Alex cared. Curling in a ball and rocking ever so gently, I wondered, *What do I do now?* I couldn't tell Mom. I wished that I could, but if I did, she'd kill me. That's not what I wanted, but neither was this.

Later that week, I told a friend. One who hadn't had a boyfriend and wanted one. She thought the whole thing was cool.

It wasn't. I didn't know how to help her see things the way I did. And if she didn't get it, who would?

Afterwards, I didn't want anyone else to know, so I didn't break up with Alex. Because no one knew, everyone treated him as they had before. I know this sounds crazy, but I kept having sex with him because, well, I was no longer a virgin. So what did it matter? I stayed with him a few more months, took all my inner turmoil, and squished it into two spring-loaded words: "Oh well."

I repeated them often with a shrug.

# I JUST WANT TO BE HAPPY

Thing is, from the moat in which I fished, choices came with a price. Guys date-raped and cheated. Slept with my *friends*. And without boundaries and a healthy support system, I didn't know how to protect myself. Boy did I need someone to lock me in a turret, cut off my hair, and hide the key in the belly of a dragon. Trouble was, I didn't live in a fairy tale and happily ever after wasn't looking likely.

After Alex, sex came easily.

"Who cares that you're not a virgin anymore?" that lying voice whispered inside, nudging me into promiscuity. Once my virginity was gone, I spiraled out of control. Even though it didn't feel good, I gave myself away for free, piece by piece.

Is that true? No. How could I give away what I never really had?

Because I believed that I had to have sex to keep a boyfriend, I buried my emotions, anesthetized them with drugs, and pretended I didn't care.

*It didn't matter*—the trail of lies continued—*how many men or how many times.*

Enter stage left: Tony. Hot and popular, with just the right amount of lost doggishness. Since he was a senior, I knew who he was, but how did he know me?

"He thinks you're cute," my friend said on the first day of our junior year. "He and Mike want to take us out after school. Ple-e-ease say yes."

Four hours later, in the backseat of Mike's Camaro, Tony leaned over and kissed me. I flinched in surprise, then snuggled closer. Drawn to his good looks and disarming smile, I lost it when he winked at me and fell for him like only a sixteen-year-old can. That's when I confided in him. I told him my dream. "I just want to be happy."

"Me, too," Tony nodded as he passed me a joint.

"Wow!" I smiled. "We both want the same things in life."

From the little that Dad knew about Tony, that he was a party animal being raised by a single mom, Dad didn't like my choice. "When looking for a husband," he advised. "Check a man's genes."

"Don't worry, Dad." I giggled. "I totally checked out his jeans."

\* \* \* \* \*

We dated off-and-on my last two years of high school with more break-ups and reconciliations than I'd seen on any soap opera. Every time he cheated on me "by accident" or I did the same to get back at him, we'd split.

As I packed my bags for college, Mom caught me off guard. "Promise you won't go to church?"

*Wha-a-at?*

"Cults abduct students from college campuses." She looked me in the eye, and I made the easiest vow ever: "I will NEVER STEP FOOT in another church *aslongasIlive*." After all these years of making me go, her request seemed odd. But so did a lot of things. I had no plans to attend church, and now I had permission to quit. *Woo hoo!*

Don't get me wrong. I believed in God, but after the parental control and manipulation, I didn't want Him telling me what to do, too. And why would He be any different?

At seventeen, I spun off like a whirling dervish, taking those heavy expectations and flinging them like a Frisbee.

# THE STORY I WASN'T
# GOING TO TELL

W hen I left for Louisiana State University, I thought my relationship with Tony was over. But a month later, the receptionist at my dorm left a note on my door: "Your boyfriend will be here this weekend."

*Huh*, we talked on the phone all the time. He never told me he was moving south.

At home for the holidays, I told my mom. "We're going to get an apartment, but don't worry, we'll get married."

Her face dropped. Because of all her thou-shalt-nots, I'd assumed she'd be glad we had wedding plans. But she shook her head and begged, "Please don't."

*What?* There is just no pleasing that woman.

And now I had Tony, whose desires played a mean tug-of-war with my parents' expectations. I thought I'd thrown them away. But nope. I attended accounting classes for Dad while cleaning twelve houses a week to pay my half of the bills with Tony while dulling my angst by smoking another joint.

"You're *living in sin*," Mom accused, since we were still not properly married.

When things like that bugged my conscience, I found a way to justify what I was doing. It probably had something to do with Dad always telling me I did everything wrong.

Texas was a common-law state. Once I signed Tony's last name as mine on a car I bought, we were married. That was easy. Even though I'd always dreamed of a big ceremony, so much for fairy tales, right? He and I lived out our addictions happily ever after; well, not really. If you've ever straddled a fence, you know it flippin' hurts.

Here's the odd part. Dad knew we fought over Tony's drinking, so what did he give Tony for Christmas . . . a beer stein. Tony and I chuckled—a practiced, brittle sound. Not a laugh at all. We didn't have the nerve to do anything else.

If Dad would just give Tony a chance, he'd see the good, wouldn't he?

Deep down, I didn't admit it to myself then, but I wouldn't have wanted a life of addiction and all that came with it for my daughter either. I would have tried to peel her away from that lifestyle and everyone in it. Who wouldn't? In reality, Tony and I were both broken in different ways and, of course, our families were, too.

Most Friday nights, we partied with our neighbors in the apartment complex as the weekend stretched before us like a cat preening in the hot sun. The smell of marijuana-laced the air as Led Zeppelin, Tony's favorite band, blared from the stereo speakers. Those were the sweet moments.

We were having fun, doing laundry in our third-hand mismatched washer and dryer, and hosting dinner parties with two and a half forks. We were happy, except on *those* nights . . .

Like the time we visited friends for dinner. At a previous gathering, I'd confessed. "Pills and alcohol are not a good mix for Tony."

Did our host think I was kidding?

While I hung out in the kitchen with his wife, he slipped Tony a Mandrax, which is a downer. When Tony started slurring his words and lost coordination after only just opening his second beer, my eyes landed on our host. "You didn't."

Red-faced, he laughed.

"We've got to go," I stood.

"No, you don't," he shook his head.

We both realized it was too late when Tony fell to the floor, digging through his pocket for his keys. I looked back at our host. "Would you mind driving us home?"

"You'll be all right. You're just fifteen miles down the road."

"Asshole," I muttered under my breath on my way out.

I hated those nights, wondering if we'd make it home. I loved Tony but not the cost of his addictions. Unfortunately, they came as a package deal.

Over and over, "It'll never happen again," echoed throughout our home. But we never quit partying. Even after an AA meeting, the cycle continued. I'd never thought about how long it had taken to get this messed up, and how it might take more than one meeting to break free. I thought we had given it a chance.

Too many times, I'd said, "Promise-promise-*promise?*"

He'd agree and things would settle down for a month or two. Those were the quiet weeks, when he brought me flowers, took me to dinner, and only had a beer or two. Those glimmers of hope kept me hanging on. We went where I wanted and did what I asked. I got used to life like that. But of course, Tony got sick of yielding. He hated conflict, so he'd agree with me, then do what he wanted behind my back. As he drank, I lost the upper hand. I ignored things for a while, hoping *it* wouldn't happen again.

The *be right backs* turned into nights out. Tony got trashed and didn't come home. I'd retaliate by temporarily moving in with whatever friend would take me. For seven and a half years, we cycled. From best behavior to here-a-slip/there-a-slip down the lo-o-ong slide of barely-holding-it-together until another blowout. Then we'd get back up and do it again.

Thing is, we didn't know how to do *healthy*. We did our best, and for a while, that was enough, until BAM! I drove my car into a ditch. I'd been hounding Tony. Thursday afternoon, I met him at the door after work. "Haven't got it yet."

"What?" He squinted into the sun as if he didn't know what I was talking about.

"My freakin' period!" I reached for another cigarette.

"What do you want me to do?" He pushed by, dropped his keys on the counter, and reached for the pot to roll a joint. "What's the big deal? If you're pregnant, we'll have a kid."

"Now? Are you kidding?"

"Why not?"

"I'm working my ass off to get through college so I can get a better job. Who'd take care of a kid so I could do that?"

"I would!" He put both hands on the counter, leaned in close, and tried to kiss me. I drew back. We dealt with this like everything else, with drugs, alcohol, and humor—an odd brand of humor.

The next afternoon, I sat on my neighbor's porch quelling my fears with Margaritas when Tony pulled into our driveway. The UPS guy followed and jumped out of the truck with a box. I went over, signed, tore open the package, and laid aside a new copy of *Weird Things You Never Knew Existed*. I rummaged through the wrappings, and plucked out something extra, a double F cup bra.

Tony spit a mouthful of beer across the porch. "What are *you* going to do with that?"

I gave him the look, put everything back in the box, and set it on the floor. Without a word, I marched into the kitchen to make another drink. Two and a half hours later, Tony slipped away from the crowd that had gathered at our neighbors'. He scaled the fence behind us and climbed the microwave tower.

On the way back over the railing, an electric jolt threw him to the ground. I didn't know any of this until my neighbor took me aside and said, "Your man just cheated death." He pointed to the top of the tower where the giant bra waved in the breeze like the flippin' flag at Dollywood. Proof he'd made it to the top.

Once I saw Tony was up and walking, I grabbed a half-empty gallon of wine off the table and my neighbor. "C'mon, we're leaving." Inside my '76 Cougar, I clutched the steering wheel and shook my head, "I can't do this anymore."

I watched as the guys congratulated Tony. He must have asked where I was because one of them pointed at us and he started in our direction. That's when I shoved the key in the ignition and stepped on the accelerator.

We roared down the road.

Fifteen minutes later, my friend and I crawled out of a ditch. Instead of leaving my vehicle there for the night, Tony got in his truck to retrieve it in an attempt to gain my forgiveness. I slept at the other end of the hall that night.

After work on Monday, I pulled into the driveway. My neighbor stood on her front porch, waving, "C'mere," then stepped inside her kitchen as I jogged across the lawn.

Without making eye contact, she rifled through a drawer. "Can I get you some Kool-Aid?"

"Naw, I'm good." I stood with my hand on the doorknob. "S'up?"

She finally looked me in the eye. "Tony left. Quit his job and left."

"Left?" I gasped as if the air had been sucked from my lungs. I slumped into a chair. "Left." *It was the same thing he did last time I told him I was pregnant.*

# MY KIDS DON'T
# DESERVE THIS

On my own, at home, I didn't want to think, didn't want to feel, and barely wanted to breathe. I reached for the couch to steady myself, eased down onto it, and leaned back. I folded my knees to my chest, wrapped my arms around them, laid my chin on top, and closed my eyes. *Shit!*

Inside, emotion shot through me like a cue ball breaking on a pool table—click-clack-clash-sh-sh—from one stage of grief to another. Denial, anger, bargaining, depression, acceptance[3] were all duking it out in my head at the same time.

How could Tony do this to me? How did I let it happen, not once, but twice?

When I was seventeen, I got pregnant. After promising to stick around, Tony left. A friend of mine had scared him as she told him, "Her parents are going to drag your ass through court!"

She meant well. But after that, I was alone. Guilt weighed heavily on me.

No adults knew, but I felt like everyone at school was laughing at me behind my back. I didn't have anyone to grieve with. I didn't really have the words, anyway. Not just about his departure, but also for what I chose to do with my baby.

On top of all that, my heart still loved Tony, even though the rest of me felt totally humiliated. I tried to bury my pain, but that never works. It always leaks out somewhere.

In my hometown, abortion was a form of birth control. One girl laughed at me because I was so upset. She'd had five. Five! I didn't want to have one, but what else could I do? At least, that's what the voice in my head kept repeating before it threatened, "What if your parents find out?"

The disapproval and death of their expectations was more than I could bear. I took care of it. I got rid of my consequences and had a hard time admitting that I'd terminated a pregnancy. I even pretended everything was fine as giant blood clots filled the maternity pads in my underpants.

Six months later, Tony came back and said, "Why'd you get rid of the baby?"

Seriously? "Because you fuck'n left!"

When I heard he was coming home, I couldn't stop myself from getting excited. I took him back without any consequences for what he did and felt betrayed by myself once again.

And now it was happening a second time.

I screamed into the empty living room, "You wonder why I don't want kids. I do. I want three, two girls and a boy, Ashley, Julian, and Andréa, just not like this because how could I take care of them by myself? And I gotta be ready because you *LE-E-EAVE!*"

I took a deep breath, let it out slowly, and crumpled before whispering, "And I can't abort a baby, my baby, not again."

There, I said it.

Listless, I got up off the couch and rounded the bar, opened the cabinet and reached for the Texas-shaped ashtray on the top shelf. *Good, enough pot to roll a joint.* I fished around inside the coffee cups searching for rolling papers and finally found an old pipe. Back on the couch, I grabbed the lighter on top of a pack of Virginia Slims, stuffed the pipe full, and lifted it to my lips. The pot crackled and the air filled with the old, familiar smell. I took a giant hit. I leaned my head back on the couch, closed my eyes, and held my breath longer than I ever had before.

"You're always high," a friend had recently said. "But I don't see any difference in the way you act. Why do you smoke pot?" Until she'd asked, I hadn't really thought about it. For years I'd smoked four, maybe five times a day. Again, her question echoed. *Why?*

The answer was simply because getting high takes the edge off, dulls the pain of the constant agony of never living up to everybody's expectations, or even just my own.

For a while, I can ignore the ache of past rejection and over-look that massive emptiness inside. What the hell was that? My voice bounced off the hollow, dark walls of a cavity nothing could fill. Not drugs or alcohol, men or friends. The thing seemed big enough to hold the freaking world. How could I be so empty?

I had lots of acquaintances I called friends, but still, I felt lonely in the middle of parties. Instead of enjoying who came, I'd focus on who didn't and take it personally. *They don't like me.*

And Tony, I loved him, right? I must if I keep taking him back.

But if I was honest with myself, I got back together with him the first time he left because I thought I could reverse the effects of his rejection by regaining his acceptance. I could become somehow *unrejected*, as if that makes any sense.

In front of my friends, I felt like an idiot. Why weren't they calling me on my stupid decisions? If I was helping them, I'd like to think that's what I would have done.

But staying with Tony was my choice. That's what I wanted. No one telling me what to do, right? I'd planned to spend the summer with him after he came home. Then I would leave like he had left me. I just didn't expect him to follow.

It's not like I regretted our years together. If we didn't wind up in one hot mess after another, it'd be different. Now I felt like I'd wasted seven years trying to make it work. And I struggled because I'd been raised that you only marry once. You *make* it work. That's what God wants.

Was I even married? All this time I'd justified our relationship as common law, but was it? If I left, did I have to get divorced when I never even got to have a wedding? *Shit!*

And what is normal in a relationship? How do you know when it's time to leave?

I sat back on the couch and rocked back and forth, hummed, then sang Brahms' Lullaby. "Lu-la-by-y and good-night, la la la la, la la la, la la la la."

\* \* \* \* \*

The next day, Tony returned.

Yup, *again* he left thinking I was pregnant. And *again*, he came back. And *again*, I breathed a sigh of relief. What was wrong with me?

I wanted to change, but I didn't know how. Every year I'd write *quit smoking* on top of my goal list. And *cut back on pot.* It was illegal and living an illicit lifestyle gnawed on me. I tried ignoring the ongoing stress, but it stole my peace. I'd stopped taking LSD and hated the way cocaine affected us—maybe not the buzz, but the look that came over Tony's face. As we ran low, he'd push past me to our stash of cash.

"No!" I'd scream. But I couldn't stop him. Not when he got like that.

So, here we were, seven and a half years after that ride in Mike's Camaro, living under the same roof without any real connection. I'd gotten my period. I wasn't pregnant, just late. That Friday night, like every other week, we went to dinner, sat across from each other, and made small talk. This flippin' carnival ride wasn't doing either of us any good.

I wanted to stop, but how?

What I know now but didn't know then was that it's possible to change. AA and programs like them have helped a lot of my friends who've wanted to quit. Those last words were key. I didn't say it was easy, but it was possible.

I tolerated a few more cycles till I sat stuck to the couch, rooted as if my life depended on it. Maybe it did.

Shivering, I pulled myself up and walked down the hall into the spare bedroom and leaned into the closet to reach for a blanket. That's when I heard it. Someone whispered inside my head, "You can choose this lifestyle for yourself, but your kids don't deserve it."

I froze. The voice sounded different from the me-I-was-used-to. Who was it? I didn't know, but the words rang truer than any I'd ever heard. Stuck in a whirlpool for so long, I didn't know of a life preserver that could save me until I heard those words. *My future children.* I'd never thought about them before, not in this context. Immediately, I quit trying to figure out where the thought came from and reached for a suitcase instead of a blanket.

I cared about Tony. I was sorry—downright heartbroken—but I couldn't change him or change myself for him. I loved him as only a twenty-four-year-old, codependent drug user could, but our plan was to be happy, and I wasn't. For the first time, I decided to *be there* for myself. I wasn't sure how, but I was ready to give it a go.

Out of habit, I rolled another joint and smoked it as I packed up my knickknacks, my music boxes, and my salt and pepper shaker collection. *The Legend of the Sand Dollar* stopped me. I'd bought the little box on a weekend away. I looked down at the story and read again about how sand dollars have a star in the center. Just like the one the shepherds followed to find Jesus as a baby. They also have four holes like the nails that held Him to the cross. A Poinsettia was on one side, the kind of flower used to decorate at Christmas—the celebration of His birth. And an Easter lily was on the other, the blossoms churches honor Him with in death. "Now break the center open and here you will release five white doves waiting to spread goodwill and peace."

"Peace please!" I sighed as I read the poem's ending. "This simple little symbol Christ left for you and me to help spread His Message through all eternity."

# WANDERLUST, THE
# DADDY-APPROVED
# ESCAPE PLAN

So, I moved home to Boston. Trouble was, so did Tony. But since I was living with my parents, he stopped turning up late, and drunk, like he had been after I left him. I knew I was doing the right thing, but now what? I couldn't stay with my parents. We'd kill each other. And Dad must have been getting to me because I was beginning to believe I needed a purpose or a pat on the back. Or maybe a kick in the right direction?

Then it happened. I got one from Tony.

On a night out with friends, I ran into him at a bar. As he followed me into the ladies' room, I hissed, "Get away from me."

"I just want to dance." He held out his hand.

"I left, remember? No more!" I pointed my finger in his face then slid back into the crowd, scanning the bar for my girlfriend as I bit my lower lip. *Where'd she go?* Suddenly Tony grabbed my arm and spun me around. Time to get out before it got ugly.

"I want to talk to you!" he screamed.

"I'm done. Get it?" I wrenched my arm free from his grasp.

And as if in slow motion, he reached over my head, tipped his beer, and emptied it. Gobsmacked, I dropped my jaw and glared at him as a stranger stepped between us. "The lady asked you to leave her alone."

Then it happened. Who threw the first punch? I don't know, but at last my girlfriend whisked me away. I blubbered into the front door at home well past 1:00 a.m. Dad sat in his brown recliner in front of the TV, as usual. He barely noticed me 'til I parked myself in front of him on a stool. He batted his hand as I wailed, motioning me to get out of the way so he could see the screen. "What do I do, Dad? I left him, but he keeps following me."

"Who?" Then it registered. He had a chance to keep me apart from Tony, but how?

Nervously, Dad glanced around the room. "You, uh, like to travel. Want me to help you go somewhere?" And there it was, my pat on the back!

"Yes, I do." My anguish vanished, just like that. Wow, Dad and I agreed on something; that hardly ever happened. He matched the thousand dollars I'd saved and suddenly I had a nest egg! Right there and then, it started my wanderlust.

As my motivation grew, so did my number of jobs. I maxed out at eight doing things like catering, house cleaning, and hosting home parties selling lingerie and sex toys. Dressed as a French maid in fishnet nylons, I ran past Dad on my way to work one day. He did a double take. "You look like a professional, but we won't say what."

Whatever. I made a hundred dollars an hour. The cash piled up pretty quickly.

Six months later, I'd saved three thousand dollars for the cost of the trip to Africa, plus eight dollars a day to spend while I was there. I didn't think I'd need a lot in the jungle or the desert.

After working so hard, I needed decompression time. I cleared my schedule and took *thinking walks*. That first night I smoked a joint behind the house. Then I sprayed Opium perfume to cover the smell in case I ran into anyone as I headed to Rock-hill Cemetery, my playground when I was little, a place to make out in high school, and now a dog park. With the family Sheltie on a leash, I shuffled through fallen leaves.

Was I doing the right thing? Since I grew up always being told I was doing it wrong, I always wondered.

Unwrapping a package of Necco Wafers, I pulled out the chocolate ones and the strong minty ones. Munching through the roll, I'd treat myself every now and then with one of my faves. A brown one, then a pink. There behind my grandparents' graves, that's where I saw the first rabbit. An eastern cottontail. His stare penetrated me with a knowing look. I didn't think much about it—not until it happened three weeks in a row and on walks in totally different towns. It looked like the same rabbit, but I'd never noticed bunnies in this part of the country.

By the third time, I got goosebumps. The presence of the little guy filled the space between us. I know this sounds crazy, but I wondered if he might be God.

Who else could inhabit a rabbit? If God created nature, He must have the power to do that. The more I thought about it, the more convinced I was that only God knew where I'd be, and He came. But why would He visit me? I don't know, but it didn't freak me out. Inside this rabbit, God wasn't all up in my face telling me what to do. He was just there, and He seemed to approve of, I don't know, everything? Me, my plans, and thinking time.

I told my friend. "Yeah, right!" she laughed. "You were high."

Yeah, but this had *never* happened before. And I wasn't looking for God, but I didn't mind. In fact, I kind of liked it.

The experience sparked something. I began to notice things like the skinny pamphlets Mom left by the toilet. *Our Daily Bread*, God books. Did she leave them for me? You know, it was some sneaky way of sharing her faith because it worked. Every time I sat down, I grabbed one for a quick read. Each time, the words spoke directly into the situations of my life with uncanny timeliness. I'd glance at the ceiling, half-expecting to see God peeking through the corner of the roof. Maybe I should have asked for direction. Aside from putting Tony in my rearview mirror, I wasn't sure what I was doing as I threw my pack into my sister's car to catch my flight to Africa.

She rolled her eyes and pointed at my new pink high-tops, "I can't believe *you* are going to camp for six months and *those* are your Africa shoes."

# RE-ENTRY

A nd already, here I was on the plane heading home.
"Put your tray tables up and return your seats to their
upright position." The flight attendant's announcement startled
me. "We'll be landing in New York shortly."

Home for dinner with that upcoming face-to-face with Dad,
my stomach twitched. Both comforting and unnerving, but like
Truth said, he and I had common ground. A desire for me to find
something meaningful to do with my life. Now if we could only
agree on what that was.

"Do you write?" Truth broke into my bleary stupor as we
taxied to the gate.

"Avid letter writer," I searched my bag for my passport. "I
always want to know what happens next."

"No, Sweetie. Do you journal? Write articles?"

"Funny you should ask. I always knew I would, but what
would I say?"

She laughed. "Why don't you take your sneakers off and rest?
Stop trying to please everyone. Because you know you can't,
right?" She grabbed my hand and put the rest of her M&M's into
it, then looked more deeply into my eyes than anyone ever had.
"I'm thinking about your quiet nights under the stars. Why don't
you take some time to listen? I wonder what you'd hear."

Truth's suggestion lingered in my mind long after she passed
through customs ahead of me.

What else had she said? "You don't need it, but you have my permission to choose your own path."

"With wild abandon," I said to myself on the flight from New York to Boston. "If I'm going to do what she suggested, I'm going to do it full-on." *What would that look like?*

Then, ready or not, I burst through the entryway of the international terminal at Logan Airport. Lights, camera, and (after the laid-back lifestyle in Africa) way too much action, caused me to blink then shiver as the February chill embraced me. In front of me were too many faces, with people waving signs. I squinted at the crowd. Mom grabbed me first. As she buried her face in my braids, she spoke through tears. "At last!"

Victoria, my younger sister, clutched me in one of her bone-crunching hugs. And Catherine, the youngest, at twenty, said, "Waiting for you to get home took forever!"

Not one for emotion, Dad gave me an awkward squeeze and mumbled, "Welcome back, Lamb."

The happy-to-see-you looks combined with knowing-you-could-have-died hugs were quite different from the bon-voyage on the African tarmac only hours before. After the long flight and the drive from the airport, I stepped inside my parents' house and grabbed the cat as she ran past, taking a deep breath of the cold on her fur. *Mm!* This was another sharp contrast from the burning-trash smells of Africa. Scamper wriggled free and raced to her bowl without any idea how good she had it.

I ran hot water in the tub for my long-awaited bath and emptied a box of Mr. Bubbles into it. Favoring my left hand, I peeled off the bandage with my right as bits of glass bubbled out in pus. I undressed and eased down into the water, thinking about all the times my African travel mates and I had itemized things we missed. Hot baths always ranked at the top of my list.

Now I thought about what I longed for from Africa. I ran to meet the mailman every day, looking for letters from Kathy, Clive, and Shane. After four months of always being able to turn to my friends, it was weird to be without them. No one else understood the life-changing experiences we'd shared.

As far as people at home were concerned, I'd only been gone a few months. But I'd returned a different person. Not only having grown in my understanding of other cultures, now I was also a vessel of mixed emotion. Grateful to be alive but grieving. Glad to lay eyes on loved ones but pining. I lifted myself from the water, ran a finger through the thick brown ring in the tub, and reached for a towel.

The busy pace of the East Coast was no longer my normal. Friends rushed past, "How was your trip?" No one stopped long enough for more than the anticipated, "Great!"

At a bar one night, I met a guy and gave him my phone number. On the way home, I said to Victoria, "I hope he calls."

"He won't," she gloated.

"Why not?" I smacked her in the arm.

"When you went to the bathroom, he asked me how we could be sisters when I'm white and you're black."

"*What?*" With the braids in my hair and darker skin tone, I'd changed, not only inside, but outside. "He doesn't want to go out with me because he thinks I'm black?" Again, the disparity— no, the outright *prejudice and discrimination*. They were easier to name after being on the receiving end.

I missed sitting by the fire, conversing and connecting in Africa.

Of course, I wanted—even needed—to talk about what happened. Not only about the slower pace or the absence of schedule, but about the camel we tasted, and the pyramids we scaled. I wanted to talk about the puddles we squatted beside as we counted hundreds of butterflies, the ferns we stroked which curled their fronds in response to our touch, and the accident that took my friend's life. I wanted to recall how one moment I ate dinner with her, and the next, it seemed, I attended her funeral.

The amalgamation of emotion heaped into a mound I didn't recognize, but Mom did. Having battled depression, she strategized to spare me from what she knew too well. *Ffflt*, she let the shades fly. "C'mon, get out of bed. First stop, Aunt Chic's house. I told her you'd balance her checkbook and take her shopping. She'll pay you. Then you and I can go to Friendly's for peppermint ice cream."

Weirdly enough, Mom became my new best friend. With her help, I transitioned faster than I would have on my own. She really did love me. And I wanted her to take care of me, save me, and tell me what she thought. It's just that I hoped she could do it without bossing me around.

I appreciated the way Truth, my safe-to-share-with stranger, wanted to know my desires, saw me like no one else had, and offered depth in relationship. She helped me realize I'd rather *go deep* in meaningful one-on-ones any day. I wanted to know and be known. Truth stepped in, listened, and named what she saw rather than saying what I wanted to hear. She wasn't afraid to state the obvious and identify things others didn't dare. Amidst the constant roar of the plane, her quiet voice helped me hear my thoughts. Even own some for the first time. Truth made me realize how cool it is to be heard—not only my words, but also my heart; even when it's a little scary. I suppose all that is easier without a long-term investment.

Home with the ones who loved me most, I didn't tell them I wished I could get back on the traveling horse and ride off in another direction. The only thing stopping me was money. I didn't have any.

Without someone ordering me around (because that was NOT what I wanted) I didn't know what to do. Why didn't I get Truth's number? I'd planned to slow down and listen, but in the familiarity and busyness, I forgot about that. And about working on common ground with Dad. And God. After all He'd done, it's as if I left Him lying under the bed like a discarded teddy bear.

Who am I kidding? I treat my childhood stuffed animal Ted better than that.

# WILD ABANDON,
# HERE I COME!

A few weeks after I got home from Africa, I sat on the stool in my family's apartment-sized kitchen and attempted to figure out my life with Dad during his lunch hour. Dressed in his usual work attire, a white shirt and black pants, he shoveled a ham sandwich into his mouth as he spoke. "You can't travel your life away. It's time to grow up and get a job."

So much for a daddy-approved escape plan. Wanderlust taught me who I was and who I wasn't. I wasn't ready to give it up yet. I guess living my life with wild abandon was going to include standing up to Dad.

From his bolo tie, a Tiger Eye stared me down. For a minute, I pretended I was back in Africa, face-to-face with the king of the jungle instead of just the king of my jungle. Blah, blah, blah, then "fuck around" got my attention. Dad always said *damn*, but never *fuck*. And I didn't hear that word back then like I do now. We said *fuck*, but not to Dad. For him to say *the f word* out loud to me in conversation, well . . . he meant business. "You got lucky with your back, but when it comes your hand, we need to do what we can to fix it."

Sure enough, I flippin' broke my back! I got a compression fracture on my T12 vertebrae. *How the heck was I still walking around?* Apparently, that happens. I asked the doctor, "What do we do now?"

"We let it heal on its own."

I liked that plan because I'd purchased trip insurance, but the mounting American medical bills consumed the payout fast. I didn't want to owe Dad for bailing me out, though he wouldn't have required that. And I didn't want him to remind me of his help in the years to come, though he wouldn't have done that either. I guess I struggled with pride as much as with him.

The problem was that the various tests and subsequent surgery cost a lot with no guarantee of returning feeling to my fingers; nerve damage is like that. My parents and I finally agreed. "Let's schedule a study and see what the doctor recommends."

Two weeks later, Mom and I waited for the nurse to take me back to a room.

"Elizabeth Bristol?"

I followed her down the hall and into a room with a technician. I sat on an exam table as he hooked my hand to some wires. Then I watched him step inside a glass booth. Like in a hearing test, I was to lift my forefinger as feedback. But this time it was because an electric jolt zapped my wounded hand. *What the heck?* As the pain intensified, I almost lifted a different finger. Instead, I kept my cool. I signaled as before, though now I gave him *the look*, expecting him to stop. But he didn't.

When the test was finally over, I whimpered and lurched my way down the hall to Mom, my new place of refuge. She got up from her chair and raced over to hug me as the receptionist called out the next victim.

"Irene Whitmore."

Irene couldn't peel her eyes off me. I knew she was worried she'd come back out in worse shape, like me. I attempted a weak smile. She looked from the administrator waiting for her to the door, as if she might bolt. They need two separate waiting rooms for that procedure.

* * * * * *

At home that night, Sue called. She was the driver's girlfriend and my bulk-food mentor from the Africa trip. "Oy, mate!"

Just the pick-me-up I needed. "Where are you?"

"Connecticut on Saturday."

"Are you kidding?" I scrambled for a pen and some paper.

"I'm interviewing for a cook's position on a charter sailboat heading to the Caribbean. Can you meet for lunch?"

"Better believe it." I squirmed with more than a little jealousy. "The Caribbean?"

"I'll tell you about it when I see you, and I want to know every detail about Africa after I left—the accident, who's hooked up, everything."

Ah, I sighed as I hung up. She knows the players in my stories and wants to hear them. I thought Saturday would never come.

As I walked in the door of the address Sue gave me, I heard a man's voice say, "The job's yours if you want it." I rounded the corner and saw that he looked like the human version of a nautical figurine which you'd find in a novelty shop.

I smiled wistfully, happy for Sue as she introduced us. But over lunch I could barely focus as she told me about the offer and all the travel it included. While I re-acclimated into small-town life, she was off on another adventure.

Heading back to the parking lot, we passed Captain Bill on the street. He looked at me and said, "With a crew of four, we could sure use help. Do you want to come?"

*Sail. To St. Thomas?* I grabbed Sue. "Is he serious?"

"I am!" He winked.

Like a *get out of jail free* card, his words caused an instant dance party. I took them home with me. Driving up I-95, the travel bug surged through my veins, but there was also that familiar struggle. Should I stay and get the stupid operation the hand doctor recommended, or go and let it heal on its own like the spine doctor said we'd do with my back?

The trip seemed like a no-brainer, yet after the accident, the thought of another adventure scared me a little. Thing is, I didn't want to side with fear. At home I walked round and round the lake behind our house, dithering. It never occurred to me to ask God.

Two days later I called Captain Bill. "I'm in, if the offer still holds?"

"Sure does! Did I tell you the owners of the boat are producers for Universal Studios? They've invited us to be their guests at the grand opening of the amusement park in Florida."

Woo hoo! I called Sue. "I'm coming!"

Then I went looking for Dad and found him watching TV in the living room. I stepped in front of him. He motioned for me to get out of the way until I said, "I'm not having surgery."

"Dammit," he glanced up from his chair, "what are you thinking?"

"I'm not going through a painful procedure they can't promise will work."

He grimaced with a wisdom and disappointment I didn't understand.

I turned on my heels. Decision made, I climbed the stairs two at a time. Then I heard a voice in my head, "Don't go!"

I stopped, but just for a second. After all the warnings I'd experienced with God in Africa, you'd think I might have stopped and listened as Truth had suggested. I hate to admit it, but I kept God at a distance. Why? With so many people telling me what to do—well, two—I didn't want another. I convinced myself that *fear*, a familiar wrestling partner, was attempting to scare me away from fun, and I packed a bag.

Just because I'd experienced an accident while traveling, I told myself, it didn't mean anything would go wrong this time. So, on May 13, 1990, my sister Victoria drove me to Connecticut. As Victoria, Sue, and I stood next to the boat, the voice in my head grew louder. With my backpack on, I wavered. "I don't know what to do."

"Please stay?" Sue begged.

"Make up your mind." Victoria dangled her keys. "I've got to go. Comin' or not?"

"Ple-e-ease?" Sue mouthed.

The internal battle raged on. Needled me. As I said, people think I'm brave. I'm not. I hate when someone rocks the seat of the Ferris wheel. But more than that, I hate to let fear get the better of me. Against the advice of the voice in my head, I got on that boat.

Fear could go to hell.

# DARK AND STORMY NIGHTS

On the boat, Sue and I spent that first day doing what seemed like a meaningless task: varnishing. Wax on, wax off. I was just like the boy in the movie *The Karate Kid* who'd asked his teacher to show him how to fight. He'd spent days taking orders and working like a slave until he finally exploded. "We had a deal! You're supposed to teach, and I'm supposed to learn."

"Not everything is as seems," his teacher said, as he lunged at the boy. The kid responded with defensive moves that had become automatic—strengthened through the repetition of the monotonous tasks. "Look eye," his teacher said, "always look eye."

That was my problem. I'd stopped "looking eye" with God, my new instructor.

I'd slid back into self-reliance as if I knew better than He did. But that didn't mean He'd abandoned me or stopped sending messages. In fact, He was about to put the puzzle together; I just didn't see it coming.

\* \* \* \* \* \*

After work, Sue and I made our way around the corner from Pilot's Point Marina to a local pub. We hopped onto a couple of stools at the bar next to the dance floor across the room from Captain Bill. The bartender arched her brow in our direction. "Two of those funny concoctions?"

Sue nodded then turned toward me, "You'll love these. Dark rum mixed with ginger beer and bitters." With the sky as clear as could be, that first drink, a *Dark and Stormy,* went down way too easily.

Six years older than I was, Sue had gained my trust in Africa. Now, eight months later, in another country, on a different bar stool, I continued looking up to her as she told me how the sailing gig came about. "When I taught school in Australia, Simon, my husband-at-the-time, bought a boat. After we separated, I joined the Woollahra Sailing Club and spent weekends racing with guys who needed crew."

"So, fill me in." I leaned closer. "Why's this boat in Connecticut if they charter out of St. Thomas?"

"Last year," she began as she glanced around to make sure Bill was out of earshot. We'd learned quickly to be careful what we shared with him because he didn't think the same as we did, often surprising us with his reactions. Even though we weren't one of his girlfriends, he was possessive. "They beached the boat," she continued, "You *never* want to do that."

"What happened?"

"As the wind and waves rose," Sue lowered her voice and got her storytelling on. "Bill and the crew stayed on board, glued to the radio's ongoing report about Hurricane Hugo heading their way. They held out as long as they could. At the last minute, he released the anchors and steered toward shore while his crewmembers hung tightly, bracing for a collision."

"Did he tell you that?"

"No, I've been piecing things together from different sources. After the storm, the crew went to a shelter. Locals welcomed the shipwrecked survivors, offered blankets and snacks. Over a hundred people died in that storm which caused ten-billion-dollars-worth of damage. Bill and Andre, our first mate, flew to Connecticut toward the end of the refit and hired the new crew, you know, when we met for lunch. As soon as the marina gets the insurance check, they'll release us to go."

"Just out of curiosity," I grabbed her arm. "When's hurricane season?"

"Starts next week."

"You better be joking!" I hailed the bartender. "Two more, please, and I wouldn't mind if they were doubles." A catchy beat initiated our move to the dance floor. I slid from my stool, glad to ditch that conversation.

*Hurricane season?* As I passed Captain Bill, I heard him brag, "I found four pretty girls to crew for me." Was that the standard he used to hire? Uh oh!

By closing time, Bill's rental car bulged with people. Among the mix, I looked down and wondered, *Is that my arm or someone else's?* Unfazed by the lack of room inside the car, Kim, the stewardess, grabbed hold of a windshield wiper and climbed aboard. She crawled onto the middle of the hood, leaned back, and yelled, "Woo hoo!" as we careened from the parking lot.

"I'm goin' out," I told Sue. As Bill drove, she and I climbed through the car window to join Kim. Trouble was, now Bill couldn't see a thing. Somehow, we made it back to the marina. The car lurched to the side as he pulled the keys from the ignition and got out. Should this have clued me in to how the trip would proceed? Probably.

With beers still in our hands, free of all inhibition, Sue, Kim, and I helped each other stand on the hood of the car to shine moons at the boys.

"I want to go for a swing!" Sue pointed to the boatlifts. We pulled up our pants, scrambled off the car, and raced across the cement. Scaling the ropes, we sat side-by-side and swung our legs, propelling ourselves over the water. That's all I remember.

The next morning, Sue and I woke up in my bed together, which was a surprise to us both. I rolled over to face her and she said in a muffled voice, "Oh good, it's you."

It was often a shock who ended up together at the end of each night.

The days passed, one blending into the next while we waited for the harbormaster to release us. From nine to five, Sue and I formulated menus and shopped for the thousand-mile, three-day trip down the coast. At night we hit the bar and got to know the crew members on all the boats. And just when we thought we'd never leave, Captain Bill gathered us together, Andre, Kim, Sue, Karen (one of Bill's girlfriends) and me. Bill smashed a bottle of champagne over the bow, "We've got the paperwork. We leave in an hour."

"Waste of good alcohol," I muttered to Sue as we circled the harbor saying good-bye. "Why not a toast?"

"It's tradition, for safe travels."

"Well, then." I clapped my hands. "I'm all about that!" But every fiber in my being cringed when I remembered the warning, *Don't go!*

Sue spun around. "I know this is scary for you. We're going to be okay."

At 3:00 p.m. we motored out of port toward the Gulf Stream with a fancy meal and a movie scheduled for the night. By 7:00 p.m., the rocky seas triggered nausea in one of us, then another, like a mean game of dominos. The kitchen, or "galley" as Bill kept reminding me, held two-thousand-dollars' worth of food. But the swell of the sea coupled with the smell of puke? Well . . . none of us ate dinner that night.

"You okay?" Sue stopped to check on me as she came out of the bathroom and climbed up over my head to her bunk. Avoiding eye contact, I groaned. What had I gotten myself into?

Since the owners weren't on board, we slept in the five staterooms of the main living quarters. Writhing in my double bed, I pressed my stomach up against the corner of the boat, hoping to distract myself from the pain. The uneven rock of the sea tortured me as I longed for sleep in the palpable darkness. I hated those nights, the lack of control and the power that the ocean held. Then and there, I promised God—not Fred-up-close-and-personal, but God-at-a-distance, "You can have whatever You want if only You keep me safe."

If God could control everything, He could have stopped the waves. But He didn't. On those nights, I saw Him as the ocean, an inimitable force I couldn't control and didn't trust. Used to charming others in order to get my way, I was beginning to see that a relationship with God wasn't going to go down that way, and it scared me.

The next morning, two hundred miles out to sea and five thousand meters deep, Sue and I stood alongside Bill in the engine room amidst the nauseating smell of diesel when he said, "Afraid I got bad news. Saltwater leaked into the tanks last night and contaminated the fuel. Now we can't use the CD player, the shower, the electric flush toilet or the motor. We're on a sailboat, we'll sail."

Thing is, there was no wind.

In teams, we stood watch for three hours at a time, keeping an eye on the boat and our surroundings, as well as looking out for pirates. Seriously. Pirates were a dangerous reality. In the first couple of days at sea, we barely made headway. The boat drifted one boring knot after another. "Look at this." I showed Sue the points I'd plotted on the map at the navigation table after our turn. "I think I did it right. But something's wrong?"

"Let's see." She re-plotted. "Uh oh, Bill's going to kill us."

I raised an eyebrow. "What?"

"Remember how mad he got when the Gulf Stream swept us north on our last watch? And when the headsail fell in the water? Well, we're about to catch his wrath again. Somehow, we just made a big circle."

We snickered. What else could we do?

Then Sue looked down and noticed I had my leash on, the harness I wore which attached me to the boat so I wouldn't fall overboard. She laughed again, "What are you wearing *that* for on a flat sea?"

"Because!" I smiled shyly. *I didn't want to share what my gut was telling me. Things were going to get worse.*

Andre and Kim relieved us. We tread the three steps down into the saloon, sat at the dining room table, and created a rationing plan by listing our food on a calendar. "Since we have no electricity," Sue perused her notebook, "the freezer won't keep anything frozen. So, we'll cook and eat that stuff first."

"Since we only provisioned for six days," I bit my lip, "what do we do after, fish?"

"We don't have any poles," Bill informed us as he passed through the cabin. "And from now on I'm banning you two from going on watch together."

Kim bent her head into the saloon. "Did you guys notice the bird on deck? It was a beautiful thing with peach-colored hair almost, instead of feathers."

Sue and I raced up top. Kim joined us.

"What should we name him?" she asked.

"Albert," I didn't think before I spoke. "Albert the albatross."

"Wasn't there a story about that?" Kim put the binoculars down.

"Yeah. *The Rime of the Ancient Mariner.*" In the epic poem, when the breeze stopped, the albatross who had accompanied the ship keeled over, and all the people died of thirst. The story fueled my fear. I instantly regretted the memory.

"Let's take really good care of that bird!" I insisted.

But, sure enough, he got caught in the ropes and died the next day. After his death, we had even less wind than before. Half the trip from Connecticut to Florida had taken two days; the rest crawled into weeks.

You'd think I would have been ready to pray by now. Why was it that I had stopped talking to God? Oh yeah, I didn't want anyone else telling me what to do.

In Africa, I enjoyed His presence. He saved my life at least twice and was totally there for me. But oddly, I didn't want to *need* Him. Used to my own independence, I didn't know how to depend. I saw it as weakness. I was grateful for His help, but I did things He wouldn't approve of, and I wanted to keep doing them. I didn't want Him hanging around, cramping my style, so I thought I could continue straddling the fence. Living my way till I needed help. I thought I was doing just enough to gain what I imagined necessary for His approval. Just enough to pay Him back so I could have the best of both worlds—freedom *and* help. The funny thing is He never bossed me around. He treated me like a friend, but I used Him like a genie in a bottle.

* * * * *

On day thirteen, a ship loomed on the horizon, the first evidence of another human being we'd seen. "We're saved, right, Bill? They'll rescue us?" I asked.

"The ship's too big to pull up alongside." He stared at the map, without the nerve to look me in the eye.

"Can't we radio them and ask for fuel?"

"No, we'll be okay," He ducked downstairs.

"If this isn't the ultimate case of a guy not wanting to ask for directions," I complained. But when Bill found out Sue had a radio operator license, he changed his tune. Suddenly he insisted she call. *What? Was he out here without a license about to bypass help because he didn't want to get busted? You've got to be kidding!*

After making contact, it turned out Bill was right. They couldn't help. So, we continued peeing in buckets, collecting rainwater to drink, and bathing in the sea. Well, not me. The water, so clear I could see barracudas circling below, made the decision to not bathe easy. For thirteen salty days, I wore the same clothes. I had others, but changing took energy, and get-up-and-go charged a premium. For those who swam, Bill advised, "Grab hold of the rope as you jump in. Even though we only drift, you don't want to float away."

That morning Karen stepped to the side of the boat in her skimpy bikini, looked over her shoulder, and smiled at Bill who'd been ignoring her all day. *Great, what are they fighting about now?* She leapt into the sea. Either she ignored his warning and hoped he'd rescue her, or she missed the rope. The current yanked her sideways.

"Swim," I yelled, "fa-a-ast!"

We screamed. She panicked. Quickly, and in slow motion, the distance between us grew. "Je-su-u-us!" Was I swearing or praying?

No one moved. I thought Bill would. Nope, he screamed more than anyone else. Finally, Andre, who had the scar of a shark bite across his chest, jumped in. He battled the sea and saved the flailing girl, bringing her back to safety. We pulled them in, all of us shaken.

Breathing a sigh of relief, I stretched my head and shoulders, trying to relieve the pain in my stress-filled body. I sat down on the seat at the rear of the boat, leaned back on the cushions, closed my eyes, and whispered, "Thank You."

That afternoon, I don't know how we got away with it after Bill's ban, but Sue and I stood watch. She steered the boat, and I sat behind her. Looking out over the sea with binoculars, I noticed a circle of fins. For a minute, I couldn't speak. I grabbed her arm and pointed. "*Sha-a-arks!*"

Having spent summers on Cape Cod, I saw the fake fish in the Martha's Vineyard harbor as they filmed the movie *Jaws*. My nerves were already shot. It didn't take much to freak me out.

How would we fight off a shark if it ate through our boat like the one in the movie?

Just then, dolphins—not sharks—emerged from the sea and surrounded the boat. Sue and I grinned at each other. Leaping and diving, their enthusiasm reminded me how to laugh as they swam alongside, ushering us. It didn't seem to matter where.

Then, early the next morning, back on watch together, Sue put her earphones on and let out a scream, "Listen!"

"If you're due at work by eight-thirty, you've got twelve minutes and that traffic out there is awful." The radio had been out of range for days. Finally, a voice other than our own reminded us of everyday life. For a minute, everything seemed okay. Great, even. A world filled with risks and excitement and dolphins, compared to being stuck in traffic and late for work.

I pointed toward the horizon. "Land ho!"

I couldn't stop chanting until everyone sleeping down below came to see. Bill tried the two-way radio, the one that worked within a twenty-mile range and picked up a signal. Within minutes, he'd contacted an ex-girlfriend and said, "She's flying some fuel out to us."

"I take back everything I said about you, Bill!" I jumped up and down and hugged him at the same time. "Will we make into port in time for happy hour?"

"We'll try." He smiled.

"I know where to go," Kim started planning. "We'll start at the Ocean Deck where they serve oyster shots."

"Sounds good to me," I surveyed the sky and finally caught sight of a small plane. We waved while Bill spoke into the radio, "I see you!"

As we watched expectantly, the plane positioned itself over us. The door opened and two square boxes fell from the sky, splashed into the water right next to us, and flippin' burst into flames! I'm not kidding. We ducked and gripped the rails as the boat pitched. Then I peeked over the side and watched my hopes fizzle as the rest of the fuel burned off.

Plans changed by the minute. We couldn't sail in. The water was too shallow and the current too strong. Andre volunteered to swim in and get more fuel, but the seas picked up, gearing for an afternoon squall. *Shit!* Lightning and strong winds threatened menacingly. Was there too much wind for the sail? The boat tipped. I braced myself, holding tightly to anything that didn't move as water flooded over the side.

"He's over-canvassed," Sue shouted.

*We're going to flip!*

Bill and Andre rushed past, trying to do the work of six sailors while we girls leapt out of the way. "Just give us something to do." The boys yelled at us as if we were useless, but they were the ones who'd thought it was a good idea to weight the crew with inexperienced newbies.

*Shit! Shit! Shit!*

Kim didn't like the way Andre was treating her and, in the middle of the crisis, a lover's spat ensued.

"Stop it!" Bill yelled, "or I'll throw you girls overboard right now."

"Try it!" Kim spun around.

Thank God Sue pulled her aside. "We're almost there. Pull it together and we'll laugh about this at the bar tonight."

Bill screamed into the radio. "Snake, I need your help!"

In what seemed like an eternity after our cry for assistance, a boat surged through the storm. Snake's long ponytail whipped in the wind as he grabbed two red canisters of fuel. His tattooed deltoids bulged out from under his muscle shirt as he heaved one canister up on each shoulder and leapt from his boat to ours over the tempestuous sea. "Where's the party tonight, Babe?" he said as he strode past Kim. Sue rolled her eyes.

Still mad at Andre, Kim smiled and said, "You tell me."

"We've got work to do," Bill interrupted and finally gave us jobs.

The wind and waves rocked us unpredictably. I tried to steady myself as I poured diesel into a tiny hole on the side of the boat without a funnel. The precious liquid splashed all over the place, but the hopes of happy hour in Daytona kept a smile on my face.

"How long has it been since we've had a drink?" *I didn't have the energy to calculate, but it seemed like months. Had it only been days?*

Filled with fuel, the boat no longer held us hostage. We motored into Ponce Inlet Marina late that night. As usual, lassoing the bollard on shore with the mooring line and pulling ourselves into the slip proved to be a problem. With one last fight, we docked and stood on dry land for the first time in weeks. Bill called a taxi and we jumped in, instructing the cabbie in unison, "To the nearest bar."

As everyone raced to place an order, the laser lights stopped me in my tracks. I blinked, waiting for my eyesight to adjust. Slam dancers pushed me back and forth like the waves at sea. The drunken crowd of partiers looked vaguely familiar, like we were, not so long ago. But now, I struggled to relate. The precariousness of life had stolen my . . . was it innocence? No, that was taken long ago. But something had happened.

As I reached the bar, Kim yelled. "Dark and Stormy?"

"No, no more dark and stormy nights for me, thanks. I'll take a beer."

"And a shot coming right up," Kim ordered.

"Nope!" I insisted, "just a beer."

As I sipped, I held onto the bar, watching the rest of the group raise a shot and toast, "To Snake, our savior!"

Wait, the only one I'd ever heard called *savior* was Jesus. And in the Bible, a snake represented the devil in the Garden of Eden—the opposite of a savior.

# HE-E-ELP!

I'd had enough! After the harrowing journey to Fort Lauderdale, I'd packed my bags and fully intended to opt out of the next leg of the trip. I called my friends who lived locally and begged them to rescue me. In the marina, Sue and I sat on deck, waiting for their arrival. I broke the awkward silence, "I'm sorry, but I can't live like this. Scared all the time."

Just then, a yellow Camaro drove into the lot; two girls got out and waved like crazy ladies. I jumped up and ran to greet them, inviting them onboard. "Have a seat and let me get you a beer."

And just like that, with the sun warming my skin, the boat gently bobbing, and friends who wanted to know the story, all became right with my world. On the edge of their seats, they asked, "What happened next?" cheering when they heard how we'd overcome another obstacle.

It turns out that our story made great entertainment. And the weird thing was, the more I spoke of the danger, the less it freaked me out. Terror's ugly face morphed into that of excitement and made me question why I'd packed my bags, seducing me for another kiss.

After a few drinks, Bill caught me at a weak moment. "Why don't you stay?"

"Why wouldn't you?" one of the girls asked me. "You love adventure!"

I looked to Sue who didn't say a word but tried hard to hide her smile. She knew the cracks in my armor.

"Well," I said, "I've made it this far. I might as well."

Initially, I was glad I stayed. The owners of the boat flew in and showed us their gratitude by wining and dining us at every bar in town. They had money and knew how to have fun. If they wanted a pizza at sea, they didn't hesitate to call for delivery, even though it'd take a helicopter to get it to us. They sailed with us for four perfect days, and then we dropped them off at Grand Turk Island and headed toward our final destination, St. Thomas.

No sooner were we back at sea, though, when my nightmare resurfaced. Another storm rolled in. Thirty-foot waves taunted, "Toy boat. Toy boat. Toy boat."

"Three on deck at a time." Bill changed our watch assignments—three hours *on*, three hours *off*. We never had enough sleep, especially with the extra calls in between.

"We've got a problem." He woke us and herded us into the engine room. "Bilge pump's out."

I turned to Sue and mouthed, "What?"

She whispered back discreetly, "The thing that puts the excess water back in the sea."

*That can't be good.* I looked at the pool we stood in as Bill busied himself checking fuses and flicking switches. Then he turned toward me. "Get the vacuum. We'll reverse the water through it."

As if I knew what he was talking about, I found the vacuum cleaner and handed it over. Sue plugged it in. Bill muttered as he fiddled. He couldn't get the hose connected. "Dammit," he shifted gears. "Get buckets, anything that'll hold water."

In minutes, we'd formed a fireman's brigade. Bill handed the full stockpot out the door of the engine room. In his cabin, Andre reached for it and passed it to Kim up the stairs. She gave it to Karen in the cockpit, and I took it from her to hand it to Sue who threw it back in the ocean bucket after bucket. We worked like this till our arms gave way.

Seeing the futility, Bill called it. "Andre, you and Kim take watch. The rest of you get some sleep while I think of another plan."

"Are we gonna sink?" I asked Sue. Too tired to answer, she shrugged and shook her head as she led the way to our quarters.

The next afternoon, two sudden shifts of wind and a squall hit. They slammed us back then forth, holding us hostage at a ninety-degree angle like a gang of bullies on a starboard tack. More asleep than awake, Sue and I made our way back up on deck in response to Bill's screams. Books flew from the shelf with another bang on port tack.

On deck, the sails thrashed in thirty knots of wind and driving rain. Bill pushed me out of the way as he leapt back inside the cockpit and filled the remaining sail with air. "The mainsail's ripped," he screamed over the noise of the storm. "It has to come down."

In its place, we raised the spinnaker.

Finally, the wind and the waves died down. Bill sewed the seam of the mainsail inside the cockpit while I slipped away and returned with a snack, oranges. I peeled and passed them around. "We need to eat, keep up our strength."

"Why're you all wet?" Sue asked.

"Water's up to my armpits in the kitchen. I mean, the galley." A laugh caught in my throat when I saw the alarmed look on Sue's face as she swiveled toward Bill. He ignored her and kept right on sewing, so I tried to do the same. An hour later, another gust of wind snapped, and Bill summoned us back on deck because the spinnaker tore right across the middle.

As long as Sue didn't freak, I was good. She was my rock. This time, though, I saw my fear mirrored on her face. When Bill asked her to cover the helm, she refused, "I can't do it, and I'm not going to pretend I can."

"Well, who else is there?" Bill retorted, and that's when I lost it. Screaming in my head, I stumbled downstairs. Through the porthole in the ceiling, I could see him dangling from the mast out over the now dark sea. I shook my head. *We're never going to live through this.*

Bone-weary, I crawled into bed. With the boat at a ninety-degree angle, I planted my feet shoulder-length apart, braced myself against the wall, holding tightly to the bunk above so I wouldn't fall into the sloshing water below. I pulled my lips over my teeth and bit hard when that threatening voice inside took up a chant, "We're gonna die. We're gonna die."

The boat rose, pitched, and then fell as the bottom dropped out from underneath us. I placed my weight on one foot then the other, the only version of rocking or self-soothing I could muster. Just when I thought we were going down, we crashed. I crumbled. *The boat can't handle this. It's going to fall apart.*

"God, if You save me, I'll do whatever You want!" I whimpered in desperation.

As if I had hit a switch, a presence filled the room. With my eyes open, as if dreaming, but awake, I saw Jesus. I saw him not like I could see Sue lying in the bunk above. Not in physical form, but ethereal. And to my surprise not spooky at all. *"OHMYGOD!"* I said, *"It's YOU?"*

What was it, another dimension?

"No one else could be *here* like this." I gulped, as understanding flooded me. "You've been here. I tried to get away, but You've been here the whole time!" I could see it clearly.

The calm, glowing One smiled, and all of a sudden, I knew. It hadn't been fear telling me not to get on the boat, scaring me away from the fun. It was Jesus trying to spare me the agony of this trip because . . . because He loves me? Yes, He loves me!

And there I'd stood, as if I'd had my hand on His chest, pushing Him away. *What was I doing?* Seeing Him now, I realized we'd been stuck in this pose a long time. I hadn't wanted Him to go in case I needed Him, but I hadn't wanted Him to come inside and control me.

Ever so patiently—suspended in time, but oh-so-very-present—Jesus held out His hand and invited me to dance.

"Yes," I yielded, and something so much more peaceful than peace settled inside even though the storm still raged, and the circumstances hadn't budged. "Let's dance."

Embraced in His arms, I fell asleep—even in the midst of those crazy waves.

* * * * *

The next morning, I rubbed my eyes. What was that bright light? Sun shone through the porthole and filled the room. As I sat up and looked around, the boat rocked gently on the tranquil sea. "Sue," I screamed, "Wake up! We're alive!"

*Had everything been a dream?* Definitely not, but something inside had shifted . . . had changed. I plucked my flip flop from the water as it floated past, high in a way I'd never been before, but I knew why. It was because of Jesus! The catastrophes of the last few days were under control, His control, and I didn't mind that at all.

Miracle of miracles, Bill had actually contacted the Coast Guard. They came and towed us into Puerto Rico. Turns out, our propeller got caught in a fishing net. The guardsman winked at me as he said, "I can't believe you lived through the storm with all the water in the keel along with the six-inch hole in the exhaust system."

Thinking I was making eyes at him, Bill got cranky and misread the situation. But nothing bothered me that morning, not even him. Joy bubbled through my body like supernatural champagne. The calm, shining sea reflected my soul. And I know it sounds corny, but I knew it then. Nothing would ever be the same.

# STRADDLING THE FENCE

It takes a while to get sea legs, but the same goes for land legs after you've been on a boat for a couple weeks. Little did I know, my new friendship with Jesus was like that, too.

In a grand display of appreciation, I climbed over the side of that sailboat and, on quivering knees, kissed the ground. Or rather, the dock. A holy moment. Bill grabbed our passports and dealt with the customs' agent then drained the excess water while we cleaned. Then we went to celebrate.

Sue and I staggered as we attempted to race each other to the bar then to the restroom. "Last night," from inside the stall, I confessed, "I prayed."

"*Prayed*?" She chewed up the word and spat it out.

"Yeah, no big deal." A twinge of betrayal shot through me like a fishhook caught on something. I hated that I hadn't stuck up for my new friend. I wanted a do-over, but instead, I ushered Sue to a table. "Don't know 'bout you, but I'm way past ready for a beer!"

At the bar, Bill sat on a stool arranging my flight home. I'd made it this far, but I was done. For real, this time. He shifted the receiver away from his mouth and whispered, "If you want, you can stay in St. Thomas with my friends who play back-up for . . ."

I shook my head. "I don't care what band." His name-dropping no longer impressed me. I wanted to put my feet on solid ground and move on. Bill got the message and booked a taxi to come at 4:00 a.m. the next morning. And just like that, it was over.

* * * * * *

I landed in Massachusetts, intrinsically changed and surprising even myself with the different choices I made.

As I got dressed to go out with friends, I moved my fishnet nylons to the back of my underwear drawer. Then I winced when one friend asked me to repeat the tale about the time I won the dirty joke contest and got my picture taken with my favorite stripper. I didn't want to tell those stories anymore; I had something better to share. Thing is, I didn't think they'd want to hear. And I didn't have the guts to bring it up.

I didn't want to keep the most important thing in my life to myself, but I'd only told a rare few about the Presence of God I experienced in Africa. As long as my anecdotes were cool and mystical, minus Jesus, my friends liked them.

I got that. I knew what it was like to run from God. Only a few years back, I'd cold-shouldered an ex-boyfriend who tracked me down to tell me about his conversion. *Great, you found Jesus.* I rolled my eyes. Thought he'd completely lost it. Now it freaked me out because I thought, *That's what everyone's gonna think about me.*

How was I supposed to be this new self in the middle of my old world? And why does conversion look so drastically different on the other side of the decision? I meant what I said to Jesus on the boat. But without the urgency of the moment, and if my situation hadn't been so dire, would I have prayed?

No, but it's not like I regretted it. What happened between us was more than a promise. Although I didn't understand everything, I knew for the first time in as long as I could remember that I had peace that didn't come in a bottle or a rolling paper. Jesus had my attention, and I wanted to know what He had to say even if no one else did.

There was no going back.

But what did having Him in my life really mean?

Since I'd promised God on the boat that if He saved me, I'd do what He wanted, it was time to do what my grandmotherly seatmate, Truth, suggested I do after the flight back from Africa. If I wanted to find out what God wanted, I needed to listen.

I went back to Bethany Congregational Church and looked for answers. I even attended Bible study once. Boy, did that give Mom a hot topic of chitchat when I wasn't yet ready to spread the news. She met me at the front door with a big smile on her face, "How was it?"

"Fine," I said, pushing past.

"Your cousin called." I froze, mid-step. I knew the one, my party pal. I imagined a snippet of their conversation. And sure enough, disdain filtered through the phone when I rang him back. "So-o-o you went on a date with *Jesus?*" He sounded like Sue after I'd told her I had prayed.

Turns out, Jesus can be a real showstopper.

I needed to talk to people about life with Him, but no one I knew wanted to hear. I was afraid of losing friends, so I wasn't all chatty-Cathy about my newfound faith. I still had to live in this world with my family and, hopefully, my friends. They meant a lot to me, probably too much. So, I'm embarrassed to admit it, but a whole lot went on inside before it ever came out of my mouth.

I hid my relationship with Jesus until I met a new friend at a temp job, Brenda, a Christian who invited me to a conference.

# GOD REALLY DOES LOVE ME!

I sat in the audience with Brenda at that conference for Christian women three months after I got home from the Caribbean. The speaker read from the Bible:

> Then Jesus got into a boat, and His disciples followed Him. Out of nowhere, a vicious storm blew over the sea. Waves were lapping up over the boat, threatening to overtake it! Yet Jesus was asleep. Frightened (not to mention confused—how could anyone sleep through this?), the disciples woke Him up.
>
> **Disciples:** Lord, save us! We're going to drown!
>
> **Jesus:** Please! What are you so afraid of, you of little faith?
>
> Jesus got up, told the wind and the waves to calm down, and they did. The sea became still and calm once again (Matthew 8: 23-26, TV).

"That's the same thing that happened to me," I said. "*I was you of little faith!*"

The speaker went on, "You can have a relationship with Jesus."

Up until my vision on the boat, Jesus, Fred, or whoever, had been on the periphery of my life through intuition, coincidence, and dreams. Lately, though, we hung out, took walks, and I know some would think I was crazy, but we talked. It was like chatting with a friend, only silently. I'd be thinking about something, and since God's God, I assumed He could *hear* me, so I'd ask Him what He thought. And here's the weird part, I'd pick up a book, a box of cereal, or catch a random conversation at the gym and hear what felt like His next line in our conversation! It was wild.

It didn't seem coincidental. The circumstances would line up with what He said and confirm something for me. As I experienced Him in this way over and over, I trusted Him more and more.

Then one night, He said, "Thanks!"

"For what?" I couldn't imagine why God would ever thank me.

"Hanging out."

I got goosebumps. Started getting them all the time, enough that I began calling them Godbumps. Then I saw something in the Bible: "When you call on me, when you come and pray to me, I'll listen. When you come looking for me, you'll find me. Yes, when you get serious about finding me and want it more than anything else, I'll make sure you won't be disappointed" (Jeremiah 29:12-13, TM).

That's what was happening!

"If you died right now," the speaker at the conference said, "do you know where you'd go? With this prayer, you can be sure it'd be heaven."

I always wanted to know for certain, but boom! Say a little prayer and you're in? Is that how it works?

"Is there anyone here who's never said the *sinner's prayer?*" The speaker peered around.

Tentatively, I raised my hand. In my own way, I *had* invited Jesus into my life. But with Dad's, "You're doing it wrong," still echoing in the back of my head, I wondered, *Had I really?* Just in case, I bowed my head, closed my eyes, and prayed something like this with everybody else:

God,

I messed up. Sorry. Forgive me? Thank You for sending Jesus to die in my place, to pay the penalty I deserve for the wrong I committed. I want to go to heaven. Thank You for saving me and hanging out. Help me become the person You want me to be.

I opened my eyes and Brenda surprised me as she pulled me into an embrace. "I remember when I got born again."

*Is that what I just did?* With family and friends, we had a subtle understanding; a little church was okay, as in attending funerals and weddings, but you didn't want to be one of those crazy born-again people with God all over everything. And I'd already been pushing it.

"I tell you the truth," said the speaker, "no one can see the kingdom of God unless he's born again" (John 3:3, paraphrase of the Bible).

Oh yeah, she said *that's* the prayer that gets you into heaven! I let that sink in. The words of the Bible confirmed I'd specifically done what I needed to in order to spend eternity in heaven. A weight slid from my shoulders.

How come they never told us that in church?

Back home, I stole away to the cemetery where I could think. Ever since my experience on the boat, I'd been talking to God. And this might sound crazy, but I assumed He'd reply. It never occurred to me He wouldn't. After all, conversation is key to connection, right? So even before anyone told me I could have a relationship with Christ, I pursued conversation with Him.

Each time God and I conversed, I heard, "I love you," inside. Full of angst and questions, I'd come to Him wired as usual, ready to jump in deep until He said that. Then I'd ease down on a log and look over at the lake. I'd be unable to speak as peace washed over me yet again, taking my anxiety with it. Each time my insides quivered, you know, like they do when someone says, "I love you."

God hadn't just given me a ticket to heaven. He wanted to be a part of my life.

Inside, a movie clip played of me as a little girl. I twirled around the yard plucking petals from a daisy. "He loves me! He loves me! He loves me!" The words took root.

Soaking in His Presence, I smiled. "We don't need a specific prayer to start a relationship with You, do we? When we're ready, You're all over that. You want connection even more than we do."

Now it was His turn to smile. How did I know that? Good question. I had that warm feeling inside. Do you know how it is when you feel totally loved and accepted, enjoyed even? It was like that, so that's how I pictured God in my mind's eye, smiling as I heard, "Yup, I'm right here, anytime you want to chat."

"Our friendship is more intimate than any I've ever had," I told Him. "Almost scary, but so not. It's utterly amazing, and I don't think I've ever said the word *utterly* before. So, if this is *born again* . . . bring it. But can You keep me from being one of those Christian weirdos?"

# BALAAM'S ASS

Little did I know, I'd just begun a love story. Or maybe a love-hate story? Not with God. He and I definitely had a thing going, and I wasn't two-timing Him. I was just beginning to connect with His people. My brothers and sisters in Christ. And that didn't always go down as I expected.

Starting with the speaker at the conference, even though I didn't know her name and we never talked one-on-one, I found myself grateful that she encouraged me to have a relationship with Jesus as she spoke to the group. I thought that's what I was doing, but she helped me to see I wasn't crazy. Other people were doing it, too.

From her, I got the idea that I could find a community, a church where I could get to know God, alongside other people. I found one, but at each service I crept in late, sat in the back, and peeled out the door as soon as it ended. I suppose I wasn't likely to meet anyone while acting like that. It's just that I liked God and wanted to learn more about Him, but Christians hadn't always known what to do with me, and I like my friends to be authentic. I hadn't always found that in church.

Not long after the conference, I stepped inside Creekside Community Church, one I'd passed a dozen times. In the lobby, someone reached for my hand and put a program in it. I opened the door to the sanctuary and was greeted with an electric guitar. Yes! I stood tall and scanned the room to find its source.

That's when my story got a little love-at-first-sight action as I laid eyes on the hot bandleader with the long, blond hair. Then and there I decided *this is my new church*, which is kind of weird because blonds didn't usually do it for me. As they say, though, God uses everything.

That's as far as it went with the guy, though. I didn't know how to do relationships in church. I didn't even have the guts to talk to him. I just admired him from afar and became highly motivated to attend for the first time in my life.

The Sunday morning concerts reminded me of a nightclub. May not be for everyone, but the music shifted something inside me. My problems slipped away, at least for the moment. After forty-five minutes, I was ready to listen. A pastor dressed in a suit stepped up to the lectern and read from the Bible. Explained things. He made me want to know what the book said. I'd tried reading it before but, no offense, it was mind-numbingly boring. I'd always put it down.

At home, I'd scrounged through the bookshelves in my parents' bedroom, in my room, and even the basement. Finally, I found the Living Bible which Bethany Church had given me for confirmation. It was in a box under my bed where it had lain dusty and abandoned for years. I pulled it out and flipped through it, unsticking the pages.

Around that time, my co-worker Brenda said, "You've got a Bible, right?"

"I do." I brought it into work and showed her. "The chapters confuse me. They don't flow from one thing to the next like most books."

"You know there's an Old Testament and a New."

"A what?"

She opened the Bible and held one section, the Old Testament, in her left hand and the rest of it, the New Testament, in her right. "Each," she flipped through the pages in her left hand, "contains many different books." She showed me Genesis, Exodus, and Leviticus, which are whole books in their own right. Altogether the Bible contains sixty-six.

"Where's the part about Jesus?" I asked her.

"His story's so important, four people talk about Him in four different ways in the first books of the *New* Testament—Matthew, Mark, Luke, and John. You might want to start with John. He was good friends with Jesus."

I took my Bible home and read a little before I fell asleep each night. We conversed, God and I, through the book. The words answered my questions.

I'd been wondering why the Bible seemed so boring before, but now it was like a magnet. What changed?

1 Corinthians 2:14 says: "People who do not have God's Spirit do not accept the things that come from his Spirit. They think these things are foolish. They cannot understand them, because they can only be understood with the Spirit's help" (ERV).

Ah, and how did I get God's Spirit in me?

"When you heard the truth, you put your trust in Christ. Then God marked you by giving you His Holy Spirit as a promise." (Ephesians 1:13, NLV).

So, when we choose to become His, God gives us "the Holy Spirit like an engagement ring is given to a bride—a down payment of the blessings to come!" (2 Corinthians 1:21-22, TPT). And all of a sudden, the Bible makes sense because the Holy Spirit, now inside us, explains it to us.

Yup, with His Spirit in me, the Bible read my mind and put my thoughts to poetry:

You have explored my *heart* and know *exactly* who I am;
You even know *the small details like* when I
take a seat and when I stand up again.
Even when I am far away, You know what I'm thinking.
You observe my wanderings and my
sleeping, *my waking and my dreaming,*
and You know everything I do in
more detail *than even I know.*
You know what I'm going to say *long*
*before I say it* (Psalm 139:1-4, TV).

"Wow," I beamed. "When You talk to me like that, God, I get it! All along, I knew You watched me. It used to freak me out. But now, I'm glad You have Your eye on me. I guess it's because I trust You. I know You understand my heart and the reasons I do what I do in a way no one else can, not even me. Before I believed *in* You, now I *believe* You."

Big difference, believing in God's existence didn't affect my life. I still struggled to figure things out and made a big mess. But when I believed Him, through both the Bible and the words He impressed on me, my heart changed.

Brenda knew I wanted more. She invited me to church and then to her Wednesday night Bible study. When she picked me up for work one morning, she said, "How 'bout if we meet one afternoon a week, just to talk?"

*Just to talk?* Something didn't feel right, but I said, "Okay."

In our first get-together, we sat in the conference room at work. As I leaned in closely, she actually said, "Let's talk about how you spend your money."

*Who asks that?* I sat back in my chair and thought *makes me think of a cult.* And that's when the *hate* part of the relationship with the body of Christ kicked in. "Nope," I stood. "I don't think so. Let's go."

I couldn't wait to talk to God that night. "I like my new church with the hot guy and the cool music, but I'd rather study the Bible with You." I think He smiled until I started to explain what I hated. Turns out, God's not about hate. He didn't get mad or anything, just said, "Why don't you let Me take care of this?"

What a great idea! Instead of stewing over everything, I let go. In this case, my angst disappeared. Brenda and I still worked together, even carpooled, without any more issues.

And weirdly enough, the pastor at my new church started talking to us about how we handled money. Again, I took the topic home to chat with God. I found out He can go where no one else can and get a whole different response from me. I got excited about tithing, giving money to the church, and others in need. And normally, truth be told, I'm pretty frugal. As I gave, it seemed like God stretched the money I had left. It went further.

When I follow Him, benefits ripple like a stone thrown into a pond, affecting not only me but also everyone else in the mix. That made me want to throw rocks all the time.

Each night, God and I played my new favorite game. Before I turned out the light, I randomly opened the Bible wherever it fell, put my finger on a page, and read.

One night it said, "I have loved you with an everlasting love. I have drawn you with loving-kindness" (Jeremiah 31:3, NASB). I snickered, then I saw a scene on an internal canvas: God sitting at a drafting table with long, silver hair pulled back into a ponytail, wearing glasses and an earring, drawing a picture of me!

I thought about Jessica Rabbit, the seductive cartoon in the movie, *Who Framed Roger Rabbit*? I imitated her by leaning back and breathlessly echoing her words. "I can't help it. I was drawn this way."

* * * * *

Eventually, I joined the activities committee in the singles' group at church, hoping to find new friends who shared my faith. Instead of a progressive dinner, we planned an aggressive one. We ate each course of a meal at a different table with a new group of people, getting to know each other. Another night, we sped around town, kissing 7-11 clerks in a Polaroid scavenger hunt. Who knew good, clean entertainment could be so much fun?

At a team meeting, one of the other committee members caught me off guard when she said, "I'm moving to California to go to seminary." The hesitant look on her face reminded me of my own reluctance. Would I do that? I liked to think I followed God full-on, but was I turning up my nose because inside, I was saying, "E-e-ew!"

With the best façade I could muster, I smiled weakly, congratulated her, and made for the door. Laid rubber in the driveway as I said to God, "Don't get any ideas. I'm on your team, but I'm not switching over to all-things-Christian, like books and music. Seminary, don't even think about it!"

*I thought I'd do anything God asked. Thought I was all in, but I guess there was still a little hesitation.*

The story in the Bible where God speaks through an ass came to mind. In Numbers 22-24, God's people, the Israelites, move in next to the Midianites and the Moabites. The M&M's get scared 'cause they've seen God protect His people. They hire Balaam to put a curse on God's people. Excited about the money they've offered to pay him, Balaam goes to God, explains the situation, and asks God to curse His own people.

Of course, God says no.

Balaam hangs his head, tells the M&M's to leave without him.

They depart but return with even more money, so Balaam has another visit with God. This time God says, "Go ahead, but do only what I tell you."

I get it. Balaam's human. He hoped to use the gift God gave him and come home with some cash. He tried to renegotiate instead of just doing what God said. I've been there.

God put a little rebar in Balaam to help him out—blocked his path three times with an angel. At first, only his donkey sees it. The prophet gets angry and kicks his faithful steed (I hate that part.) The burro speaks up. For real, the donkey talks. Balaam still doesn't twig until the animal reminds him, "Hey, I don't usually speak, do I? Sto-o-op hitting me!"

And—BAM—God turns on the light!

A huge angel right in front of Balaam says, "I've come to oppose you because your path is reckless. If she [the donkey] hadn't turned away, I'd have killed you by now, and spared her" (Numbers 22:32-33, paraphrase of the Bible).

"The dumb ass speaking with a man's voice forbade the madness of the prophet" (2 Peter 2:16, AKJV).

\* \* \* \* \* \*

Right away, Balaam gets it. "I'm sorry, Lord. I sinned. If you want, I'll go home." But with the fear of God in him, Balaam's ready. He'll do the right thing now.

Okay, I wanted to do God's will. But if He asked me to do something crazy, like go to seminary, I might need to borrow that donkey.

# GOD PROMISES, HE'LL NEVER LEAVE

Still trying to figure out what incorporating God into my life looked like after the conference, I didn't know exactly what I wanted. But like a wild animal that had acquired a taste for human flesh, I wanted it badly. *Ew.* Where did that creepy analogy come from? Along with the cool God stuff, something else was happening. It was like I was in a spiritual battle.

\* \* \* \* \* \*

"Ru-u-unning with the devil-l-l." My younger sister, Victoria, cranked up one of our favorites. We sang along as I climbed into the passenger seat of her Dodge Charger. With a map of the US and enough peanut butter to last a month, I raised my fist. "Let's explore this country and find a new place to call home."

"Need anything before we hit the highway?" Victoria said as she drove through Foxborough, Massachusetts.

I choked back an unexpected sob as we sped through familiar territory one last time. "Geez, how many times have we walked through this center of town?"

A breeze blew through the open window, carrying the scent of fall. With its first tinge of color, nature confirmed a change as we turned onto I-95 North, venturing into a new season where transformation might just embrace us, too.

Normally my thoughts flowed right out my mouth, but after a recent fight with Victoria, I was on best behavior. "What do you mean, you don't think we'll have a good time?" she'd roared at me the previous Friday night at El Torito's while drinking margaritas and munching on nachos.

"I'm just sayin', you might have more fun travelling with a friend. We've had our differences lately."

"As long as you keep *Him*," she drew a capital H in the air with her finger, "out of our conversations, we'll be fine."

How would I do that? I didn't want to exclude my new man from anything. Leave God waiting for me in the pew at church? No, I wanted to get up and have coffee with Him, bring Him to work, and debrief as we walked the dog, but Victoria wasn't the only one who felt this way.

So, I ran each thought through a filter in my mind. If my thought had something to do with God, I took a hit off my coffee instead of sharing it. I got pretty quiet.

Victoria pulled up to the ticket booth on the Mass Pike. The guy inside reminded me of my friend Dave, a Wolfman Jack look-alike with long silver hair and a goatee. Dave had just gotten out of detox. On a rare occasion, I'd admitted my faith to him as we talked. I didn't want him to judge me and walk away, but he needed a life preserver to know how others got by. So, I told him my story. He groaned. "I'm tempted to say, *oh no, they've got you, too*, but in AA, I confess my need for a Higher Power every day. I don't want to own that, but it's true."

On the outside, I looked at my feet. Inside, I cartwheeled. My declaration freed me—not only because I'd shared my truth for a change, but also because he'd validated what I'd said with the recognition of his own need for God. I didn't want to admit my lack of control either. It's hard to lay down power you think you have in order to trust an invisible spirit.

* * * * *

After driving for three days with minimal conversation, Victoria and I had made it to South Dakota. On Interstate 83, heading west toward Mount Rushmore, I needed to get out of my head, and we needed an adventure to bring us out the other side of this awkward silence. I dug out the AAA guidebook and leafed through. "Want to go to a ghost town?"

"Sure," she nodded. "Lead the way."

"Take this exit and follow the signs."

"K." She hit the blinker, took a right up the twisty dirt road, and turned into an empty parking lot. "There's no one here. Is it worth a stop?"

"It's off-season and mid-week." I opened the door and hopped out. "Let's stretch our legs." We peeked into a run-down shack in the deserted mining town. "As the post office," a placard on the door read, "this building served as a community center. Everyone gathered here to share the news as it came in on pony express."

A signpost with a pointing finger directed us "to the mine" in a font I'd call *dripping blood*. We mimicked the Twilight Zone's scary movie music "doo DOO doo" as we hiked the half-mile up the path.

Then, *the* spookiest sound I have ever heard pierced my soul.

Chills raced up my spine as the hair on the back of my neck rose. Victoria and I stared at each other. Then we peeled down the trail, into the parking lot, and jumped in the car. I thrust the key into the ignition, punched the accelerator, and maneuvered the vehicle onto the road.

As we sped down the mountain, fumes of smoke billowed up behind us as the brakes screeched. I had to pump those suckers to get the car to stop as we careened into Rapid City. We were safe, right?

We rolled into Otto's Garage and jumped out. "What happened to you?" the mechanic joked. "Looks like you seen a ghost."

I shook my head, but not very convincingly. "I think our brakes went."

"Got my work cut out for me today. I won't be able to have a look 'til mornin'."

"No worries," I said, grabbing my bag from the back seat and handing him the keys. "We'll stop by then."

Up the road, Victoria and I checked into the Hotel Amber Inn after grabbing a six-pack of Bud in a convenience store. We turned on the TV and made a couple of sandwiches, avoiding eye contact and conversation. Two beers later, in the middle of *The Wizard of Oz*, I peeked at the elephant-in-my-mind. What was that—eerie howl or evil laugh?

Wait! I put my hand up. I didn't want to know.

I've always been drawn to the unique, the wild, maybe even the dark side. Why? I don't know. I guess the spiritual has always attracted me in one way or another. As a kid, I piled onto the couch with my cousins. We'd pull down the shades, turn on the thirteen-inch, black and white TV, and tune into *Dark Shadows*, the cheesy 60s soap opera about a vampire. Then, we'd grab each other from behind and squeal, "Boo-o-o!"

Back when we were eight and ten, Victoria and I rested our fingers on a Ouija board indicator. "Who-o-o does Steve Malcolm like?" Then we stared into a mirror with a babysitter as she recited, "Spirits of the dead, please bring up . . . "

*Was all that bad?*

A newish sensation ebbed at my conscience. Was it a you-should-know-better vibe? No, it was more like a let's-talk-about-this from God. Was I in trouble? Afraid of conflict, I cracked open another beer and pretended to watch the movie. Of course, I'd experienced conviction even before praying the sinner's prayer—even before I was trying to live God's way.

Now that I was, how would disagreement with God go down? I didn't want to find out. I dug up an old pair of invisible blinders and attempted to ignore Him, even though He stood front and center in my mind.

He let me because He never makes me do anything I don't want to.

\* \* \* \* \*

A week later, in Los Angeles, Victoria dropped me off at a friend's apartment for a few days. Lacy, a college friend from Texas who'd moved west, always knew where the party was. On our way out that night, I said, "What do you mean this place is *undercover?*"

"The club meets weekly in an unadvertised venue, moves from space to space. To get in, you've got to know someone who knows someone." She raised and lowered her eyebrows a few times. "If you know what I mean?"

"Not really." But on a Sunday night, I entered what looked like any other nightclub and a man, or maybe a woman, quickly pulled me inside and closed the door. As my eyes adjusted to the dark, I noticed a giant, Latino policeman standing off to the side. "If something happens," I whispered to Lace, "he might be a good person to know."

"Let's hit the bar." She led me by the hand. "Think we might need a few drinks for this."

"We are Siamese twins," I whispered. "You take a step. I take a step. Got that?" We crossed the empty room and hopped onto a bar stool next to the only other patron in the place.

"Agreed, how 'bout a shot?" She opened her purse and pulled out a cigarette.

"Can I borrow one of those? I'm trying to quit, but not tonight."

Two hours later, when we turned from the bar to find a ladies' room, that same cop stood behind us, whip in hand, poised to strike a woman chained to a post. She danced seductively and waved her naked butt in his direction.

*What kind of place is this?* I winced, but not because of the tequila. As we passed cages of men dressed in leather underwear, one wrenched the rubber bars apart and reached out to grab me. I jumped back and ran for the door marked Ladies. It turned out to be one big toilet stall crowded with people doing God-knows-what. I grabbed Lacy's arm and dragged her out of the room, then out of the club. "We gotta go."

"What's wrong?"

I pulled her toward the parking lot. "We just gotta go."

In the car, I put my hands over my face and rocked back and forth. As Lacy turned the key in the ignition, I lifted my head and peered in the rearview mirror. "Make sure no one follows us."

"You're scaring me," she said. "What's the matter?"

"I had a bad experience. Tonight brought back . . . well, more than a memory." I shivered.

In her apartment, Lacy got me a glass of water and rubbed my neck. "Feel like talking?"

"I can't. I promised I wouldn't ever say anything."

"You're a good friend." She let out a sigh of relief. "How 'bout we go to bed? Everything always looks better in the morning, right?" She grabbed a pillow and blanket from the hall closet and laid them out on the couch for me before disappearing into her room.

The memory wouldn't leave though . . .

\* \* \* \* \* \*

On my way to Africa, I'd spent a week in England. After a day of pub-crawling, a guy we knew took us to a recording studio at midnight. My two English girlfriends curled up on the sofa inside the front door and passed out. He and I went upstairs and had another beer. Nothing seemed out of the ordinary until we came down. Hundreds of people had filled the place.

"An acid house party," he said. An illegal get-together, the craze in London at the time.

As if in a bad dream, I went from room to room. "Where're the girls?"

I was drunk, but nothing like the guy who held his hand in front of his face, gazing at it with glazed eyes, or those dancing naked. Back at the front door, I found one of my girlfriends just as cops, or Bobbies, burst through the door.

"Bloody hell, what's this?"

I pressed into the crowd, not wanting to leave without the other girl. A copper grabbed me from behind. "You've got to go," he said.

My memory skipped to the girls' flat. As I lay on their settee, worried about our missing friend, sleep wouldn't come. I wanted to fight, but who and how?

*I gotta quit living this way before someone gets hurt.*

The next morning, my friend turned up. *Thank God!* I reached to embrace her, but she pushed me away. "I need to be alone. You two go."

*Go?* Not knowing what else to do, we left and went on another bender. We knew something terrible had happened, but what could we do? Hours later, I remembered the drinks we'd had on the roof the day before. And panic rose as I pictured the friend I'd left behind climbing the stairs to that roof, walking to the edge, and scaling the ledge.

"N-o-o!" I screamed as I tried to shake the vision out of my head, the image of her on the ground after having jumped. Then my mind took me to another ledge. Surrounded by darkness, *I* stood on the edge of insanity. Somehow, I knew that's what it was called. Teetering, I reached out, but there was nothing to hold onto. *What would I do if she jumped?*

"We gotta go!"

Entering the neighborhood, I leapt from the cab and raced ahead, took the stairs two at a time. Inside the flat, she sat at the kitchen table just as we'd left her. I wrapped my arms around her rigid frame, buried my face in her hair, and wept. I knew in my heart we were just in time.

\* \* \* \* \* \*

A year later and miles away in Lacy's apartment, I sat at another kitchen table, trembling. Safe, on the other side of trauma, I bawled. What was it about the night that triggered that memory? The fear, the evil, I didn't want a life filled with these kinds of events. So, I cried out, "Jesus, I need Your help! I think I opened a door to darkness. Maybe even a couple. Can we close them, please?"

Reaching for a tissue, I blew hard when His quiet, gentle answer calmed my heart, "I'm here anytime you need Me and I'll never leave" (Hebrews 13:5, paraphrase of the Bible).

Tension slipped from my shoulders as I crossed the room and lay down in His peace at last.

# STRUGGLING TO BE A GOOD
# GIRL WITH MY BAD SELF

The next morning Victoria picked me up at Lacy's and we began the final leg of our trip to Colorado. Without a word, I sat in the passenger seat, map open on my lap and eyes staring out the window.

As Victoria and I wound through the mountains in bumper-to-bumper traffic, the car broke down. We pulled off the road. Immediately, a cop knocked on the window. "You're vapor locked," he said. "In about fifteen minutes, when the car cools down, it will run."

Victoria and I mirrored body language, as we shrugged at him and giggled, "Vapor locked? Beam me up."

"Liquid fuel changes to gas in high altitudes when cars sit in traffic," the cop said. He backed away and went to help the people in the next stopped car.

Vapor locked, what a great phrase. Maybe God was doing the same thing to me? Giving me a moment to regroup before settling down in a new place. Where was I with this new faith?

I was good with it, but I didn't want to lose myself in the transformation. I still had some old ways of doing things, and I wanted to keep them.

Would I do anything God asked? I wanted to say yes, but I still couldn't be sure.

Since we each had friends in Colorado, Victoria and I agreed Denver seemed as good a place as any to perch for a while, so we signed on with a temp agency and I bopped around the city trying new churches. Meanwhile, my social life jerked me from side to side like a carnival ride as I made new friends and reconnected with old.

At an outdoor Easter sunrise service in Red Rocks Canyon, I wrapped my down comforter around myself and yawned. I turned to my new Christian friend I'd met at water aerobics and said, "I can't remember the last time I got up this early, never for church!"

On the stage, a lone violinist drew her bow. A ballerina stretched on the barre and an artist set up an easel. I took a deep breath of the cool morning air and smelled coffee! Where? I poked my friend, then pointed at two people lying in sleeping bags off to the side. "If we come next year, we're doing that." Just then, the sun peeked over the horizon and the service began.

Later that week, I met up with Kathy. My tent mate from Africa had just moved to Denver from Canada to get her helicopter license. She met me at a bar that featured stupid human tricks, where I was aiming not to drink quite as much as I used to. Kathy did not feel the same way. As she stepped into a sticky Velcro suit, I canvassed the crowd, riling everyone up. "Ka-thy! Ka-thy!" Like a prizefighter, she waved, then jumped on the spring-loaded platform, did half a somersault, and stuck to the wall by her backside, upside down. She not only jumped once, but over and over, winning the Velcro-fly contest and demonstrating how to do it to the drunken guys lining up behind her who just jumped at the wall face first, hoping to stick.

How was I going to merge my faith with my friends?

I wondered that over and over as I sat across the hot tub from the naked Playgirl model we brought back from the bar. Partying like this didn't feel right anymore. In the past, I might have slept with the centerfold guy, but I no longer wanted to have casual sex with strangers or wake up in unfamiliar beds to search for my clothes and do the walk of shame. I shook my head to keep thoughts from landing like birds on a wire swooping down for a natter. Since I was cutting back on my form of escapism—getting high—I didn't know what to do with these thoughts and feelings. I needed a new way of processing emotions.

Well into the next day, I avoided God. I'd asked Him to help. Now I needed to let Him. Embarrassed, but missing Him, I finally pulled up a chair. Whether a relationship is with a person or with God, it takes time, energy, and honesty.

"Thanks," He said.

"For what?" I looked down at the floor of my apartment.

"Coming back so soon." Wow. That conflict resolution went better than any I'd had before.

About that time, my new Christian friend showed me a list of Bible characters along with everything they'd done wrong: Moses murdered. King David slept with another guy's wife. When she got pregnant, he sent her husband to the frontlines of the battle to get killed! The list went on. By the end of it, I breathed a sigh of relief. I wasn't alone. It turns out a lot of God's people blew it time and again, and not only does God forgive, but Romans 8:28 says, "We [can be] confident that God is able to orchestrate everything to work toward something good *and beautiful* when we love Him and accept His invitation to live according to His plan" (TV).

How cool is that?

I wanted to include God in my decisions, to ask for help when I needed it rather than wait until it was too late. Then it hit me: I don't have to do anything I don't want to. I didn't get that before. Trying to keep everyone happy, I often did things I didn't really want to. Like sit in that hot tub with the male stripper. Since I wasn't going to fool around with him, what was I doing? I didn't want to tease the boy.

As this *new me* emerged, I felt as if I was walking a tightrope. I didn't want to come off too churchy after having been there/done that right alongside them, and I didn't want to lose friends. But I could no longer deny God. How did I quit people-pleasing around others and just plain *be there* for God, my friends, and myself?

Of course, it wasn't long before I got a chance to try. The following Saturday night, I sat in another bar watching a different friend enter a seductive banana-eating contest after she'd had too many beers. Instead of climbing onstage with her to do my own impression of a you-know-what, I squirmed. I had chosen to no longer live this way—eating bananas alluringly, sending not-so-subtle messages to the men in the audience, and waking up with a hangover and a groan when I remembered what I'd done, if I recollected it at all.

Instead of ignoring God, I turned toward Him. "What do You want me to do?"

My not-at-all-bossy God said, "I love you. Let's get her off the stage and take her home."

"Let's do it!" I smiled.

That's when it hit me. Since I'd been spending time with God, I'd been more like who I was created to be than ever before. At least, that's what it felt like. And He knew I wouldn't—couldn't—follow Him perfectly even if I wanted to. But He seemed to be okay with that.

# AS GOD AND I BECAME A WE

I sat on my couch one Saturday morning with a cup of coffee and a Bible, daydreaming. *What do I want to do with my life?* When I was eight, a relative of mine visited from Alaska. In her patchwork maxi-dress, she'd played guitar and taught us songs, then asked, "How'd you like a pen-pal?"

"Uh-huh," I nodded in response to everything she said. "What's that?"

Soon packages and letters filled my mailbox. When I saw the mailman turn up our street, I stopped whatever I was doing and ran to greet him. I would rip open whatever he handed me to find a sealskin headband made in skin-sewing class or pictures from teenybopper magazines. I traded Bobby Sherman and Donny Osmond for David Cassidy, and that's when I made up my mind: I'm going to Alaska one day.

On the couch, I snapped out of my reverie in search of a refill, and realized I had a question for God, my new partner, *Had one day come?* I took a deep breath, exhaled loudly, and began to hum my theme song, *Should I stay, or should I go now?*

"What do You think, Fred?"

Those days, I usually called Fred the more conventional "Jesus" or "God," but this conversation was important. So, I came to Him with my own term of endearment. Inside our place of connection, I trusted Him to say *no* tenderly if He said it at all.

Waiting for His reply, I picked up the newspaper and dug through it until I found the travel section, the only segment I ever read. The entire portion featured the bears of Brooks Lodge in Katmai National Park, *Alask-a-aa!*

"We're go-o-oing?" I clapped my hands. "We're going!"

I danced for days before settling down, then I turned back to my new favorite verse: "I know what I'm doing. I have it all planned out. Plans to take care of you, not abandon you, plans to give you the future you hope for. When you call on me, when you come and pray to Me I'll listen. When you come looking for Me, you'll find me. Yes, when you get serious about finding me and want it more than anything else, I'll make sure you won't be disappointed" (Jeremiah 29:11-14, TM).

I'd half-expected God to hold me back from my dreams. Instead, He encouraged my wanderlust! All this time, I'd searched for my place in this world, Dad's approval, and whatever else; yet God had a plan? Now that's destiny. I scrunched my bucket list into a ball and tossed it in the trashcan. "Let's do this."

In the next few weeks, I gave my stuff away and connected with friends on the countdown to my adventure with God. Out of the blue, or not, Sandy an old friend from college, called. "Ple-e-ease, can I come with you?" A travel mate. Thank You, God!

Before I knew it, we drove out of the driveway with a tent and a cooler full of food. With a lot of time on the road, I stared out the windshield at the beautiful countryside, dreamt with God, and processed with Sandy. "I'm wonderin' what I wish for? You know, in life. I'd like to want a man, but I'm still a little gun shy. Maybe I want a job I love."

"A partner and meaningful work? I think that's universal." Sandy perused our map as we parked in front of the youth hostel we'd chosen for the night. I got as far as the porch when one of the guys staying there looked me in the eye and said, "Why do you do the things you do? Why are you here?"

"Well, I pray and look for signs."

"So, you think there's a divine plan or something?" He rubbed his hands together as he looked at the others 'round the table. "We've got another perspective."

I set my pack on the floor and joined them.

"Boy, did you pick the right one of us for that conversation," Sandy said as she shuffled past. Hours later, I didn't want to step away, but I had to pee. "Sorry, guys, I'll be back."

In the kitchen, Elias from Sweden said, "I heard you talking. What d'you think happens when we die, life after death?"

I smiled as I pulled out a jar of peanut butter and some bread, offering him some. "Well, sort of. I believe in heaven and hell, eternal life." I stuck two pieces of bread in a toaster. "And I think it takes a relationship with Jesus to get to heaven."

"Why do you say that?" Elias asked.

"Well, the Bible's my standard, and I see it there in lots of places, like where Jesus says, 'I am the way and the truth and the life. No one comes to the Father except through me' " (John 14:6, NIV).

The conversations, one after another, connected in a way that felt important even if I didn't totally understand how; each pointed me in the direction of this one guy as people kept asking, "Have you met Malik?"

"I don't think so. Who is he?"

"He's not easy to forget." Elias snickered. "He's the black guy wearing a bra and carrying a purse. He gave you directions on the phone and was super concerned about whether you got here or not, kept asking everyone if they'd seen you."

"Where might I find him?" I took the first bite of my sandwich.

"Holding court out back." Elias pointed.

I found a chair and joined the party. Two, maybe three hours later, the gathering had dwindled down to Malik and me. He told me about growing up with a controlling father and his stint in Africa as a missionary. It was *a calling*, he explained. Then he told me of the sex abuse at the hands of a man who'd said, "I targeted you because your father's a pastor."

*Ugh!* I doubled over as if I'd been punched. "And now," he said, "I'm getting a sex change."

Elias was right. I wouldn't forget Malik, but not because of his bra and purse. I just loved him—I couldn't help it. Even after all the harm he'd experienced by Christians, he didn't resent me but answered my questions with incredible candor. I wanted to give him a hug. "Would that be okay?"

Sheepishly, he smiled, "Of course."

"I'm so sorry!" I said. "I know I wasn't one of the ones who hurt you, but it bothers me when people misrepresent God. He so loves you and hates what happened. If it's okay, could I pray for you?"

He nodded.

"Dear Sweet Jesus, I know you feel Malik's pain because I do, too. Please heal his heart, and bring him peace. It's in Your name I pray."

After coffee the next morning, Sandy and I loaded the car and stared back at the hostel. No, I wouldn't forget. While my pain and experience was different from Malik's, it also came from a place that seemed like it should have been safe.

As Sandy drove, I pulled out my Bible. I had a few questions. By now, I'd been a Christian for a while, a couple of years. I had gay friends. I also knew that some of the verses in the Bible call homosexuality an *abomination.*

Yikes. So, as a Christian, what did I do with that? "Lord?"

"You love," God responded without missing a beat.

"I can do that!" I smiled. "In fact, I think You put special love in me for Malik because I haven't cared about anyone like that, well . . . since that little pygmy."

We drove on through Alberta, British Columbia, and finally landed in Alaska. In Anchorage, my final destination, Sandy and I parted ways. She took a bus and then a ferry, heading south toward Skagway while I sat in the 5th Avenue Mall at the food court munching on sesame chicken, listening to other people's conversations.

"Excuse me." A girl stopped at my table with a plate full of reindeer sausage and eggs.

"Wanna sit?" I brightened, hoping for company.

Instead, she said, "Can I take a chair? Looks like you have more than you need."

"Yeah, sure." I took a deep breath and let it out slowly. My pen pals were the only Alaskans I knew, and they lived on an island 986 miles away. We'd never actually met face-to-face. "God," I said, "those pictures of Alaska in the newspaper. That *was* You, right?"

That sense of peace I was getting stopped me from panicking.

After lunch Mom sang into the phone. "Happy 30th birthday to you-u-u!" before she said, "You hate the cold. Why don't you get in the car and come home?"

My back stiffened. I'd actually considered the idea until she suggested it. Instead, I spent the rest of the day applying for jobs and renting a room off Boniface Parkway. Then I walked to the nearby library to look at the *Help Wanted* postings. Inside, I slunk into a chair next to a mom with two kids and opened a newspaper, biting my nails off one by one. She said, "Lookin' for a job?"

"Yup, just moved here." My leg jumped up and down as if it had a mind of its own.

"You will love it!" She tied her daughter's shoe. "My husband's in the military and I told him, 'I've followed you all over the world. When you get out, we're coming back here!' "

"What's so great about it?" I set the paper down.

"It's gorgeous and not as crowded as everywhere else, but we have everything we need. Super friendly people. We don't even lock our doors. And if you like adventure, you'll never run out of things to do."

"Ha!" I sat up and leaned in. "Now you're talking my language."

"When's he coming?" her son whined.

"Don't worry." She picked his jacket up off the floor. "He's on his way."

"Who?"

"Famous Amos." She reached into her purse, then handed me a flyer.

"The guy on the bag of cookies *is real?*" Sure enough, just then, the black man in the white suit strode through the door with chocolate chip cookies, my favorite. He handed them out like communion wafers, but with milk instead of grape juice. I sat back in my chair, closed my eyes, and smiled. "God, You know exactly what to get a girl for her birthday. Thanks!"

Back at my new place, the answering machine blinked. I pressed *play* and listened to the message: "We'd like to offer you the admin job you applied for this morning at The Anchorage Heating Company." Ha! In one day, I found a place to live *and* a job.

Wait, what happened to work *I'd love*? As I pondered that thought, the phone rang. "It's Pam," said a friend from high school. "I'm in town. I just got your new number from your mom. Can we get together?"

"Absolutely!" We met at F Street Bar and Grill where I filled her in on my fresh start.

"Sounds like God's lining everything up for you." Pam caught sight of herself in the mirror behind the bar and primped.

"You think?" Hm. A new job *and* a new apartment? I guess that could be Him. As He and I became a *we*, life wasn't boring like I'd expected it would be. All this time, I'd searched for happiness. Maybe His plan included more than that. "Okay," I said, "I'll stay a year. See what happens."

"That's what I said." The waitress set our drinks down. "Twenty years ago."

"Twenty years?" I sipped my beer.

Then Pam put a cherry on top of everything. "If I move back up, can we get an apartment together?"

"Yes, please?" I threw my arms around her.

Just then, one of the eight-guys-to-every-girl that Alaska was known for at the time sauntered over. Like the bumper sticker says: "The odds are good, but the goods are odd." He licked his finger, touched the sleeve of my shirt, then his own, and tilted his head toward the door. "Let's go back to my place and get out of these wet clothes."

Not even tempting, but still my favorite line.

# STAGES

A few months later, I killed someone. Well, just in a play. I'd joined a theatre group to meet people and ended up performing in an improvisational murder mystery as an auto mechanic who'd had a sex change, starred in X-rated movies, and murdered someone.

Usually a volunteer behind the scenes, I took the acting gig because I heard the group was down one due to a family emergency. Without much thought, I agreed to step in. It was totally out of my comfort zone, both the performing and the actual role. I didn't feel like I could quit, though, after giving the director my word.

So, there I was at play practice, screaming unconvincingly when I found the dead body. I might as well have been saying "baa, baa" like a sheep calling for its mother instead of screaming like I would if I discovered a corpse in real life. At that moment, I wasn't the only one thinking, *This show must _not_ go on!*

Offstage, Chance, an Irish lesbian with a test-tube baby, sometimes worked as a counselor. The rest of the group twitched nervously until she stepped in. "Can I teach you how to emote?"

"Yes, please," I said weakly.

Chance took a deep breath, pulled herself up, and planted her four-foot-nine-inch frame in my face. I scrunched down to meet her gaze as she belted out, "I slept with your father."

*Whoa,* I flinched. Then recognizing the game, I matched her one for one. "I forgive you."

She pushed her glasses up her nose. "I killed your mother."

I inhaled deep then exhaled slowly. "You didn't mean to."

Just that afternoon, I'd confided in her, "My family shows physical affection to our animals rather than each other." Chance stepped back, filled her lungs with air, and used it against me. "I drove over your cat and killed her *on purpose.*"

For a minute, time stood still. I couldn't breathe. Then deep inside, the latch on a gate—one that had been closed for a very long time—creaked open. Torrents of emotion gushed up from the depths. My body convulsed as I unleashed the kind of tears that I hadn't cried in over fifteen years. Abruptly, play practice ended.

"I'm sorry," Chance repeated. "Will you still ride home with me?"

Sobbing, I nodded as I grabbed my stuff and ran to the car. After we dropped everyone else off, I admitted, "My emotional baggage keeps getting in the way. I don't mean to, but after trying two therapists, I still mask my feelings. Somehow you got through. Will you counsel me?"

"Let's finish the play first." She reached over for a hug. "If you still want to do something after, we can talk."

I marked my calendar to call her the Monday after the play ended.

In the seven years since my break-up with Tony, I'd wondered about counseling, thought maybe an investment in the right person could help me get to the bottom of a few things. Chance didn't come packaged how I expected, but I decided to take a risk. Like I said, I'd tried others but didn't connect with them.

"Why are you so angry?" She sat on a couch opposite me in her living room when we met for our first session.

"I hated the manipulation I experienced growing up. When I got into trouble, Mom pointed to the back hall. 'If you're going to cry, you know where to go.' The isolation sucked, so I suppressed my frustration and buried my anger."

After each counseling session, God and I dissected our conversations. In a tangled web of my emotion, we circled round and round, coming back to each issue from different angles. God helped me make changes in my life based on new understanding, like when I whined, "Tears, what good are they?"

"They're My gift." He smiled.

I learned that when I express emotion, I release it. Like a pressure cooker, I let steam off when I say what needs to be said, confront when I'm angry, cry when I'm sad, own my bad when I'm guilty, and apologize when I'm sorry. At first, tears usually accompany them all. But after a while, not so much. I gain the ability to keep a clean slate and maintain healthy relationships with clear communication. It's actually pretty amazing.

I bawled over Hallmark commercials and movies, for friends going through hard times, and finally for myself. I found healing and the courage to speak as I owned my emotions.

The following Monday night, Chance and I picked up where we left off. Upon her recommendation, I belted out a primal scream on my drive home from work every day for six months. I released a beast in my car. Because my current angst drew reinforcement from the depths of my history, further down than any physicality, my body could only muster a cry like that once a day. It needed recovery time.

I shared this experience with a friend. Unaware that she'd try it, I didn't warn her. "Do a test scream first." She lost her voice for three days.

I screamed and screamed until the day my pit of anguish dried up. I could hear the difference. I can give you a good ole yell when I get mad, but my reaction no longer connects to a boatload of emotion stored up from years gone by.

I only wish I gave my rage a pen, paired my cries with explanation. These days I shriek on paper, writing until I have nothing left to say.

While I was doing this, I struggled. I didn't want to detach from my loved ones. I wanted to connect and go deeper with them. But these changes altered me. Not only could my relationship with God distance me from people I cared about, but so could this personal growth. *Ugh!*

That's when Chance nearly pushed me over the edge. "You might want to take a hiatus from your family? Orphan yourself to find out who you really are."

*Huh.* I used to joke about my conscience being in my mother's southern accent, sounding more like her than me, but neither of these things made me laugh just then. The concept of owning my thoughts and establishing a voice . . . *my* voice?! For that reason alone, I put the plan into action. I took a break from the relationships I thought could stand it.

"Mom, you know I'm in counseling. I'm gonna take Chance's recommendation and step away from the family for a month. Everything's fine. I'll give you an *emergency* number you can call to check on me."

"WHODOESSHETHINKSHEIS? I'm coming up there!"

"Mum, please don't." I ended the call and rang Chance. "WhatdoIdoifshedoes?"

162                                                        *MARY ME*

"You reiterate your need for space and refuse to see her."

Chance had obviously never met my mother. I hung up the phone and turned to God. "You know I'm not trying to hurt anyone, but Mom's response reminds me of why I need to do this. Please, can we do it without a drastic showdown?"

Mom didn't come. And I didn't see it then, but these days, if I were in her shoes, I'd get on that plane and go have a face-to-face with my kid. I get it now.

But I don't regret the freedom I gained in the break. I do, however, regret how it alienated Victoria. I never imagined how much this would hurt her or how long she'd hold a grudge, no matter how many times I begged her forgiveness. I hate that she felt abandoned and wish I could fix that, but it's a mistake I can't undo.

I don't blame Chance. I own it, but I see that I may have taken the control I'd let my mother have over me and given it to Chance as my counselor. Walls went up and came down as I learned how to take that control back and how to keep it, but that wasn't why I came to the counseling chair. I wanted a man in my life, and frustrated with my choices and past experiences, I needed a new skill set.

What straight woman chooses a lesbian counselor for this? I did after having been wounded by men.

"Thing is," I told Chance, "I crave depth in relationship, but I keep my sneakers on in case I need to run. And my passport, I carry that puppy with me everywhere, even to the convenience store. Carpe diem, right?"

"Sweetie," she smiled, "your fear of commitment causes you to miss out on intimacy in relationships." *Whoa,* that was my takeaway for that session.

As usual, I got back to my apartment and had a test to pass. A friend had left me a voice mail. "Do you want to go to Peru with a theater group?" She might as well have said, "Want to run?"

When I called her back, she upped the ante. "If not South America, I have a friend who needs a house-sitter in St. John for the winter. Take your pick."

I hung up the phone and turned to God. "Now that I'm trying to stay in one place, why are the opportunities so enticing?"

"When you follow Me, you face resistance and temptation. Of course, the offers are good." I refused them and clung to Him like never before.

As I tried to fathom the mysteries of intimacy with God, I realized Mom focuses on logistics and news, swims through life like a snorkeler skimming the surface. Dad's aloof, never wants to know anything. And Tony, my long-term love, hid in addiction. My deepest connections had been with friends until this supernatural thing with God.

Before the break with my family, Mom said, "You don't think Chance might try to convert you, do you?"

"To homosexuality?" I scoffed. "No!" But after Chance's recent invitations to volunteer with her at different events, I wondered. On my way home from the Snow Queen Ball, I said to God, "I'm thirty-two, single, and haven't had a relationship in years. Am I gay?" *Wait!* I put my hand up. "Don't answer that yet."

Like rabbits on hormones, my emotions ran wild. I drove home, drew a bath, and lowered myself into the hot water, now begging, "Please don't let me be gay! No offense, but my homosexual friends don't have it easy, and I've got enough to deal with right now."

God knew. But I had to own some hard stuff I'd never admitted before. I wasn't ready to talk, not even to Him. He didn't say a word, but His peaceful presence never left.

The issue of homosexuality wasn't a hot topic back then, not out loud like it is today. I had relatives who were gay, but we never talked about it. Of course, silence speaks volumes.

Was I afraid I'd get ostracized? No.

Because of so many close friendships with women and the pain I'd experienced with men, I don't think friends or family would have been surprised if I told them I was gay. In fact, some of them may have accepted me more easily coming out as a lesbian than as a Christian.

With all the anti-gay rhetoric associated with Christians, *God won't like it* never occurred to me as I sat in that tub, adding hot water 'til I shriveled like a prune. I'd already confessed to Mom, "I used to play *I'm the husband* with my friend Karen when she spent the night."

With zero shame, Mom admitted, "I did, too. Lots of kids explore. That doesn't make us gay."

No. And I'd wanted a man and kids. Was that still true? Yeah, I think. I mean, I loved my girlfriends. We think alike and have similar interests. Was I a lesbian and I didn't even know it?

No, I'm not attracted to women like I am to men. I guess I could try. But if I were gay, I'd be drawn to them, right? I drained the tub and started over.

After an hour and a half, a subtle assurance spread through my chest and out my extremities like a hot oil treatment. I love women as friends, but that doesn't make me gay. I want a husband, I'm just wounded. I don't know how to have a healthy relationship with a man.

I crawled from the bath with a sigh and said to God. "Thanks for being here."

* * * * *

"You smile at women all the time," Chance said at our next meeting. "I want you to smile at a man. Can you?"

*That's easy,* I thought as I left her house.

However, fifteen minutes later, I understood what she meant. As women passed by on the sidewalk at the Loussac Library, they smiled big. When I checked in with my face, I realized there was a giant grin on it. Chance was right; these women responded to my initiation. One weary woman accepted my face as if it were a glass of cool water and she a thirsty camel. *What the heck?* I drew back.

Then I spotted a man up ahead and screwed up my courage, *I can get my homework done.*

The struggle began. Men often perceive a smile as an invitation. I wasn't ready to deal with those consequences. I handpicked an elderly gentleman I could handle if he tried anything.

The following week, Chance raised her left eyebrow. "Now have a conversation."

When I consider a man *safe*, like family members, friends' spouses, or others who shouldn't make sexual advances, I relax. A little. Other men require precautions, depending on the situation. Different tactics.

A friend gave me her ticket to the opening of the Out North Contemporary Art House. I went. In the gallery, I recognized Steve, a guy who fell into my *safe* category because of previous encounters in the theater group. I wandered over. "S'up?"

We chatted easily, got snacks, and sat down for the one-act show when I realized, *I'm doing my homework!*

On the walk to the parking lot, Steve told me about his dog and said, "I've got him with me. Come say 'hi.' " He opened his car door, and the dog jumped out. I reached down and scratched the base of his tail for two seconds. Instantly, the dog ejaculated on the sidewalk. Steve *Siemen's* dog—I'm not kidding, that's his name—flippin' ejaculated on the pavement!

Steve followed me to my car as if he thought I had a magic touch and wanted me to use it on him. He kept asking, "What'd you do to my dog?"

"Nothing!" I jumped in my car, mortified. As I drove away, I asked God, "Is there a spiritual attack on my relationships with men?"

"Yup! What are you going to do about it?"

"I'm going to fight back!"

# THE HOLY SPIRIT

"I'm looking for a church," I told Chance.

"Why would you do that?" She wrinkled her entire face.

Like most of the others in my life, she didn't get my desire to spend time with God. Whenever I did, I wanted *more*. More cool connections too-coincidental-to-be-serendipitous, more knowings, more healing. I just plain wanted more of God, whatever that meant. I was ready. Or maybe not. But I was willing.

Yielding to Him was way more fun than I'd expected, and there was more. I knew it.

After I'd returned home from the boat trip in the Caribbean, the lady at the conference had said, "We all need a personal relationship with Christ."

So, there were others out there who had one. I just had to find them.

On Sundays, I church-shopped. In the congregations I visited, I discovered community and tradition but missed God's presence. If not in church, where could I find like-minded people who wanted to get to know God better? I needed a spiritual adventure team.

I broadened my search. I read bulletin boards, skimmed newspapers, and volunteered. As I trudged through the snow in the Fred Meyer's parking lot, an insert slipped from the Anchorage Daily News I carried and fell to the ground. I leaned down to pick it up, *Community school classes for spring, hm?*

I called my new friend, Minerva, from the theatre group. "Wanna go to a goal-setting class?"

The following Tuesday night, she and I met at Chinook Elementary School in a classroom full of small desks huddled together in the middle of the room. "Tonight," our leader handed out paper, "we're going to make collages of everything we'd like included in our lives."

Minerva sat across from me. Squished in those tiny chairs, we cut words and images from magazines and glued them onto poster board. After half an hour, she announced, "Done!"

"You're kidding?" I stood up and stretched, walked over, and looked at her page. There were three big pictures—a man, a baby, and a house—her dream couldn't get any clearer.

On the other hand, my page, crammed and full, revealed the clutter in my head. "I want to taste the variety of life," I told her. "I don't want to fit on a page."

Who was I fooling? As much as I wanted to let people see *the real me*, I hid. Even from myself.

In a meditation group I found in that same flyer, that teacher took us through a guided reflection. Jesus smiled from the corner of my inner field of vision, surprising me. I waved like a shy kid looking out from behind a curtain onstage, hoping to find someone paying attention as she waited for her presentation to begin. Then I buried a grin in my armpit.

When I used to get high or sleep around, I cringed when I thought God was watching me as if He was spying on me. Now, I liked how Jesus, my big brother, kept an eye on me and protected me.

"Imagine a rod connecting you to the core of the earth." The teacher read from a book. I sat bolt upright, wriggling. Jesus laughed. Not at me, but with me. I smiled sheepishly.

"You must have a fear of commitment?" The teacher offered a brilliant deduction as if it wasn't so obvious. Commitment was already on my list of issues. A struggle for sure, but God and I would get to it.

Weekly, I attended Adult Children of Alcoholics. Not because my parents drank, but the ACoA laundry list resonated. I wanted the same healing their members did. So, as a group, we confessed:

- We became approval seekers and lost our identity in the process.
- We are frightened of angry people and any personal criticism.
- We have an overdeveloped sense of responsibility and it is easier for us to be concerned with others rather than ourselves; this enables us not to look too closely at our own faults . . . [4]

Was I getting carried away with gatherings? I don't know, but I felt sure I'd find more of God in a class titled Angels. Instead, the teacher confided, "I had sex with the Archangel Gabriel." *Ew.* That didn't feel right. I didn't go to the next class.

In the *Course of Miracles*, I got a strong, get-up-and-go nudge. In the middle of winter in Alaska, with coats and boots piled on the floor beside me, it felt disruptive to leave. But the Nudger wasn't taking *no* for an answer. God had a personal course in miracles for me; apparently this wasn't part of it, so I quit arguing, picked up my stuff, and excuse-me'd my way out.

So far, by process of elimination, my spiritual quest revealed more of what I didn't want than what I did. So, I kept seeking. I studied chakras and *The Celestine Prophesy.* I read two hundred and ninety-eight books, everything from Louise Hay's *Affirma-*

*MARY ME*

*tions* to Shirley MacLaine's *Out on a Limb,* while John Bradshaw's books-on-tape led me through one guided meditation after another, dealing with my inner child. At the same time, I read my Bible and compared everything to my anchor.

And that's when I found Faith Christian Fellowship.

Every other week, I visited another church, then bounced back to this non-denominational gathering that met in an auditorium. Again, I loved the concert and the opportunity to pick from different services. The pastor, like the one at my last church, dressed in a suit. He stepped behind a music stand and lightened things up a bit as they do in a comedy club before the opening act. We studied the books of the Bible, chapter by chapter, without missing a line. Drawn to this guy's explanations of the linguistic and cultural background, I sat enrapt and gravitated to this group of Evangelicals. They validated my experience by constantly making sure, "You *do* have a relationship with Christ, right?"

I did! And because of that, they accepted my wild God stories.

That's when I started hearing about the Holy Spirit. Growing up in Bethany Congregational Church, I'd heard of Him, but I didn't think He'd have anything to do with me. He seemed far away. I understood Jesus because He's a man. I prayed to God the Father because that's how Jesus prayed. And as each became real, this probably sounds crazy, but I made time to read the Bible and ask them questions. Then I waited for responses.

In John 14, I read about how Jesus told His disciples that He was going on ahead to be with God and prepare a place for them. When His friends panicked, Jesus consoled them and promised to send the Holy Spirit, a part of God, to be with them. He is the Spirit of Truth, the Counselor, the Comforter, and the One who teaches and reminds them of His words. The piece of God that communicates with us inside.

Wait, I had to camp there for a minute. That's what Fred does. Then it struck me. Fred's the Holy Spirit? No wonder I wanted more of Him.

# PUT DOWN YOUR DISHTOWEL

- Work on my issues, *check.*
- Find a spiritual community, *check.*
- Love my work. *Jesus, how do we get there?*

After teaching me how to emote, Chance encouraged me to step in the direction of my dreams by listening to my heart. Over and over, it kept saying, "I hate my job at the heating company!"

"At least you have work." My friend from home, Pam, had flown back east, put her affairs in order, and now we celebrated her return to Anchorage with dinner at Subway and a movie at the dollar theatre.

"You're a hard worker, Pam. Don't worry, you'll find a job." I slathered mustard on my ham sandwich. "But let's stop settling for whatever comes along and hold out for more. Something with purpose and meaning."

"And heat's not meaningful in Alaska?" Pam looked at me like I was an idiot. "Aren't you glad we don't live in an igloo?"

"I *am* grateful for our new apartment and a place to plug the engine block heater of my car in so it starts every morning. And I love my new volunteer job." I was painting the old ladies' nails at the nursing home on my lunch hour, listening to their stories about the olden days. Pearl ran from her husband because he kept making her have backstreet abortions. As a single mom, she had moved up from Washington and fueled planes in the war.

"I went to church with Pearl on Sunday. We were the only ones in the whole chapel at the care facility who weren't on stretchers or in wheelchairs. Afterwards, that little lady with the big purse teetered down the hall toward the cafeteria asking, 'Can I treat you for lunch?'

"As we settled at our table, she glanced sideways and signaled with her head for me to do the same. I looked over at an old guy hooked up to an oxygen tank who was chasing peas around his plate. Pearl said, 'He's staring at your legs!' "

Pam laughed. "He probably couldn't see that far."

"I know, right?" I wiped my mouth. "Hey, maybe I should work with old people?"

"But if you left your job at the heating company, you'd miss the FedEx guy—the one who looks like a stripper. And I've never heard of another place that lets you drink beer at your desk or listen to books on tape. Your job is perfect, don't rock the boat."

"I can't stay." I shook my head. "I need to help people."

The next day, I tried to explain it to Chance. "It isn't my co-workers or the admin tasks I don't like. I just need something more."

"When will you quit?" Chance had a whole different take on this than Pam.

"I'm afraid of leaving a paycheck," I vacillated, "until I have another."

"I'll cut my fee in half," she offered, then helped me list my expenses: food, gas, rent. We came up with a budget and set the wheels of change in motion.

After our session, I pulled up in front of a housesitting job. A new gig to make extra money. I grabbed Princess the pampered toy poodle and prepped her for a walk as I daydreamed about my ideal profession. Home health care? Maybe.

"My turn!" one of the kids across the street squealed over the sound of a lawnmower. As I locked the front door behind me and inhaled, I could smell *Mmm, freshly cut grass.* Down the street, a pit bull broke free from his owner and made a break in my direction. Not usually leashed to a poodle, it didn't hit me that he was making a beeline toward me.

I opened the gate, stepped onto the sidewalk, and *ba-bang!* On his hind legs, the pit bull's forelegs landed on my chest. I staggered back as he panted in my face and did the only thing I could to get the poodle out of his grasp: I held tightly to her leash and swung her up over my head. In slow motion, I turned my face away from his dog breath to check on her. No! My furry little dependent dangled from my hand like a limp rag.

Huffing and puffing, his owner caught up and worked hard to pull the dog off me and gain some semblance of control. I grasped the trembling poodle, held her closely, and backtracked into the yard as she gasped for air.

That night, I had dinner with Alan who rented a room from Princess's owner. I told him what had happened. "Why do you think you're here?" He cut a large piece of salmon in two. "Even though I'm her roommate, I don't want to be responsible for her seventeen-year-old dog. She'd freak if something happened."

Quickly changing the subject, I told him about my job search. "What do you like to do?" He handed me a plate.

"Take care of animals." Shoot, I didn't mean to bring that up again. Refusing eye contact, I searched my brain. "Um, I like to shop, run errands, care for the elderly, and help people write their stories."

"That's your job description." He pointed his knife at me. "Go get a business license."

"The list of things I like to do is my job description?" I perked up. "Can I make a living doing that?" It was definitely worth a try.

Within a month, I'd made a plan, printed flyers, and gone to a class at the small business development center. Then I birthed *Service with a Smile* with its vague name because I bristled at the thought of being labeled or limited to a piece of me that could be criticized and rejected, leaving me isolated, lonely, or unloved.

There it was again. The reason I included, well, everything I had to offer.

I accepted almost any job, passing out candy at the mall as the Easter Bunny and dressing as Barney for a kid's birthday party. As my friend drove past The Fork and Knife, he nodded toward the dancing utensils out front and told his family, "Better wave. You know who that could be!"

In all the imitations, I discovered I am not a clown even when I'm wearing the costume. Why was that different than the others? Well, I could copy the TV show and get away with my impression of the purple dinosaur or love on the kids as the Easter Bunny, but people expect more from a clown. They expect goofiness, tricks, and persona. Without that, I felt like a fraud. I found out that in my pursuit for happiness, authenticity was essential. I needed to be true to myself.

As I practiced making balloon animals in the birch syrup booth at the Saturday market, an elderly black woman teetered over, surrounded by two large bodyguards. I held out a taste. "A hundred gallons of sap boils down to one to make this unique Alaskan product."

"I'll take a bottle." She reached into her purse for twelve dollars. We made our exchange, and she moved on. Seconds later, a young reporter shoved a microphone in my face. "What's she like?"

"Who?" I restocked samples.

Simultaneously, everyone around me yelled, "Ro-o-osa Parks!"

*How did I miss that?* If I hadn't been so busy working eighty-four hours a week, I might have noticed it was *Rosa Parks Day*, and she was our guest. Afraid of too little income, I took on too much work until everything around me kept reinforcing this point.

Working at the bank the next day, I sat with my first mortgage loan clients. The wife squinted and wagged her finger at me as she tried to place my face. "I know you."

"People always say that." I evaded her question, hoping she'd trust me without realizing I was a temp who didn't really know what I was doing. "I must have one of those faces."

"God must have liked your mold and made a bunch of you." She smiled.

*God?* I flinched, then blushed, trying to focus on her paperwork when the unexpected mention of His name brought Him front and center. I'd been asking for more of Him. Then I ran ahead and left Him in the dust. I got so dang busy I went AWOL. It's like God wanted a word.

Was I in trouble? I kept my eyes down and hoped He'd move on.

Why hadn't I talked to God about these work decisions? I guess I didn't want to lay too much on Him. He's God and all, but I didn't want to max Him out and lose Him as I'd done to some of the men in my life. As always, He let me choose and slipped into the shadows as I spent my attention on the people in front of me.

After I re-financed loans, I typed invoices for another company then rushed to a third client's house. Balancing her toddler on my hip, I retrieved her son from karate. Then I showed up late for Minerva's party and heard that same lady from the bank say, "I told you I knew you!"

"She has a hundred jobs these days." Minerva hugged me. "If she doesn't watch out, she's going to turn up at the bank dressed like the Easter bunny." *Great, how was that for instilling trust in the clients.*

Minerva was right, though. It was too much. In over my head, I needed to cut back.

In the Bible, Jesus hung out with Mary and Martha. When He visited them, Mary sat at His feet, lingering on His every word. Martha scurried about, waiting on Him hand and foot.

Standing in the kitchen with her hands on her hips, Martha looked out the door at Mary in the living room, just sitting there like she had been all day. Scowling, Martha shook her head and picked up a dishtowel.

If I could peek my head in and ask, "You okay?" she might raise her voice, hoping someone in particular heard her diatribe as she gave me an earful.

How do I know? I *was* Martha.

When I got too busy, I set my relationships aside. Like when I lived with Tony. With a house-cleaning business, college classes, and the work in my own home, I'd pass him for a quick kiss each morning with a bite of breakfast in my mouth while loading books on my body as if I were a pack animal. All day I'd run before returning exhausted and bedraggled that night, snapping like a turtle, making myself as unattractive as possible, and hoping against hope that he didn't want anything because I had nothing left to give.

Now, with twelve jobs, I'd done the same thing to God. With no time together, our relationship grew distant. We were becoming disconnected. I growled at Him after finishing work at *Service with a Smile,* noting the irony.

Princess's roommate was right. Caring for that poodle, or anyone else, came with responsibility. To feel good about what I did, I needed enough time to do it well. It turns out, I wasn't just looking for work but a vocation—maybe even a calling.

When Martha finally had it with Mary, she took Jesus aside. "Would You *please* tell her to help me?"

Instead, Jesus gave Martha a talking-to. "One thing is necessary. Mary has made the right choice, and it will not be taken away from her" (Luke 10:42, HCSB).

I'll bet Martha didn't appreciate those words at first, and neither did I when I realized God wanted me to put my own dishtowel down and spend some time with Him.

But God didn't want for me to be just a Martha. He wanted to Mary me.

Still avoiding God, I drove up to the University of Alaska to stare at the alpenglow on the mountains a few minutes before meeting with Chance. God startled me. "This is your last appointment." *No, it isn't!* I shook my head, started the car, and drove to her house, trying to ignore what I'd just heard.

But five minutes later, Chance crooked her neck and confirmed. "We're done, right?"

"No!" I disagreed.

"Counseling happens in layers," she said. "That doesn't mean you can't come back or that others won't help you along the way."

"Yeah, yeah, yeah." That was not what I wanted to hear. Back home, I landed on the couch. "God, if Chance isn't going to help me, who will?"

"Maybe I want to?" He said. "How about if I help you slow down so you don't show up at the bank dressed like the Easter bunny."

*Hm.* I smiled, sat down at the computer, and composed a letter to God, even though He was right there. In my mind, a letter made my intention official. Contractual even.

> God,
>
> After all You've done, how did I forget—You have a plan!
>
> I'm so sorry I didn't come to You for a job. You're right, life's been too busy. I need work that covers my bills and helps me to grow spiritually, but not too much that we don't have time together.
>
> What do You think I should do?

That Sunday at church, an ad in the bulletin read: part-time receptionist needed for summer.

"No!" I shook my head and said to God, "I definitely do not want to be a church secretary."

But like a child tugging on the hem of my dress, the ad caught my attention three weeks in a row. On each occasion, I saw the letter I wrote to God in my mind as if He was saying, "You-u-u as-s-sked."

Finally, I dropped off a resume. Taking one last glance before I slid it under the door, I noticed I'd accidently brought in my *fun* one which listed face painter, hot dog vendor at football games, and slave at the Renaissance Festival. No office experience listed; I smiled.

In the interview, the office manager said, "Why do you want this job?"

"I don't!" I wrinkled my nose. "God keeps bugging me to apply."

# BECOMING REAL

At home, a week later, I hit the answering machine *play* button. "This is Cindy at Faith Christian Fellowship. We'd like to hire you." Be-e-ep. "This is Cindy, the one you interviewed with last week. Call when you get in." Be-e-ep. "I'm looking for Elizabeth Bristol. Is this the right number?"

*Crap, I got the job?* After I applied, I went away. Since I'd told Cindy I didn't want the position, I didn't think to tell her I'd be gone. As I perched on the edge of the couch, I couldn't deny how the ad had grabbed me after I wrote God that letter. So now, I didn't want to say *no*, but I didn't want to say *yes* either. For some reason, I didn't think I'd actually have to take the job. But how could I decline? I consoled myself; it's only for the summer.

Then *What-the-heck-am-I-doing?* and *You've-got-to-be-kidding-me!* swam through my mind like two sharks in a tropical fish tank. The largest one eyed me warily as if to say, "Who are you now?"

I know, right? A church secretary. I frowned. Was God outing me as a Christian?

Then it hit me. I wanted to be authentic. By holding back, I presented a façade. My whole life I'd aimed to please people. Now I wanted to follow God, but not like some sort of robot with mechanical movements and glassy eyes, mindlessly agreeing in monotone, "Yes, boss."

God could've made us clones, but He didn't. He gave us free will. And He kept bringing me into situations like this where I had to own my truth. I felt like I was jumping out of a plane without a chute, ditching the me-I'd-known-for-almost-thirty-years for this new me-I-didn't-totally-get. At the other end of the transformation, would any of my friends still talk to me?

In this church where I now worked at the front desk, 800 people attended each of the four services. It wasn't long before God showed me how I freely gave haphazard advice to the people who phoned us. He didn't like it. Because not only does God care for me, He loves everyone else, too.

I'll never forget the call. As a writer, I should include the specifics to build up the problem the caller had as a titillating scandal, but I don't remember that part. As church secretary, God gave me spiritual amnesia. I listened to calls of a personal nature every day and forgot them because it wasn't the details that mattered. It was the person, always the person. And protecting their confidentiality was essential.

As I replaced the receiver in its cradle, God said, "Think about what you just said."

The hair on the back of my neck stood. I shivered as my old captors, Mr. Fight and Mr. Flight, took up their familiar stance and temptation.

"Ru-u-un!" Flight yelled while Fight dangled a pair of boxing gloves in front of my face. I looked up at God. Then, like a wronged child awaiting a scolding, I assumed the position, head down and eyes fastened on the desk while my stomach did cartwheels.

Instead of punishing me, though, God downloaded understanding through a series of I-statements:

- I speak as a representative of the church now—of God.
- I need to stop spouting off simple answers to complicated problems I know nothing about.
- I don't have kids. Why am I giving parenting tips?

Blushing, I realized flippant advice could change a person's life in the wrong way. I had access to counselors and could connect the callers to them. Why hadn't I?

Tears puddled in my eyes. Then it's like God hugged me from inside. I don't even know how to explain it, but His love made me want to bring Him every single one of my problems right there and then. "I'm so sorry," I whispered. "I can't do this, but You can."

"We can!" He promised.

That's when the Velveteen Rabbit came to mind. A stuffed animal *made real* by the love of a child.

> "Real isn't how you are made," said the Skin Horse. "It's a thing that happens to you. When a child loves you for a long, long time, not just to play with, but REALLY loves you, then you become Real."
>
> "Does it hurt?" asked the Rabbit.
>
> "Sometimes," said the Skin Horse, for he was always truthful. "When you are Real you don't mind being hurt."
>
> "Does it happen all at once, like being wound up," he asked, "or bit by bit?"
>
> "It doesn't happen all at once," said the Skin Horse. "You become. It takes a long time. That's why it doesn't happen often to people who break easily, or have sharp edges, or

who have to be carefully kept. Generally, by the time you are Real, most of your hair has been loved off, and your eyes drop out and you get loose in the joints and very shabby. But these things don't matter at all, because once you are Real you can't be ugly, except to people who don't understand."[5]

*OHMYWORD,* that's what God was doing; making me Real with His love. And there's nothing quite like God calling you *beautiful* when He knows all you've done, thought, and said. Acceptance like that changes me. As I bask in His care, I morph. For Him, I don't have to tone it down or be someone I'm not. As I yield, He molds me into my truest self.

Did it hurt? Well, like the wise, old Skin Horse admitted, "Sometimes."

But God strengthens me so I can take it, whatever *it* is. And I found out how strong I could be after I'd been broken. While going forward is sometimes hard, I'd never choose to go back.

That night, I went to dinner at a Thai restaurant with a friend. As I sipped a beer, I thought I saw one of the girls from church scowl at me from across the room. *What?* As if at a sporting event, I looked at the marquee in my mind. "Should you be drinking?"

*Oh, C'mon!* Was that God? I couldn't be sure.

I didn't want to run my question by my friend in case she agreed. And I didn't clarify with God, either, probably for the same reason. I saw nothing wrong with a beer or two, but then I thought about my friends in AA. As a new employee of the church, some could recognize me before I noticed them. I didn't want to dangle a beer unknowingly in front of someone who was trying to abstain. So, from then on, I decided that I'd still have a beer. Just not in public.

Is that hypocritical? I hated hypocrisy, but I wasn't ready to quit drinking, so I made a concession. I'd stop getting high. Weirdly enough, God had never given me a hard time about that even though it was illegal. And when I asked Him to help, all I can say is that He gave me amazing grace. I've heard others say the same thing, but I know plenty of people who haven't had that experience.

Why does God do things one way for some but not for all?

This may not reveal my best *aunt-ing* skills, but when my nieces were little, I learned quickly I could bribe one to do just about anything with chocolate, but not the other. We're like that—unique. Again, I remembered how "God causes all things to work together for good to those who love Him" (Romans 8:28, paraphrase of the Bible). Maybe working everything out in one person's best interest looks different than it does for another.

It's like when we used to complain as children when we didn't see that our parents were doing what was best for us. You know, like a little boy saying to his mom, "You're so mean. You never let me eat all the candy I want!"

God certainly doesn't do things the way I would, but He can see things I can't.

No matter what, addiction's horrible. On my own, I'd tried to quit smoking cigarettes 976 times, and I don't think I'm exaggerating. Sometimes I stopped for years, but I craved them the whole time.

When I gave up through God, He even took the desire.

Then once, during a stressful time, I picked them back up. It'd been so easy to stop with God, I figured I'd go another round. After two weeks, He warned me. "You know how hard this can really be." My grace period was over, and I haven't had a cigarette since.

Hanging out with God, I'd quit all the other drugs I used to do except pot, and I got down to smoking it once in a while instead of all the time.

"People use God as a crutch." My friend smirked as she handed me a joint.

"'Spose we all lean on something." I took my last hit ever.

Drugs, my off button, had caused me to forget the day's problems. They'd helped me to relax. But in this process, I no longer wanted to escape. I wanted to quit and just needed help.

Finally, I said, "God I can't do this, will You help?"

When I asked, He flicked a switch like He'd done with cigarettes. Over and over, I'd tried to give up. My resolution never took until He did something; I don't know what, but it worked. With other things, it hasn't always been so easy. So, I have to stay close to Him for the help I need.

I think God likes us to depend on Him.

In the past, others had taken advantage of me. God doesn't do that. Instead of taking, He gives. He gets the best *for* me instead of the best *of* me.

He's not a crutch. He's a flippin' superpower!

# THE UNFORGIVABLE SIN

I wanted a man in my life. A healthy relationship unlike anything I'd had before, with love, intimacy, and real connection—but without sex. I wanted to walk my talk by doing things God's way this time: no-sex-before-marriage. Was that even possible? I didn't think so.

I still believed the lie: *If I want to keep a boyfriend, I have to have sex with him.*

So, how did I get one without doing the wild thing?

Instead of asking God, I usually avoided men or chose the ones I could control. What was I thinking? I hated when someone did that to me.

Why did I think I wanted to be on either end of that?

I needed authenticity in my relationships with men, too, to be able to communicate in healthy ways like God had been showing me. I wanted to be able to cry and work through conflict with words without people-pleasing. I wanted to stand up for myself while also encouraging the men around me to stand up for themselves. You know, neither of us controlling the other.

With the perfect opportunity to prowl, I got into Minerva's blue Taurus with a couple of friends and rode ninety miles to Talkeetna for the Women of the Wilderness Contest and Bachelor Auction. Fighting a cold, I passed on the competition and watched the others from inside the bar. As I nursed one hot drink after another, Rick, a guy I'd recently dared to date after the ejaculating-dog incident, ambled over. Because of my dilemma, not knowing how to go out with him without sleeping with him, I'd stopped returning his calls.

"What are you doing here?" I sipped my Irish coffee.

"Writing an article for the paper. Do you want to help share the women's point of view?"

I scrunched up my face. Hanging out with him all weekend would feel like I brought a date to the bachelor auction. "Don't think so."

Outside, my friends hauled water, made sandwiches, and delivered snacks to the bachelors by snow machine (the Alaskan term for snow mobile). Judging by the way *Hard Copy* and *Current Affair* cameramen followed Minerva around, she was either in the lead or had the juiciest story. Of course, what reporter could resist the thrice-widowed nanny from Texas working her way through an *Alaska Men* subscription in search of husband number four?

"My first husband died in a military maneuver." Juanita Teresa Gonzales Cobarruvias Perales Delos Santos Rangel, a.k.a. Minerva, reveled in the attention. "The second died in a car accident and the third on the operating table."

At the auction raising money for battered women, Minerva bid on five bachelors and bought two. Each bought her a drink and spun her around the dance floor.

While Rick hovered at the edge of that same dance floor, taking pictures for his article, I drank a good part of a bottle with the winner of the competition. She'd won the coolest decanter with dark liquor on one side and white on the other. Hungover, or maybe still drunk, I woke up spooning in bed with Minerva and one of those bachelors, two other friends, and a dog named Homer. Thankfully, I was fully clothed. So much for a new man.

I'd been learning more functional ways of interaction, but it's not like I could incorporate all of them into my way of doing things overnight. And apparently, in order to be part of a healthy relationship, I needed to do my fair share of work on myself.

With my tail between my legs, I avoided You-Know-Who until the long ride home. Then I closed my eyes, leaned my head back on the car seat, and called on Fred. Like the way I approach Mom with things I wouldn't tell Dad, I went to Fred instead of Jesus or God. Of course, they're one and the same; this just spared me the awkwardness of telling the one who scares me most.

"Fred," I said, "I'm sorry. Rick freaked me out. I should have come to You. Getting drunk was stupid *and* the easiest way to end up in trouble."

In my mind's eye, I saw Jesus smile. Still, I addressed Fred. "Isn't premarital sex *the* unforgivable sin? Seems like it, anyway, according to Mom. But I know the Bible says, blaspheming the Holy Spirit is the unforgivable sin" (Mark 3:28-9, paraphrase of the Bible). Jesus, the definition of patience, loved me. I could tell by the look on His face.

"What is blaspheming the Holy Spirit?" My internal voice squeaked. Did I do it?

"It's a fancy way of saying *refusing Me*."

"Huh." I chewed on the inside of my cheek. "So, the only thing that can keep a person from You is themselves?"

"Yup."

I squinted into the morning sun. "John 3:16 says: 'For God loved the world so much that He gave His one and only Son, so that everyone who believes in Him will not perish but have eternal life' " (NLT).

"I love it when you quote the Bible to Me." Jesus held His gaze, never turning away.

I blushed. "So, if we come to You, we spend eternity together. If we refuse, we *choose* eternal life without You?"

"Yup."

Like God sometimes does, He brought a recent conversation to mind that I'd had with my three-year-old niece. She has a surety in matters about God that blows me away. As we lay in her bed together, we prayed: "Now I lay me down to sleep . . . and God bless . . . " She listed everyone in her small world then asked, "How come Auntie Victoria doesn't go to church?"

"She used to." I kissed her forehead. "I guess she decided she didn't want Jesus."

With a simple yet profound observation, she pegged it. "If Auntie Victoria knew who Jesus really was, she'd want Him."

*Whoa, right?*

"I think so, too," I said. "For a while, I also thought I didn't want Jesus. But you're right, I just didn't know Him."

With those women in the car on the way back from Talkeetna, I put all these thoughts aside and opened my eyes to return to the conversation, debriefing the weekend's activities with them.

That night, at home, I crawled into bed. "Jesus?"

"Yeah."

"If there's one area in my life that really needs Your help, it's my love life. I run from what I want most: a relationship that leads to marriage. I don't want to get drunk or sleep around anymore, but I want a boyfriend. How do I date without having sex?"

"You let me help you." He smiled.

And again, incredible peace filled my body as I closed my eyes, took a deep breath, and exhaled. "Okay."

# MYSTERIOUS WAYS

The more I listened to God, the more He proved trustworthy. And the more I wanted to hear *everything* He had to say. Well, until His suggestions caused me angst. No, even then, too.

One lunch hour, I stopped at Dimond Mall. At one of the kiosks, I locked eyes onto a Magic Eye 3D picture, the latest craze in the world of trends. To see the subject embedded in a horizontally repeating pattern, you focused on your nose, and eventually the subject became clear in the background of the design. As if trying to outstare a cat, I couldn't look away even though I needed to get back to work.

Eight long minutes later, I accidently screamed, "It's a unicorn!"

People around me burst into unexpected applause. I blushed then fled with a sense of accomplishment.

That night, as I lay in bed talking to God, a shaft of moonlight shone through the curtains. Without trying, I saw another 3D picture. This time, it was candles around my room. I rubbed my eyes, but it didn't go away. Just before I'd turned out the light, I'd read, "It would be silly to light a lamp and then hide it under a bowl. When someone lights a lamp, she puts it on a table or a desk or a chair, and the light illumines the entire house. *You are like that illuminating light.* Let your light shine everywhere you go, *that you may illumine creation*, so men and women everywhere may see your good actions, *may see creation at its fullest, may see your devotion to Me*, and may turn and praise your Father in heaven *because of it*" (Matthew 5:15-16, TV).

I settled back on the pillow and grinned at God's illustration of His Word with the reflection of the candles around my room . . . until He reminded me of the way I'd hidden my relationship with Him from some of my friends. My smile faded as I turned toward the wall. "You're not always a popular subject. What if they walk away?"

I fell asleep before I heard His answer. Again, I had a choice.

That Sunday, I got to church early. At the coffee table, I ran into a cute guy who dressed in a suit, carried his Bible, and always sat up front—not the type I ever would have picked before. Continuing my attempts to talk to men, I told him about the picture in my room. He raised an eyebrow. "That would freak me out."

"Not me," I laughed. "I love weird God experiences, and I don't think freaking people out is His goal. I bet He relates to you in other ways, you know, like we do with people. My relationship with Mom is different from my connection to my boss. I guess that's part of what we mean when we say *personal relationship*, right?"

"I guess." The cute guy smiled for real. Not some fake, whatever-you-say imitation. He and I might have had a different perspective, but that didn't scare him away. I liked that.

"Remember," I said, "Jesus didn't heal everyone the same. One blind guy got his sight when Jesus spoke to him. Another was healed after Jesus made mud with spit and wiped it on his eyes and told him to go wash in the river. Don't you know a few blind guys bypassed Jesus and tried rubbing their faces in the dirt!"

These chats reminded me of when I used to smoke pot and talk to my friends about God, trying to figure Him out. But the conversations made more sense when I wasn't high, especially when I included God, too. It was like the time I went out with my roommate's friend, one of many first dates as I built up the courage for a relationship. I came home alone and went to bed. Before drifting off to sleep, I said, "God, he and I look at everything through a different lens. What's the deal?"

In my mind, I gave Jesus the relationship as if it was a dirty dish on a cafeteria tray. When I looked down to see what I handed Him in this vision, however, it was a plate of bacon and eggs. I chewed on the inside corner of my mouth as I looked at Him.

Jesus took out a giant saltshaker and sprinkled some on the food. "Needs salt!"

"Wha-a-at?" I laughed even though I didn't know what He meant.

While I waited for His answer, I dug through my Bible. Matthew 5:1 caught my attention: "You [Jesus' followers] are the salt of the earth" (NKJV). And then: "Do not be unequally yoked together with unbelievers" (2 Corinthians 6:14, NKJV).

I'm not *yoked* with him, am I?

I read the notes down below the text in my Study Bible and talked to friends at work. A yoke is a wooden harness that connects oxen. How did that apply to us?

That's when I came across the words *contractual agreement.* I thought about the lease I'd had with my roommate Pam and groaned like Ebenezer Scrooge might have in *The Christmas Carol* as he traipsed the globe with the Ghost of Christmas Past. I knew which scene we'd land on.

In her thigh-high boots and micro mini-skirt, Pam frequented Chilkoot Charlie's with her hair pulled up as high as she could get it. As she prepared to go out one night, her sister, my funky hairdressing friend from home, called her a "ho."

"I'm not a ho." Pam applied another layer of hairspray.

"Well, you look like a ho."

Pam strolled into that bar, took a look around, and whispered in my ear. "I *am* the nicest-looking girl in this place." I laughed. Don't get me wrong, Pam's a pretty lady, but it's her confidence that lines men up.

When we lived together, she'd emerge from her bedroom in the early afternoon dressed in flannel PJs and with her hair in a ponytail. She looked better that way as far as I was concerned.

One Saturday afternoon, I'd reached for the phone.

"Who are you calling?" She opened the fridge and peered inside.

"Minerva's new man. I need to get rid of my mattress. He'll take it to the dump."

"Don't bother him." She waved. "We'll wait 'til it's dark and squish it in the dumpster."

"Isn't there something in our lease that says we're not supposed to do that?" I didn't want to step back into anything that made my stomach feel wonky. This clean conscience I had was worth everything it took to get it. But I didn't want Pam to think . . . *what*? Ugh, another peer pressure thing. That I was morphing into a goody-two-shoes and no longer fun? Or that I was a chicken? Or worse . . . *uncool*?

"No one will know," Pam promised as she peeked out the door later that night. "C'mon, the coast is clear."

We dragged the thing down the hall, onto the elevator, through the garage, and pushed it into the garbage container. Easy peasy-ish, except that it didn't fit. We sprinted across the parking lot and back up the stairs.

As I pulled into the lot the next day, I looked over at a mound of snow. Then I did a double take and watched kids sledding on the flippin' mattress. My cheeks burned. The following day, the elderly receptionist lugged the thing through the slush and back toward the dumpster. *Cripes!* Instead of jumping out to help her, I parked, ran inside, and told Pam. "I'm calling Minerva's man."

"You can't do that now." She warned. "They'll find out it was you and you'll *really* get into trouble."

As I lay in bed, flashing back on the memory, my stomach queased over. Is that even a word? Verb form of queasy. The Bible says we *reap* what we *sow*. Some might call it fate or karma. Either way, I didn't want anything else boomeranging back at me. It was time to plant some God seeds. "Is that why You gave us a conscience?" I asked God. "To help us follow Your direction? It never feels right when I don't do what I know I should. From now on, I'm going to. My friends can do what they want. If our relationships shift, well, You and I can figure that out later."

God smiled. Then He reminded me of the yoke thing with another verse: "Place my yoke over your shoulders, and learn from me, because I am gentle and humble. Then you will find rest for yourselves because my yoke is easy and my burden is light" (Matthew 11:29-30, GW).

In my mind, I saw Jesus put His arm around me, lean in to hear what I had to say, tilt His head back, and laugh, all the while holding me gently. Then it hit me. "*Your arm* is my yoke? Cool. Now do the saltshaker and the guy."

"He doesn't share your faith. If you marry him, you'll be yoked together in a contractual agreement. The relationship needs salt, or faith, on his part so you won't be unequally partnered."

"So, You want me to marry a Christian?" I sighed as pictures of coupled friends flashed through my mind. Some partnered with people of different faiths, others with someone who shared their beliefs. Dating a man of another religion hadn't mattered to me before, but then again, neither had my faith. Now that it was important, I definitely wanted to share it. "Hm, the church has a singles' group. You gonna hook me up?" I grinned. "Just like You did with the job?"

# MR. RIGHT?

Now that my job at the church was settled, I itemized what I wanted in a man. At a goal-setting class, as the leader provoked us. "Tell me the color of his eyes and what he ate for breakfast."

At thirty-three, with my biological clock ticking, I listed, "long hair, loves God." (Yup, in that order.) I would like him to have a career as a caregiver, to work out, and to be laid back. And no kidding, a live specimen strode right through the front door of the church and up to my desk.

Of course, lots of men could be described this way, but that day, I didn't see it.

Sizzling hot in a white Oxford shirt tucked into a pair of snug jeans, Jim flashed his extra-white smile. He looked like Jesus! "I'm looking for the singles' group," he said. "Can you help me?"

"I can!" I wanted to say, "help you right back out that door before anyone else gets their hands on you." But instead, I came around the front of the desk and uttered the only thing I could think of, the stupid cliché. "Are you new in town?"

Was God answering my prayer? Because I'd take this guy.

Then, of all times, I had tickets to visit friends in London. If I could have, I would have postponed my trip. I didn't want anyone scooping him up while I was gone. I thought about him most of the time I was away. Dreamt about him, even. He was too good to be true. He was a male model, wore his sweater tied around his neck, and pulled the top layer of his hair back into a ponytail while the rest hung long. *What if he was gay?* "Please, God, no." Should I have put heterosexual on my list?

"What do you think?" I asked my old roommate at Heathrow airport. I hadn't mentioned it to anyone in Alaska. With a lot of gay friends, she was the perfect person to ask.

"No." She nodded with confidence. "Not if he's going to church, I don't think so."

"Yes!" I screamed, banking on her answer.

I wanted a man in my life. I wanted this one. Of course, he'd make me happy. He'd bring proof to the world around me that . . . *what?* A hot guy like him wanted me?

*Ugh, get over yourself, Bristol,* I thought to myself.

On a double-decker bus I daydreamed, imagining my life free from parental pressure once I had my own kids. That's meaningful, right? Enough to gain Dad's approval and put that mark on the world he'd always encouraged? I would give birth to two girls and a boy, Ashley Dawn, Andréa, and Julian. Then I'd have done my part with Mister Gorgeous, the embodiment of my list. I closed my eyes and smiled when a memory surfaced. I tried to push it away, wanting to keep thinking about Jim, but the flashback stood firm. Sometimes, God talks to me through remembrances of the past, so I turned my attention to Him and took a virtual trip back in time to a Renaissance Fayre. Wenches danced to medieval instruments as I stepped into a booth for a turkey leg. Back at the jousting match, my friend was beside herself. "I just saw him!"

"Who?" I wiped the grease dripping down my chin.

"The man of my dreams, my husband, the father of my children, the one I'll spend the rest of my life with. I haven't seen him from the front yet, but when he gets out of the bathroom, I'll point him out."

I laughed out loud. On that bus in London, I said to God, "But I've seen Jim from the front!"

Hoping to slide in under forty, married with kids, I had seven years left. But was Jim the right guy? And did I want to get married? After running for eight years from the relationship with Tony, I thought I did. But after the lying and cheating from men in my past, I wasn't sure about any of this. Even after having hung out with God almost as long, I was still learning to trust Him. He hadn't disappointed me, but I hadn't let my guard down either.

So, why couldn't I stop thinking about Jim's dark eyes and perfect smile? That settled it. I went back to Alaska and angled up to him in the singles' group at church. "My friend's celebrating her fortieth with a 'thankful' party next week at the musk ox farm where I volunteer; wanna go?"

"What's a musk ox?" Intrigued by an animal he'd never heard of, Jim agreed and picked me up in his little red sports car the following weekend. Then he posed by one of the prehistoric-looking animals that jumped on all fours when it wanted to scare predators away. I couldn't wait to add the picture to my photo album and show him off to friends.

"Mmm, you smell good," he complimented me.

"Lagerfeld cologne." I took a whiff of my wrist. "I couldn't find a perfume I liked."

"Men's cologne?" he asked. "You need a perfume."

*Really, why?*

Inside the bungalow, overlooking the backside of the farm, my friend offered us a glass of wine. I accepted. Jim said, "I don't drink." Cool, I had a designated driver.

He sat down at the table and made me a blue origami crane with some paper he found there. I mingled. On the way home, he said, "You make friends easily. I admire that. I like that you connect me to others. Thanks!"

Over the next couple of months, we attended singles' events and church, hiked with my friends, and went out to dinner with the people who were the closest thing I had to parents in Alaska. On top of the Captain Cook Hotel, overlooking the city lights of Anchorage, the waiter brought our flaming dessert to the table while my Alaskan Dad focused on Jim. "You know, if you marry her, she'll eat you out of house and home."

"Jim works out daily." I gave my Alaskan Dad *the look*. "He eats no fat."

"So, you're divorced," he continued. I kicked him under the table and answered for Jim again, "Yes. Now why don't you tell us something personal about you?"

After dinner, my Alaskan Mom and I went to the ladies' room. I checked my face and dug a brush out of my purse.

"Mason Pearson," she said. "Where'd you get that? Those are $150."

My jaw dropped. "Jim gave it to me. And this ring and my watch."

All these gifts, and finally, five months later, we were going on a *date*. What made it official? I don't know, but it was Valentine's Day. Months later Jim was still a mystery. I tell everyone everything, but that's not the way he works. I studied him, learned his buttons, and made every effort to press the right ones.

When he came to pick me up, I gave him a gift.

"You made that?" he asked.

"I did." We looked down at the heart-shaped cake resembling a box of candy. Raspberries and strawberries cascaded from under the chocolate lid. I'd garnished it with mint and confectioner's sugar.

"Looks good enough to eat!" He helped me put on my coat and escorted me to the door. *Oh yeah, eats no fat. What was I thinking? What will he do with a cake?*

At the Seven Glaciers Restaurant, I ordered. "Crab cakes, an Artisan cheese plate, and Halibut ceviche."

Jim said, "I'll take the salmon, by itself."

On the drive back up the Seward Highway, he pulled off the road. We kissed a little.

Without any forethought, I blurted. "What's the worst thing you've ever done?" *What was I thinking?* Jim turned the ignition, eased the car back onto the highway and accelerated without answering. Wait, I wanted to keep kissing!

Since I couldn't take the words back, I asked. "Did you hear what I said?"

"Yup."

"And?"

"Don't want to talk about it."

That was not how I wanted to end our first date.

Well into the next week, I couldn't stop thinking about that conversation.

Meanwhile, the children's ministry cast the Good Friday Passion Play with Jim as Jesus. Two of my co-workers fought over the role of Judas, the man who *betrayed* Jesus, in order to peck my boyfriend on the cheek. *Really?*

Since I hadn't had a man in a while, I'd forgot about competition. I hate rivalry. Women pretend to be friends and prowl away from Girls Night Out, looking for my man to pounce on him when he's had too much to drink. Oh wait. That was before, right?

Again, still figuring out this new world, I pasted a smile on my face rather than addressing it with my new friends, the bunch of cats. All the while I wondered, *what is Jim hiding?*

It seems like there's always a pile of unknowns on the other side of desire.

If he had information he wanted to keep private, I wanted to be okay with that. The fear of exposing my past scared me, too. In my need to share, I wasn't after his secrets. I just wanted to be honest in a relationship I'd hoped would lead to marriage. I no longer wanted to hide my past; I wanted more freedom.

Because of my new life with God, the skeletons in my closet lost power. But I was still learning that. I wasn't yet living it. In my head, I put my dukes up. "I'm gonna tell him, Skeleton, because you're not holding me hostage anymore. You've stolen far too much already!"

But I still hadn't said a thing.

Finally, as Jim dropped me off one night, I said, "I have something to say, but I don't have the courage to tell you." I tucked a word of confession into his back pocket.

"You don't have to do this." He looked into my eyes.

"I want to. When you get home, read my note."

I thought he'd pull the paper from his pocket on my front step after I closed the door. That's what I would have done. At the very least, I thought he'd call me when he got home. I'd confessed my deepest, darkest secret. and he didn't say *anything.*

Finally, the next afternoon, I tracked him down. "Well?"

"Well, what?"

"Well, my giant confession, well!"

"What's the big deal?" he said. "You had an abortion when you were seventeen. That was a long time ago."

"*What'sthebigdeal?* It's the worst thing I've ever done." Shame caused me to flinch. If people knew, what would they think? What does *God* think? He's all about the sanctity of life. And maybe this sounds hypocritical, but I wanted to be like that, too. I wished I'd had the nerve to do something different back then.

Much later, I realized that what seemed like a lack of empathy on Jim's part probably wasn't about me. My ability to share my secret freed me. Did his inability keep him enslaved?

# IS THIS HOW IT'S
# SUPPOSED TO BE?

Growing up, I didn't have strong men in my life. And the men I'd trusted, well, that hadn't gone so well. In my new evangelical church, the guys took care of me in a brotherly way. I liked it.

On a Thursday afternoon at the end of summer, the church staff gathered in the pastor's office for the weekly meeting. We took turns sharing news. I fidgeted, "I took this job for the summer, right? Since the receptionist is coming back, I'm going to work at the Musk Ox Farm."

Surprise rippled through the group. I looked at the youth leader on my right, eager to pass the attention to him. Without expecting it so soon, he stammered, "We're, ah, playing pin the ponytail on the pastor in youth group tonight."

After the meeting, Cal, the senior pastor, stopped by the reception area and said, "Can I talk to you?"

"Sure!" I followed him down the hall, practically skipping.

Twelve years older and the first pastor I'd gotten to know as an adult, I thought of him as a spiritual leader. A father, sort of. Or a big brother. I took his suggestions to heart like everyone else did. He was a pastor, right? You could trust him. Clean-cut, he was a people-magnet who took time to mingle and really listen.

So, of course, his free counseling appointments filled weeks in advance. Mostly with women.

Inside his office, I perched on his couch. He sat back in his chair opposite me and rested his ankle on his knee. "Would you say," he held out his hands, lifting each up and down, alternately, as if they were a scale, "God thinks working with musk ox or people is more important?"

*What's he getting at?* I skirted the answer and took the question back to my desk instead of responding. Then I raged at God on my way home. "The ad for this job said *onlyforthesummer!*"

I called my new prayer group leader, my prayer mama—a Native artist with creations all over town. Without coming right out and giving me her suggestion, she poured into me. "Revelation is when God speaks crystal clear words defining something so succinctly that we're left awe-struck by His presence-infused understanding of truth. Enveloped in the warmth of His sweet presence, we hear His whispers of unconditional love and acceptance with a very personal knowledge of who we are in Him. He invites us to participate in His glorious ways and partake of the riches of knowing Christ. We know He's spoken."

Yup, that's what I wanted. Well, to sit and have coffee with Jesus and to hear what He had to say plain and clear. But as I tried to discern God's will, I didn't always know what He was saying. The continuum went from *know-know-know* it, like a dog with a bone you couldn't take away no matter how hard you tried, to "I *think* that's what He *might* be saying."

After my prayer mama and I talked, I hung up the phone and landed on the couch with my Bible. As usual, I happened across just the right verse. "Jesus said to his disciples: 'Therefore I tell you, do not worry about your life, what you will eat; or about your body, what you will wear. For life is more than food, and the body more than clothes. Consider the ravens: They do not sow or reap, they have no storeroom or barn; yet God feeds them. And how much more valuable you are than birds' " (Luke 12:22-25, NIV). I thought of old Sunday school pictures of Jesus surrounded by animals, loving them. But here it seemed to say He loves us even more. Maybe that's why I was feeling drawn to help people instead of musk ox even though I *loved* animals.

Still, I hemmed and hawed, avoiding Cal's question even though he and I talked regularly since there were only nine of us on staff and I sat at the front desk.

The full-time receptionist had taught me to write him a short poem each week requesting his sermon title. The writing, both my requests and his responses, had gotten more elaborate each week. Of course, we had work to do, but there we were, personalizing another author's ideas like my version of *The Purple Man:*

> Once upon a time, a purple pastor packed his purple co-workers into his purple vehicle and set out on an expedition. Over the purple highway they puttered until they reached the purple sea, pulled over and purchased permits for the whole purple clan. Then they piled their personal belongings onto a purple boat.
>
> The following morning, when that purple pastor crawled out of his lavender tent onto the puce-colored sand and looked toward the amethyst sunrise, he cried in distress. "This is plum crazy, we've been marooned!" . . .
>
> . . . like I will be if I don't get your title to include in the bulletin before it's printed in the morning.[6]

I taped this recent poetic prompt to Cal's door. And my new friend, Kim, poked her head out of her office across the hall, lowered her voice and said, "Something's going on."

"Growing up with these people," I said as I finished fiddling with my note, "you know how it works around here. Me, I'm just slinking around the outskirts trying to stay out of trouble."

"That's the thing." She put her hands on her hips. "I keep getting into trouble."

"You?" I laughed. "Why?"

"I schedule musicians. When a volunteer cancels at the last minute, I call Hannah since she's on staff. She must be saying something to Cal, because I've been hearing about it. And this is weird," she whispered. "You know how you and I pray together? They don't want us doing that anymore."

"*What?* Pastors don't want support staff praying together? That doesn't make sense."

"This hurts most of all." She blushed, and then looked down at her cute shoes with her lacy socks. "Cal never calls me into his office. You go in. What do you talk about?"

I put my hand on her back and rubbed it. "Well, talking to men is hard for me. As Cal stares at me and asks questions, I babble and tell him whatever comes to mind. When I get out of there, every time, I wonder why I said so much."

And even though he makes me nervous, it's kind of nice that he wants to get to know me. To mentor me in my faith. He didn't need my title reminder each week. He could make a note on his calendar. But in church, weren't we supposed to connect? Maybe that's why he set it up this way.

On my recent trip to London, I'd gone looking for a C.S. Lewis book for his collection. What was that about? I don't usually shop for gifts for friends on trips. And all that thinking I was doing about Jim. I didn't buy him anything. I guess I just wanted to show Cal my appreciation.

Around that time, Cal said, "What do you need to come on full-time?"

I winced, having no desire. Believing there was no position, since the permanent receptionist was returning, I played his game. "Vacation time. I value time with family and friends. With Service with a Smile as my own business, I don't have insurance. I have something better: freedom to take as much time off as I want."

"How many days do you need?" he pressed.

"Forty." I lobbied. *Why was I doing this?*

"Not forty-one?"

"Nope . . ." My mouth seemed to have a mind of its own.

"Done!"

*Done?* "What, are we gonna have two receptionists?"

"Yup!" He smiled and turned back toward his office before I could say another word.

I never did ask God about this. I guess I assumed Cal spoke for Him.

# CAN THIS BE MY JOB?
# OH YEAH, IT IS!

As a regular staff member at the church in Alaska, I attended more gatherings at church. While a piece of me yearned for potluck dinners to hang out with my church family, another part kept everyone an arm's length away. I still wasn't totally sure about *church people*.

Then there was Melody, one of our volunteers. I don't know what it was. We connected and never had enough time to talk about everything we wanted to. I just loved her.

On her answering machine, her father had recorded in a mock English accent, "This is Carlton, the butler. Presently Lady Melody is absent from the manor. Leave a message and she'll ring your back when she returns. Cheerio."

I beamed every time I called. But when she landed in Providence Hospital, I peeked into her room and tried not to cry. This wasn't the castle her father had described or the fairytale I so desperately wished for her. Nope, lupus ravaged her body, and she lay dying. "Come in." She smiled weakly then cleared her voice. "Have a seat."

I took a deep breath and shook off the tears I wanted to cry. I left my grief in the hall, stepped inside, and sat. I was searching for a way to relieve her pain when she confided, "You know what I miss about church?"

I shook my head. I don't know why, but I thought she was going to say something super spiritual like *the sermons*. Instead, she surprised me. "I miss when Gus, our maintenance supervisor, squawks across the stage dressed like a chicken advertising the Ladies' Spring Fashion Show."

Melody's words put me at ease. We had a short conversation that lifted my spirits and, I hope, hers. With a smile on my face, I left the hospital in search of Gus, who did so much more than take care of the church. She built water rockets and directed kids' worship until they asked her to stop because she couldn't carry a tune. At family camp, she dressed like a clown, put a fish in a blender, *and drank the water*—lampooning Saturday Night Live.

She did personas. She not only wore a chicken suit, she became *Chicken Woman*.

Back at church, Gus stood in the lobby in front of a man's business suit which was hanging on a hook. As if taking a hit off a joint, she positioned herself at the bottom of the pant leg and inhaled all the way to the top left shoulder of the jacket. She held her breath for a few seconds before announcing, "That's some go-o-ood stu-u-uff."

"What are you doing?" I whispered.

"We just got a donation." She pointed to the suit.

"Is this what marijuana smells like?" The worship leader joined us and took a whiff.

Passing by and hearing the comment, the youth leader took the outfit from the hook and held it in front of three teen-agers. "This is what pot smells like. Stay away from it. It's not good for you."

The kids snickered as they passed it around. That's when I asked Gus, "Where's your chicken costume; still have it?"

"I have two!" She smiled with a glint in her eye that told me exactly who might wear the other. "Oh no!" I backed away.

"I had one experience as a person-in-a-clown-suit, and I don't need to repeat that." But there we were the next afternoon. After cancelling a lunch date with Jim, I bumbled my way out of the church with Gus. We peeked through the suits' eyeholes and cracked each other up with stupid why-did-the-chicken-cross-the-road jokes. Then we crammed our larger-than-life bodies into a car and waved at everyone as we drove through town.

At Lake Otis and Tudor, Gus wobbled out into the intersection. She knocked on the windows of the vehicles around us and surprised drivers as they waited for the light to change. They tried to ignore her, but Gus is not easy to overlook even when she's not dressed like a chicken.

I howled, holding my stomach as she messed with people in the hospital parking lot and on the elevator, then wandered into strangers' rooms. But when she crawled into bed with Melody for a chat, I lost it. I had to slip out into the hall for a minute and let the tears fall.

"You rocked!" I told her back at work. "Let's go to the hospital every week."

In bed that night, I couldn't sleep. Never in a million years did I think working at a church could be so fun. "This is what I want to do, God. A chicken ministry."

"Wait a minute," He said. "You didn't have this much fun as a clown, remember? Today wasn't about dressing as a chicken. It was about loving Melody. And loving people looks different depending on who they are. It's personal and unique."

"You're right. A ministry like this could get really fun." I lay back on the pillow, unable get the silly grin off my face. Then it faded. Chicken Woman wasn't on Dad's list of recommendations for my future. I groaned. Was I still trying to please him? "God, all day I've been flying. All of a sudden, I feel angsty. Why? Am I trying to please the wrong father? That's it, isn't it? I don't want to annoy Dad, but if I follow You, I can trust You to work that out, can't I? Loving people is Your plan. I can't shake this because I don't have to!"

God didn't say a word, just smiled.

# WAIT, BUY A CONDO?

Some people might call God's participation in our lives *coincidence*; but because I saw His answers to my questions in the context of our on-going conversation, interacting with the circumstances of my life, I didn't see it that way. And it's not like everything He said made me jump up and down. Often, I struggled to take His advice, like when He suggested settling down. That nudge exposed my fear of commitment to Him, my church family, and those around me.

Although I thought I was finally fully committed to God, there was something scary about staying in one place. What was it? Oh yeah, it hadn't gone so well with Tony.

On the ride home from goal-setting class that Tuesday night, I told Minerva, "I want to move to Israel and herd sheep." She didn't say anything and dropped me off without so much as a "goodnight."

The next morning, over tea, I said, "God, why'd she shut down after that?"

"What do you expect? When someone's about to pack up and leave, do you get closer or pull away from them?"

Ignoring His question, I confessed. "I want deeper connections with friends."

"You can have them."

"How?"

"By making different decisions."

"What do you mean?" I scrunched my eyes closed. "Hold back from sharing?"

"No. How about giving this place a chance before you ride off in another direction."

As if part of this lesson from God, my best friend visited—the one who had to tell me when Tony left. She took one look at the place I shared with Pam and said, "You may keep your stuff in this apartment, but you don't live here."

She was right. As my old neighbor, she knew I decorated with music boxes, crafts, and knick-knacks, but that was before my battle with this fear. Now, used to house sitting or couch surfing, I didn't know what to do with a bedroom. I didn't sleep in it. I slept on the couch in the living room. I never spent time decorating because I'd only have to figure out what to do with all the stuff when the lease ran out.

But I missed personalizing my space, and Pam was moving to California, so I needed a plan. Still, I squirmed as God prodded me ever so gently in the direction of home ownership. But I'd set up house with Tony, supposedly forever, and that ended so badly. I guess I tangled *fear of responsibility* with the failure and pain of that breakup? I didn't want to get stuck in another miserable situation or find myself financially responsible for more than I could handle, so I was a little skittish about signing on the dotted line.

Could committing *with* God be different? Why not? Everything else was.

I practiced saying "buy a condo" out loud and shuddered. Then I thought about my hot new boyfriend. He encouraged the idea and offered to paint. My plan was that we'd get married and have kids.

What *was* his secret? Nothing could be *that bad*, could it?

I called a real estate agent and looked for a one-bedroom close to work. Then I daydreamed about owning something. My agent returned the call. "I have a possibility across the street from the church, a nice two-bedroom."

Two? I wrinkled my nose. Then I heard *room for guests* and nodded at God.

Three weeks later, I turned the wheel of my car into the familiar parking lot of the National Bank of Alaska. Terror gripped me by the throat. After going full-time at church, I'd quit some of the twelve jobs I'd accumulated through my business, including the one I had at this bank closing mortgage loans. Now I sat in the office where I'd previously worked and signed my name on my own set of papers while hugging ex-coworkers.

Thankfully, the impromptu reunion chased the anxiety away.

However, worry took two steps back, doubled its efforts, and came at me the next week when the Anchorage Daily News released its latest segment of *We Alaskans*. The section featured my recent trip to the bush (everywhere in Alaska that's off the road system) and showed a picture of me leaning over an evaporator in a makeshift outdoor kitchen, taking in a deep breath of the sweet aroma of boiling sap as it transformed into birch syrup.

" 'We Alaskans.' That's you now," I thought as fear cackled at me in my new living room. "You will be stuck in the same place for the rest of your li-i-ife."

In spite of fear, or maybe *to* spite fear, I nested like never before. I moved into my new home with clothes, a table, and a cat. Friends at church furnished it by giving me everything from silverware to an answering machine—and it all matched! One pulled her antique furniture out of storage and said, "When you decide to leave, we'll put it all back and be done with it."

Boy, did she know me!

When I complained about the blank walls, Jim smiled. "You've got paint."

*Yes, I do!* I pulled out a suitcase of acrylics and dug through letters from family and friends, capturing favorite lines and immortalizing them on my quote room wall. "I may only have a tent in Uganda, but you're always welcome."

Next, I turned the living room into a garden by using a white picket fence I bought at a garage sale for a fire screen. A friend also gave me a teakettle that looked like a watering can with daisies in it.

As I'd shopped for a condo, one of the things that had been on my list was a large corner where I could build a waterfall. Now that I had one, I drove to Home Depot to buy supplies, made a wooden frame with a friend, and covered it with chicken wire. Then we mixed cement right in the living room. As we dolloped the goop on, I said, "When it dries, we'll fill the basin with water, add a pump, and be done, right?"

"No!" She shook her head. "Water goes right through cement. We've got to seal it, or your downstairs neighbors could have their own little cascade."

"Why didn't you tell me that before?" I wiped hair away from my face with my shoulder since cement covered my hands.

"I didn't know your plan." She held the bucket as I scraped the last bit onto the frame.

"What do we do now?"

"Epoxy resin." She nodded, and we prepared for another trip to Home Depot. Wearing gas masks, we looked like deep-sea divers, spraying our work while trying not to inhale. Then I packed to move out of the condo while the sticky stuff dried.

As I was hanging out with God one morning, I came across the words, "Delight in the Lord and He will give you the desires of your heart" (Psalm 7:4, NIV). They glowed, like a heads-up. Wondering what He had up His sleeve, I took the gift certificate my real estate agent had given me to the pet store. She knew I wanted turtles in that waterfall, Tigger and Tucker. She'd helped me find the corner to put them in, but the man at the pet store shook his head. "We no longer sell Red-Eared Sliders. They carry salmonella."

*Wha-a-at?*

That's when a box arrived in the mail from a friend who didn't usually send gifts. As I reached inside a tin full of candy kisses, my fingers caught on something hiding in the chocolate. I pulled out a life-like statue of a turtle. What an odd gift. Who told her I wanted turtles?

Jesus! Did this new baby have red ears? In the moment it took to check, I thought, *I could add some with fingernail polish.* But of course, he did! Then I wondered, *Why didn't she send two?*

Because God knew I'd already gotten one! After the sad news at the pet store, I'd purchased a parakeet with the gift certificate and then bought Tigger, a ceramic box turtle. I put the new little guy, Tucker, in my purse and carried him around for months. Every time I caught sight of him, I smiled. He was proof! God knows my desires, even the tiniest ones. Tucker strengthened my trust in God as the nudges continued.

Next, I heard, "Let's save $10,000 a year." God had suggested that when I first moved to Alaska. With twelve jobs and no time to spend money, it was easy until I bought the condo. Now I spent money without even going out. Plus, the job at the church paid less, and I wasn't working as many hours.

"$10,000's a lot!" I wrinkled my nose. "How can I do that?"

A flyer for an equity accelerator program came in the mail showing how much more quickly I could pay off the condo if I made an additional payment each year directly toward principal. Sensing the plan was God's answer to my question, I signed up. Then I sent a little extra. Like twenty bucks, whatever I could, though I doubted it would make a difference.

But with God's help, maybe I could accomplish that goal?

The more I expected from God, the more I experienced in big ways and in small. Like when He urged, "Pray for people in the way they ask. If they ask in person, pray right there. If they ask on the phone, stop talking and pray. Don't just tell them you'll do it, pray."

I was a little shy at first, even on email, so I had a few requests waiting for my response. Every time I opened my account, they bugged me because I like to get back to people in a timely manner. Finally, I asked God, "What do You want me to pray?" I heard something like, "Dear Lord, Thank You for knowing everything she needs. Take care of her, I pray in Jesus' name." Really, it was that simple.

She wrote back later that night. "You're never going to believe what happened. This afternoon a car nearly sideswiped me. I couldn't figure out how the driver possibly missed me until I opened your email and looked at the time you sent it. You prayed for me *at the exact minute* I got spared from a horrible accident. Thank you!"

Shivers ran up my spine. If I hadn't taken God's suggestion, I would have missed that.

The following day, I'd planned to hike with a friend and her family. God said, "Don't go!"

I never cancel without reason, so it took me a minute. I stammered, embarrassed to tell her what I'd *heard from God.* Instead I said, "My intuition won't let me off the hook."

Intuition. Smintuition. "Sorry, Lord. These aren't coincidences, they're God-instances! Please give me courage to say that?"

She and I had planned to meet at McHugh Creek at 10:00 a.m. Since I'd cancelled, and they weren't rushing to meet me, they arrived *late*. Yellow tape crisscrossed the trail, forbidding them to enter. Earlier, when we would have been there hiking, a bear mauled a family. It killed a seventy-seven-year-old woman and her forty-five-year-old son.

I shivered again.

# WHAT *IS* GOD SAYING?

All my friends, both inside and outside the church, kept asking, "You say you hear God. *How?*"

I told them what I knew. But after the bear mauling, I not only wanted to hear God clearly; I wanted to learn how to follow better. I looked for a study that might have answers and found *Experiencing God: Knowing and Doing the Will of God* by Henry Blackaby. Since I couldn't find a class in progress, I called Kelly, a pretty mom I'd met in singles'. "You want to co-lead?" I asked. She agreed.

Since I'd never led anything before, the prospect freaked me out. We didn't advertise. We invited friends. Then Reenie stopped me on my way out of a church. "Can I join your group?" I froze. I barely knew her. I didn't want her to see through me, realize my inexperience, and maybe even incompetence, but who was I to say, "No, you can't get to know God with us?"

So, I smiled weakly and said, "Sure!"

We all bought workbooks and spent five hours a week doing homework, reading then filling out our answers. The book had great advice and explanation, but I needed practical application. What helped me most was the question at the end of each day's reading: "What does God want you to do in response to today's study?" As I waited to hear, I expected an answer and learned how to recognize His voice better as He spoke to my heart.

And even though I'd been asking God what He wanted me to do, more than answers came from studying the book. I'd often come to Him out of need, but imagine if you had a friend and you never just hung out or gave her time to talk; would you really know her?

I think it's the same with God. In this study, I got to know Him as we spent time together.

When we met as a group, we shared our experiences. One night, I asked Reenie what God had shown her. "I don't hear His voice," she said, "so I don't do that part."

*Wasn't that the goal?*

God stopped me right there. "You went through the entire workbook as you prepared to lead. Every time it said, 'What does God want you to do?' you filled the answer in without even asking Me."

"Oh yeah," I said to God in my head.

I continued that conversation on the way home. "You're right. I know this sounds stupid, but You know how I was raised to be independent. You're busy. I didn't want to bother You. I guess I'm used to handling everything I can and only asking for direction with the tough stuff."

"*Bother* Me? I want you to let Me help."

Hm, that was not what I expected.

\* \* \* \* \*

Eleven weeks later, Reenie, the one God brought to the group—the one who *couldn't hear*—said, "I just learned I'm not supposed to live with my boyfriend."

Okay, first, I confess. I have an *inner nun puppet*. Have you seen those in novelty shops, the ones that wear boxing gloves?

Mine looks like that. And given a microphone, she gets all holier-than-thou, as if she's perfect. She, I mean I, spouts *thou shalt nots* with the best of them. It's not pretty. This nun is easy to judge, even for me. But still, part of me agrees with her. I mean me! I was tempted to say, "If I don't get to have sex, why should you?" Of course, a real nun probably wouldn't say that, but mine wanted to. Good thing I kept my mouth shut even though my inner nun puppet lifted her eyebrow and smirked, "You didn't know?"

My mom, a lot like my inner nun, had pointed at me in the past. "You're *living in sin.*"

Yup, when I lived with Tony, I knew the Bible taught sex before marriage was sin.

But this was no place for me to waggle my finger in Reenie's face. I adored her and wanted the best for her. Who was I to judge? I'd done the same thing.

So, how did I respond? I wanted to say, "I get it. With four kids, you *need* this guy to cover your rent." Something stopped me, though, like when I quit offering flippant advice as church secretary. I wanted to give Reenie more, but what? Everything that came to mind sounded harsh. So, I stepped out of God's way and shut up. I decided to let Him take care of it and found out He could say the same thing I could. But when someone hears it from Him with His compassion and tenderness, well, it just goes down better all the way around.

Because of God's love, He doesn't coddle us. He tells us the truth and points out what's best even when it's hard. Then if we want to do as He suggests, He'll help us live into it. In order to do that, He needs our willingness, but He pretty much takes care of the rest.

"What're you doing next week?" Reenie looked around the group during our next class, the last one. "I don't know where, but I've got to move. Can you help?"

Wow, she has no idea where she's going or how she'll pay for it, but she's following God's lead. *And she doesn't even think she hears Him.*

I pulled my chin up off the floor, smiled weakly, and nodded. I looked forward to seeing what God would do as Reenie took a leap of faith she didn't even know she had. God didn't let her down. With a wiggle in her finances, her gorgeous new place, cheaper than any I'd seen, fit within her budget.

Sometimes it takes me a minute to get from knowing God's words to knowing His love. But when I do, I'm always more likely to follow. It turns out that I can hear Him say just about anything because of His love.

I aim to live by His plan. Sometimes it takes a Reenie to show me how.

\* \* \* \* \*

When I bought the condo, God knew I needed a bigger one than I was looking for because of the visitors He'd bring. Locals and out-of-towners.

One snowy night after I built the waterfall, I lit the white lights on it, turned on Irish worship music, and climbed into the swinging chair with my cat. In the glow of the fireplace, I sipped hot chocolate from a mug filled with peppermint candy when the doorbell rang. Wiping whipped cream from my lips, I got up to answer it.

Tears streamed down a friend's face as she stepped inside. Spilling her current woe, she looked around, and gasped. "Is this what you do *every* night?"

"No," I hugged her, "but you're welcome anytime."

Another night, Kelly stopped by. She's the one I'd led the group with, a sweetie with a wounded past and a weird question. "Would you be my confidante if I had an affair with Cal?"

"Our pastor? You're joking, of course!" I spent the weekend talking her out of that crazy idea.

In one four-month stretch, I had houseguests every night. Alaska's like that. All summer, friends come from *the lower forty-eight*. Year-round, others fly in from the bush. Once, I had two families staying at the same time, one in my room, the other in the living room. In the middle of the night, I came out of the extra bedroom to go to the bathroom. Trying to avoid tripping on someone, I felt my way down the hall and made a mental note to get a nightlight.

The next morning, I spent time with God before I joined my guests. My devotional talked about the Great Commission. "Go and make disciples" (Matthew 28:19, NET).

*"Make?"* The word crawled up my spine like something way creepier than the itsy-bitsy spider. I tried shaking it off, but the connotations around that word reached into my past and yanked on something, making me want to throw that Bible across the room. Like an angry kid, I lay back on my blow-up mattress in the spare room, put my arms behind my head, and glared at the ceiling as I remembered Dad chasing me across the Arnold Arboretum in Boston one afternoon.

Mom had just said, "Elizabeth, put on your hood."

I must have been about eight. I screamed, "Make me!"

Her southern blood thinner than mine, she was always putting blankets on me. Why didn't I just say *okay*? Instead, I reacted to the unspoken undercurrent between us, her hyper-control always there, fueling our own civil war.

"Ed," was all she said.

"Listen to your mother," Dad mumbled.

"No!" I stammered, testing until I saw the muscles in his neck twitch. I added, "Daddy, I'm not cold."

As usual, he took her side, "Obey your mother."

I glanced sideways at Dad then set off in a sprint. What was I thinking? He ran twelve miles a day. Halfway down the hill, he caught me and cinched the hood of my pink flowered jacket around my face so tightly that nothing stuck out but my nose. I wore the coat like that all the way back to the car, peering through the hole, whimpering.

And now, with that same icky feeling inside, I looked back at my Bible. Go and make disciples? Nope, not my style. I turned to Fred. I couldn't bring myself to call God anything else right then. I certainly couldn't accuse the Father like I was about to, but I hate to admit that I could do that to Fred. "With my abduction complete, You brainwash me into the role of body snatcher? You control me, just like everyone else always has." I clung to my ability to choose. My precious free will. It was probably my favorite gift from God, at least, at that moment. "I'm not doing it."

Fred didn't say a word. Or if He did, I didn't hear. I might have had my fingers in my ears.

Over the next couple of days, I skipped our time together. Then at church, we heard a sermon about John the Baptist. He's so bold, wearing camel fur, eating bugs, and hanging out in the desert. So *him*, no matter what anyone thought. Because of that, he's my favorite Bible character.

On the way home, Fred picked up our conversation. "Why are you mad at Me?"

"Everyone I've ever seen *spreading the good news* screamed. Well, the one woman at college, maybe she's the only one. Still, 'Turn from your wicked ways or you'll burn in hell!' " I shivered.

"John the Baptist told everyone to repent. Why do you like him?" Fred made a great point.

I had to think about my answer. "It's his passion. I admire that. He walks his talk." *Walks his talk* shot through me like an arrow as if injected with spiritual power. Once again, in an experience with God, my perspective changed.

John operated out of love. He was empowered with a willingness to die for what he believed. And he did. I wanted to be like him, sort of. Like Reenie, anyway, making changes in my life as I learned of His will.

Why? Because a friend had recently teased, "I'm not worried about missing heaven. You'll open the back door and let me in." I twitched. Of course, I'd let her in! But what if it wasn't up to me? I didn't want her counting on a lie, but I wanted her there.

So, what if Jesus did die for me—for *us*—paid what we owed and told me—is telling me—to go to my friends and family so they can have this kind of relationship with Him, too. Would I?

# . . . AND THAT'S WHY YOU SHOULD BE A PROSTITUTE

While I wrestled with God about making disciples, Pam, the roommate who'd talked me into squishing my mattress into the dumpster, visited from California for the summer. As other friends came and went, we'd gather on the living room floor, sit in a circle, and pray together.

Before a fishing trip, Pam packed. "Is it okay to ask God for a fish?"

"Sure!" I sat down. "Lord, Pam wants to catch a fish. Help her?"

Three days later, she returned with a glow. "You're never going to believe what happened. I caught a salmon *this big*." She held her hands three feet apart. "He snapped my pole and got away. So, I went to Wal-Mart, got a new pole, and prayed again. This time, I said, 'God, help me catch an even bigger fish *and* reel him in!' We went out the next morning, and in fifteen minutes, I did!"

By the end of her trip, Pam had told everyone, the fishermen at the youth hostel, the girls who hung out at Chilkoot Charlie's, and her sister, "You just have to pray."

On the plane up from Boston, her sister's ear clogged. Back at my condo, Pam rolled long, skinny strips of muslin and coated them in paraffin wax to made ear candles. She put one end in her sister's ear and lit the other on fire in an attempt to break the blockage.

When it didn't work, she asked, "Can you pray?"

"Sure!" I said. "God, please open her ear." Then I hopped in the shower. When I got out, I heard Pam in the other room. "You got to thank God! He's the one that made the last ear candle work."

I smiled, but Pam's answer was not always God. One day I came in from work and heard her talking to my friend visiting from Australia. "You'd make a lot of money and have a flexible schedule. That's why you should be a prostitute!"

"Wha-a-at?" I drew the line. "That is not happening on my watch." I turned toward Ms. Australia. "What do you think your husband would say?"

Then I stopped in my tracks. Was I *making* friends do things already? Of course, this was a joke, but other times I really did exert undue influence.

That night, I crawled into bed. The midnight sun shone through my window and the troubling question returned: what if God, at the very least, wants each of us to know He's available, and He gives us the freedom to choose whether we want Him or not?

I couldn't argue with that. Everything with Him requires choice, even this thing about making disciples. The gift of free will truly is an act of love. So, wouldn't I love my friends enough to share my experience and let them decide what to do with the information? "Yikes. Lord, when I think about it like that, I want to. But still, it freaks me out; what if they give up our friendship?"

"So, let me get this straight." I sensed God saying. "You love your friends, and you believe all this, but you don't want to share. Is that really love?" My stomach lurched as I rolled over. After duking it out for weeks, He had me.

For Pam's birthday, I bought her a Bible and had her name engraved on it. "Thanks!" She flipped through the pages. "I've been wanting one of these things. They're expensive."

I caught her attention when I pulled a bookmark from inside. "What's that?" she asked.

"It's called the Sinner's Prayer. It's made up of different passages from the Bible, like this, 'That's the kind of party God's angels throw every time one lost soul turns to God' " (Luke 15:10, TM).

"You think this prayer gets you into heaven?" She grabbed the bookmark.

I nodded. "You don't want to pray it, do you?"

She began without me. *Dear Lord.* She read ahead, so fast I wouldn't know what she said if the words weren't in front of me:

> *I know I'm a sinner. I ask for your forgiveness. I believe You died for my sins and rose from the dead. I trust and follow You as my Lord and Savior. Guide my life and help me do Your will. In Your name, I pray, Amen.*

That night, I continued my on-going chat with God. "Did Pam's prayer count? I love her. And I understand her wanting a ticket to heaven, but her prayer seemed more like fire insurance against hell than a heartfelt desire to hang out with You."

"Don't worry." God smiled. "No one comes to me with pure motives."

*Wow!* I thought for a minute. "You really do love us, don't You?"

"I do."

# ANOTHER LIFE-CHANGING ADVERTISEMENT

I n church on Sunday morning, I leafed through the bulletin. Again, an ad I'd been avoiding caught my eye. I turned the page until God gave me the look. *Uh oh, time to quit running.*

> Wounded Heart
> Tuesdays from 7:00-9:00 p.m.
> Beginning September 19th
>
> If you've experienced sexual abuse in the past and would like to join this new group for healing, please stop by the church office and make an appointment with Hannah.

I looked at God as if He stood before me, then I looked behind me. I didn't see anyone. So, I turned back, pointed at myself, and mouthed, "Me?"

*What does He know that I don't?* I made an appointment.

In Hannah's office, I perched on a chair. Dressed in tweed slacks and a long-sleeved silk blouse with a gold clasp catching her scarf, Hannah sat on the couch opposite me next to her co-leader as I twitched noticeably. "On the night I lost my virginity, I went on a date with my boyfriend. He'd invited me to a party in a motel with his band, picked me up with a big bottle of wine, and, um, we had sex. I don't think it was sexual abuse, though."

"How old were you?" Hannah asked.

"Fifteen." I answered quickly.

"And he was?"

"Eighteen."

"Have you ever heard the term *date rape*?" She leaned in.

"Yeah, but I don't think that's what it was. I didn't say no as I couldn't seem to get the word out of my mouth. When he'd tried before, this is embarrassing, I moved his hands or myself. I thought he understood I wasn't willing, but I never spoke up. And on this particular night, I was wasted. I don't remember resisting in any way."

"Wait a minute," the co-leader asked. "You feel like what happened was *your* fault. Why?"

"Well, I accepted the date. Drank the alcohol. Smoked the joints. Went to the motel. Right?"

"Well, yes," Hannah said. "But—"

"You didn't choose to give up your virginity," her co-leader cut in.

"No." I shook my head. "Was that date rape?"

"I'd say so!" She nodded. "You went on a date and lost your virginity without your consent."

"Yeah." I felt like such a fool. Tricked. Now, twenty years later, I began to see the blame might not be all mine. "Can I join your group?"

"We'll see you next Tuesday." The co-leader nodded again.

At home, I grabbed the cat and made for the couch. She purred as I stared blankly out the window. "God, I'm so sorry for putting myself in unhealthy situations where so much more could have happened."

"We've had this conversation before. You're forgiven, remember?"

I bowed my head as I replayed the meeting in my mind and curled into a ball. Why was I so reluctant to call what happened *rape*? I guess because I'd blamed myself for so long. I'd felt guilty, like I messed up royally. And not only that night at the motel, but from then on. How was it my entire fault, though, when I didn't even want to do it?

But *rape*? There was no violence that night.

"Wasn't there?" God said more gently than anything He'd ever said before.

"Wow." I stood. *My* definition of violence included physical harm. Was there another? I needed to research and to let the idea sink in before I continued the conversation. Over the days and months to come, layers of insight brought healing. "So, violence not only includes physical acts but psychological and emotional acts as well. Or words by themselves. The attempt to gain sex by coercion, by *any* person, regardless of their relationship to the victim is abuse. Even if it's *only* unwanted comments."

"Mm hm," God agreed.

Again, I crawled into the fetal position. In the cocoon of my furry blanket, I rocked. "There was an abuse of power," I admitted. "Alex invited me to a party. I didn't make that up, did I? And he knew I'd get high and drink with him. That gallon of wine came with intention."

Half an hour later, I rolled over on my elbows. *Oh-My-God!* That's when it hit me. "At fifteen, when I came home from that motel, I saw the same vision I did on the boat that night. That vision of You, Jesus, holding out Your hand and offering love. *Real* love. At the time I didn't get it. I blew You off."

"Mm hm, I've always been here," He said, "waiting for you to want Me."

Every week for a year, I met with Hannah and the group. We worked through *The Wounded Heart* book and workbook by Dan Allender. The text helped us put words to our emotions and thoughts by offering a variety of answers we could choose from. It helped us own what applied to us. After "I am feeling . . ." I checked "hopeful," "proud of myself for even looking at this," and "sad," personalizing my experience by leaving "fearful," "confused," and "desperate" unchecked. In such a vulnerable place, I couldn't have come up with the words myself. But I could place a checkmark. "I'm not sure if I've been sexually abused, but I know something is wrong." Yes! How validating and freeing it was to mark that.

Over and over, the books put words to what I couldn't. Such as the fact that victims of sex abuse "struggle and are often paralyzed by illegitimate shame. Someone else made the choice to harm them in a terrible way. But rather than place the responsibility on the victimizer, somehow in their suffering and loss of dignity, the victim places the blame on themselves and their longings. And the pain already experienced from the abuse is intensified." [7]

*Yes, it's not just me!*

Then I realized I'd been set up for abuse because I never learned how to set limits. I didn't have a healthy support system. So, I got another book, *Boundaries,* [8] and worked through that as well. Because I wish I could say this was my only instance of invasion, but it wasn't. There were other attempts and *requests* for blowjobs. Seriously, why would a man push an unwilling partner's teeth toward his, you know, his most sensitive part?

Then again, did nothing in my outward appearance seem reluctant? *Ugh!*

I wasn't asking for it. Truly, I wasn't.

Six months after the class started, a new girl joined. We told our stories again. Having built trust and gained an ability to name things, we added detail we'd left out before. I could use stronger words. "What happened wasn't intimate, loving, or good, like I think sex is supposed to be. And *my boyfriend,*" I spit the words out, "took something that wasn't his to take. I knew sex between an eighteen-year-old and a minor was statutory rape, a felony, but he was my boyfriend. I didn't want to press charges and I'd heard the stories of others who had. Since I didn't stop it from happening, the courts would blame me like they had them.

"Alex met his own needs, got off scot-free, and here I sit all these years later, still dealing with residual effects."

My knee jumped up and down uncontrollably as I continued, "Afterwards, I believed, *if I want a boyfriend, I have to have sex,* so I had a lot of sex." Two others in the group nodded. As we shared *aha's*, we saw familiar patterns in our pasts. The support I didn't get at the time, I got from them. Within the context of going so deeply, we grew in our relationships. So much so, that without realizing it, I might have begun depending on them more than God.

It was easy for me to rage at their perpetrators; why couldn't I do it at mine? So used to being mad at myself for not stopping what happened, I couldn't find my anger. Even with this new perspective of calling it date rape. I had irritation but no fury. I wanted to get to throwing-rocks-on-the-beach angry so I could deal with my emotions and put this behind me, to get to forgiveness. Without rage, what was I pardoning? Had I screamed every-thing out in the car as Chance had suggested? Having never put words to those cries, I didn't know what I'd released.

In this group, we wondered about things like that.

Did we do something to lead the guys on? That's always the question, right? And what would that be? Look at him, wear a provocative outfit, or move in a certain way? Sometimes it felt like "where along this shaky continuum are you going to pin this on *me*," because if it's not in one place, it's another—

There's my anger!

"Not that my rebellion or alcohol and drug use didn't escort me into that motel room, but that doesn't alleviate the fact that what happened was an act of violence with lasting harm. I was young, without support, and the incident destroyed trust and brought on an increase in substance abuse. I'm so grateful for this class," I ran my hand through my hair, "so I can learn how to *be there* for myself because my past decisions built on each other, piggy-backed, and catapulted me into things like an unwanted pregnancy." Again, some of the others concurred.

"While I know the healing from this class comes with me and will help me make better choices in the future, there are some things I can never get back."

I guess that's why I couldn't stop pursuing healing after we quit meeting. I wanted more, and not just for myself.

# UH OH, AM I A
# RELIGIOUS WEIRDO?

With all this healing and newfound freedom, life wasn't boring like I'd thought it would be with God.

He loves us, so life with Him is more than I believed possible, even when it's hard.

God sent His Son to die for us. And if we choose Jesus, He saves us over and over again. After working at the church for two-and-a-half years, that's how I understood it anyway . . . that my friends could miss heaven if they didn't choose Jesus.

I tried to come up with another interpretation, one I could walk away from without a single doubt. For this, I relied on my internal *peace-meter*. When I followed God, I felt good. When I didn't, my conscience bugged me 'til I backed up to where I'd gone wrong and fixed it.

A similar thing happened in my belief system. When I searched the Bible for my answers and came into a new understanding, I received peace! When I held onto a thought I selfishly preferred, not so much. Romans 12:1-2 calls this being transformed by the renewing of our minds so that we might discern the will of God—the good and acceptable and perfect will of God.

Since God loves everyone, He wouldn't send anyone to hell, would He?

Well, 2 Peter 3:9 says: He doesn't *want* "anyone to perish" (NIV). So, if God doesn't want anyone to go to hell, but He gives us the choice, doesn't He get it that some of us are going to screw it up? It's not like He comes right out and asks, "Would you like to go to hell?"

No, John 3:16 says: "For God so loved the world that he gave his one and only Son, that whoever believes in him shall not perish but have eternal life" (NIV). So, if we choose Jesus and we want to go to heaven, then we can. Ding! Ding! Ding! Peace!

Does that mean hell is the consequence if we *don't* pick Jesus? It doesn't make sense that Jesus would have had to hang on a cross if there'd been another way.

And God "gave His son." How much more could He do? Oh yeah, He gave us the choice. Maybe He loves us so much that if we want, we get to spend eternity without Him. Thing is, it seems like that might be outside heaven. And where else is there?

All this scared me beyond belief. I wanted everyone I loved in heaven, but if this was the deal, it seemed like some of them weren't headed that way. Could I trust God to do whatever it took to get ahold of them? No! Because that's manipulation, right? The one thing I'm so grateful He doesn't do. *Ugh!*

With my peace-meter clanging in deficit, I couldn't come up with an alternative. I felt like I not only had to share my faith but also needed to do everything I could to convince my loved ones of their need for Jesus.

This crucible triggered a fear of rejection, and I caved. Did I have to surrender my relationships, my greatest treasure, without knowing if I'd get them back? In the process, I eventually lost the fear of making disciples and of sharing my faith. This would have been fine if I backed down when someone didn't want to hear about Jesus, but that's not what I did.

*MARY ME*

That's when I ran into Sophia, an old high school friend. I said, "Remember how it was before we smoked pot? People said, 'Don't do drugs.' But we did. We loved getting high. Pot gave us an *off* button. All the arguments we'd had with parents, teachers, or boyfriends faded away. We laughed our butts off. It seemed like we had solved the world's problems.

"With God, it's similar. But different. Life feels better because He heals relationships and teaches healthy ways of communicating with humor that doesn't come at another's expense. It turns out God's an *off* button without a hangover!"

Much later, Sophia said, "I wanted what you described. But when you shared actual conversations with God, it freaked me out. I knew you didn't lie, so I wondered if you'd gotten involved in a cult or if your head injury in Africa caused hallucinations. Because if this was God speaking to you, I was hurt. Not by you, but by God. Why did He talk to you and not to me?

"You asked if I wanted to get *saved*. I didn't know what you meant, but I went along with it. You prayed, and I felt nothing. *Nothing!* Instead of experiencing God like you, I felt rejected."

I cringed. "Then I did the same thing, didn't I? I got nervous and ran, rejecting you in a different way. I'm sorry!"

In spite of that, Sophia has a relationship with God now. "As my family's sole source of income," she said, "I panicked when I got laid off. I screamed at God, 'Did I do something to deserve Your wrath? I NEED to know You're here!' Then, it happened. I felt, no. I heard, no. Not out loud. How do I explain it?" She searched for words. "It was like *OHMYGOD! I get it!* Immediately, everything you'd said made sense. In the pit of my gut I heard, and felt, KNEW, two words with a book-load of understanding about what they meant when God said, 'have faith.' I sensed that He meant, 'I've shown you how, now do it.' So, I pulled myself together, thanked Him, and trusted Him to provide. That's when I realized, God had talked to me before. I just hadn't known it was Him!"

About the time I reconnected with Sophia, I met Jewel. That's not her real name, but a symbol of her beauty. As I tell this story, I spare the details while keeping the heart. There was so much love. I wish I could say it was mine.

Jewel showed up for our volunteer shift at the Iditarod headquarters dressed like a model for a camping store wearing hiking boots and Gore-Tex. With a shy smile, she brushed her long hair away from her face, and we struck up an instant connection. Together, we thought with our emotions, loved with our creativity, and searched for compassionate ways to care about each other through gift-giving and adventure. Jewel transformed her empty rental into a retreat house with a room for each of us and invited me to join her on Fridays for creative projects.

As I stepped into the space she'd designed for me, I jumped up and down and squealed. The desk beckoned with a burning candle, a single flower in a small vase, and a cup of steaming water with a variety of teas to choose from. I ripped open a sachet of peppermint, stuffed it in the mug, and settled into the recliner by the window with my Bible. I leaned back in the chair, inhaled the minty scent, and watched the snowfall. Leafing through the back pages of the book, my eyes fell on the word *write*, a column heading in the index.

I smiled and looked up at the ceiling. "Mornin,' God!"

The first reference read: "Moses was there with the LORD forty days and forty nights without eating bread or drinking water. And he wrote . . ." (Exodus 34:28, NIV).

A few weeks back, *Why don't you fast and pray while you write?* wisped through my mind as I sat with God. I didn't like the idea, but I reluctantly agreed. Then I forgot all about it. I guess I'll save my lunch for dinner.

Next I read, "This is what the Lord, the God of Israel, says: 'Write in a book all the words I have spoken to you' " (Jeremiah 30:2, NIV). My jaw dropped. All my life, I knew I'd write. I had stories, but what was my message?

I knew that I knew that I *knew* this was my answer: I needed to write my God stories.

After making my decision to fast from eating lunch, I heard God's voice more clearly than ever before. At the end of the day, I raced to visit Jewel in her studio to see what she'd painted on her easel. I couldn't wait to tell her what happened, but the conversations about my relationship with God triggered her painful past.

As a child, she'd sat in church with her family, believing others knew about her suffering but did nothing to help. Where was God then?

"No offense." She smiled weakly. "Can we talk about something else? It's like you're in love and can't focus on anything but your man."

She was right, and she gave me one opportunity after another to stop, but I didn't. It sounds stupid now, but with that belief *that she needed Jesus to get into heaven*, I didn't respect her request.

"Will you stop trying to change me?" Jewel avoided my eyes, pulling a banana from her lunch bag.

I wish I could go back in time and say, "I understand why you think that's what I'm trying to do, but I love you exactly the way you are. That's why I want to hang out with you forever and the reason I haven't let up. You're right, though, change happens in the midst of it. I didn't expect transformation, but I'm not the same. I quit running from conflict and I own my bad. I forgive people! It's like I'm learning how to be the best version of myself.

Even though it's hard sometimes, it's amazing, this whole new life that never ends. *That's* what I want for you."

But I didn't yet have those words. Without knowing what to say, I said something stupid.

"Is my conversion all you care about?" She took a bite of her sandwich after I said whatever I really did. "Because if so, that's not really love. In fact, if I pray this prayer you keep talking about, will I ever see you again? Or will you just move onto your next victim?"

I bent over as if punched. In an effort to influence her, I did things The-Giver-of-Free-Will never would have. I put religious signature quotes at the bottom of my emails. With patience and kindness, she called me out again. "I asked you to stop talking to me about God."

In cowardice, I lied. I told her the quotes weren't directed at her, but they were.

Manipulation is what I'd originally expected from God, why I resisted Him, but never what I've experienced. Trickery and deceit are the opposite of His nature and never bring anyone closer. Why was I doing what I hated?

And it never occurred to me that God wanted to change me. If it did, I probably would have run from Him like she was. He's altered me—set me free from the bondage of drugs and alcohol and He's taught me all kinds of healthier ways of interaction—but only because I've agreed to it.

Love listens, accepts, and apologizes. Love offers choice. If I wanted to love like God, I needed to do things the way He did. Instead, I'd misrepresented Him and learned that *sharing Christ* simply means loving people with God, going where He leads, and doing what He says. Not manipulating or attempting to shove Jesus down someone's throat.

After plenty of conversation, Jewel and I parted ways, both wishing it could be different. I've tried to reconnect with her, but she's not interested.

If I could, what would I say? "I'm so sorry for lying and manipulating. Thank you for naming it and calling me on it. You represented love so much better than I, and I wish we could tell this story together. You could color in my weaknesses with crayons I don't have.

"I've missed you. I care for you and now, I hope, you'd even call my feelings love."

# MY PASTOR'S DOING
## *WHA-A-AT?*

On another Thursday afternoon, the church staff sat in Cal's office for the weekly meeting. As we waited for everyone to arrive, Kim shared her dream, "I don't know what we were doing at a saloon, but we were all there. When we came out, there were bombs going off everywhere. After each explosion, I saw the face of a skeleton. We jumped into two boats that were tied out front like horses, a blue fiberglass one and a wooden one. As the water rose, we pushed off and went down, down, down. I thought we were going to sink. When I woke, I couldn't move or breathe!"

"No way!" the janitor screamed, "I almost had that exact same dream."

Several offered explanations as Cal brought the meeting to order. "I love dream interpretation," he said. "Let me do some research."

Then, the following afternoon, the first bomb hit when Gus stopped by my desk and kidded about attempting suicide. Who does that, right? Gus joked about everything, but I knew enough not to take the topic lightly.

"You don't have a plan, do you?"

"I'd climb into a garbage bag in a dumpster and shoot myself in the head."

I gasped, totally unsure of what to say next. "But you won't, right?"

"No, Lizzie, I won't." She laughed.

"Promise!" I begged.

"Okay," she agreed.

I contacted Hannah and shared my concern, assuming that as a counselor, she'd help. But still, Gus wouldn't, would she? She and I had spent time together almost every day for the past two and a half years, joking at the front desk or visiting Melody at the hospital. But now I felt like I didn't know her at all. *Suicide, really?* What else didn't I know?

Pulling on pajamas Sunday night, I looked at the clock. It was too late to call anyone but early enough to read. I watched the snow flurries outside as I climbed into bed then dug through the pile of books on the nightstand.

*Bra-a-ang*, the telephone burst into my cozy night like an unwelcome intruder. Cindy from church didn't waste any time. "There is a mandatory staff meeting tomorrow at ten. Be there."

"Okay, what's up?" *Da-a-a*, the disconnected click of the phone responded. *Emergency?* NO-O-O!

* * * * * *

I know I said *rejection* is my biggest fear, but after my sister's attempts at suicide, the fear of getting the news that someone I love has taken his/her life . . . I just don't even want to go there. I was terrified the emergency meeting meant that Gus had killed herself.

The words *why didn't you do something* accused me. I would have if I'd known what.

Scared, but still not knowing what to do, I put music on and cranked up the volume. In bed, I rocked until sleep finally came. The next morning, I inched into the church, looked down the hall, and burst in tears when Gus waved at me from the other end. I ran and embraced her, hard.

"Lizzie," she laughed as she tried to fight me off, "nice to see you, too!"

"I thought," I whispered in her ear, "You know, after the other day."

Behind me, two somber church elders dressed in suits herded us into a classroom. *If she's okay, then what's this meeting about?* One of the men stood guard outside the door and watched for the rest. The other invited me to sit in one of the seats he'd placed in a circle. He paced, searching the room for something to do.

One by one, staff members filtered in, glanced at me, then away.

With the lack of our usual repartee, I hovered on the edge of my seat and stared at my co-workers. No one made eye contact. One riveted her gaze at a spot on the floor and didn't avert it even once. My leg twitched, and I chewed on the skin around my nails. The silence of the room accentuated the ticking of the clock. I looked up, 10:07 a.m.

Once eleven of the thirteen had gathered, the men in suits looked at each other and nodded. The guard stepped inside, closed the door, and took a seat next to the other. "As you can see," he hesitated before his words rushed out in a flood. "Cal's not here, or Hannah. And they won't be coming back. There's been sexual misconduct. And there are others. We want to handle everything with the utmost of care. If there's anything we can do, please don't hesitate to call."

What was he trying to tell us?

*MARY ME*

Kim cleared her throat, and in her soft-spoken manner, raised her hand. "Are you saying Cal had sex with several women of the congregation and one of them was Hannah?"

*What?*

"Yes!" The elders nodded.

*You've gotta be kidding me!* Kim pegged it. She knew something was going on. How was I so blind?

Abruptly, everyone stood. The elders avoided eye contact, grabbed their briefcases, and made for the parking lot, rushing to their day jobs in the community. In stupefied silence, we filtered out of the room, shuffled down the hall. The volunteer at the front desk said, "There's a call for you." I picked up her phone and pressed line one.

"It's Kelly," said the voice, the ex-co-leader of my *Experiencing God* class. *Was she crying?* "Can you come over?"

"I'm working." My whole world just fell apart and she wants to hang out?

"You got the news, right?" *The news. How did she know? No!* I thought her idea of pursuing Cal was, well, hers. Not *theirs.* Quickly, I ended the call and barged into Cindy's office. "Kelly's one of the women, isn't she?"

Cindy put her hand over the receiver of her phone and nodded.

"She just asked me to come over." I eased down into a chair on the other side of her desk.

"Go," she mouthed.

I shook my head. "I don't want to!"

Cindy excused herself to the caller on the phone and again put her hand over the mouthpiece. "I know you. If Judas called you after he betrayed Jesus, you'd be there."

"Wha-a-at?" I jerked then stood. On autopilot, I called Kelly, "On my way."

As I drove to her house, I thought about the beginning of our friendship, trying to piece the fragments together. She's lonely and dejected. I get it, a vulnerable and needy soul attracted to a charismatic man. How many women did that describe?

The important man responds and abuses his power. *Ugh!*

A spiritual leader. Wait, what am I saying? *A* spiritual leader? This was *Cal.* I couldn't yet go there, but I longed to hop on the highway and go somewhere, anywhere. Surely, Kelly had told Cal my response to her request for a confidante. After hearing that, I got why he didn't want us praying together. As good as he was at covert operations, he must have seen Kim's role as truth-teller even when she didn't recognize it herself.

I parked in front of Kelly's house. Dazed, I got out and traipsed to the door, lifting my hand to knock just as she opened it. We sat on the couch in her living room where we'd met for the class, and she told me what had happened. "Cal had a speaking engagement in Seattle. I flew down and waited for him nearby at a hotel. When I answered the door, it wasn't him, but the pastor of the local church. My friend up here, the one I had confided in, told her husband. He'd called the pastor and told him I'd be there."

Four hours later, I left Kelly, who was still tearful.

Before heading back to church for a meeting to tell the leaders what had happened, I made my way to the Arctic Roadrunner, my favorite burger joint, for a little self-care. It was time to deal with my own emotion, finally, and to *be there* for myself.

\* \* \* \* \* \*

"You have got to be flippin' kidding me!" I screamed in my head as I slumped into a booth. Staring at a picture of a woman who'd caught a 466-pound halibut, I shook my head, but not because of the fish. In an attempt to block the noise around me, I put my head in my hands.

This is so not what I expected from church people.

As the foundations of my faith crumbled, I could hear my sister in my head. "See?" Her face mirrored my internal disgust as I thought about the nasty duplicity we'd seen and hated while growing up in church. She'd think I was an idiot for trusting this guy. After all my wavering, I'd put my faith in this man. As a new believer, I'd brought my family and friends to church, the ones who didn't want to hear about God, and pointed to Cal as a *good spiritual leader*. Not only did he betray me, but he also deceived my people.

These lifestyles of hypocrisy mocked me. Why did I think Christians would be different? I guess I held them to a higher standard, so I had a harder time forgiving them. They, I mean, *we*, should know better. Without a gun held to our heads, we profess Christianity. If we're not going to walk our talk, then what are we doing?

My sister expects perfection from Christians. Is that my talk? I know I can't be perfect. My stomach churned. Subconsciously, I reached for my purse. For years, I'd struggled with gastro-intestinal issues. Before I hung out with Fred, I ate antacids like candy, but I no longer carried any because I hadn't needed them. *Note to self: Pick up Tums.*

"Oh yeah, Fred." In the turmoil, Fred was the only name for God I could muster. "I am so done with Christianity, this hypocrisy and . . ." I tried to say *You* but couldn't finish the sentence. Instead, I drenched my Alaskan Banquet burger and fries with an unexpected rush of tears. When I came up for air, I sniveled, "You didn't fail me. People did. Why am I blaming You, well, You could have stopped it, right?"

"How?" In my mind, He gazed at me with such compassion that I couldn't look Him in the eye.

"By refusing us the incredible gift of free will. It's too much for us! We can't handle it," I said, knowing how stupid it sounded even at the time. Who'd want a bunch of robots *worshipping* them without choice; that'd be a cult, right? "You let me make my own decisions and I chose to lean on newfound friends as if they were, well, You. Sorry."

The conversation in the booth opposite got louder as if someone supernaturally turned up the volume. I listened as two guys planned their next party in Big Lake with snow machines, a hot tub, and lots of booze.

"You want to go back to that?"

"No." I moaned. Intoxication only offered a short-term fix.

The guys' conversation quieted. Then I heard two women behind me, chatting about adventures on their bucket lists. Inside I heard, "Want to run?"

After Africa and the Caribbean, I didn't need reminding that I hadn't found home there as I had found it here with this new family—the one I wanted to punch in the face. "It's tempting, but no."

When Jesus' disciples wanted to bail, He'd asked them the same thing. "Do you want to go?" (John 6:67, paraphrase of the Bible). They might have looked from one to another before answering, "Where?"

Those were my sentiments exactly. Angry and hurt, I wanted to yell. I can do that when I call God *Fred*, but when Jesus appeared in the corner of my mind's eye and held out His arms, my heart broke.

How can He love me when I'm so messy? How can He always love me?

I put my head in my hands and wept. When I finished crying, I wiped the snot from my face and took a deep breath. "I want to run. I know You're everywhere, but if I leave now, it feels like I go it alone and I never want to do that again."

Once more, God cranked up the volume in the booth furthest away. I listened as three women complained about the men in their lives. I used to say *perfect man* was an oxymoron but not anymore.

"Jesus," I smiled through tears as I looked at those dining around me. For once, I didn't care what anyone else thought. "You are my perfect guy!"

Instantly, all remnants of the wall between us melted. Our conversation no longer stilted as my words tumbled out. "You answer my questions, reframe my perspective, and fill me with peace. No one can do half of what You can. I trusted Cal, Hannah, and Kelly, my new Christian family," I choked on the word. "And look at what happened."

"Perfection is not what I expect," Jesus stopped me. "Remember, that's why I had to die."

# NOW WHAT?

"Wouldn't you think if people committed their lives to God that they'd do things His way instead of carrying on like before?"

I stood in my kitchen pouring hot water into a mug, then handed it to Amy, a tour-guiding friend of mine with another set of spiritual beliefs altogether. "Of course, we make mistakes, but why even be a Christian if you're not going to try? And why get mad at God? I'd almost turned my back on Him, but this wasn't His fault. I guess He's easy to blame!"

"It sounds like you need a break." Amy added an Earl Grey teabag to the cup before leading the way into my living room and sitting on the couch. "Why don't you come snowshoeing with me and my friend Ruth this weekend?"

"Camping in Alaska, in December, seven miles out to a cabin you *hope* to find. Are you flippin' nuts? I remember your story from last year. You got lost, thought you might freeze to death."

A week later, Amy stopped by with a Gore-Tex jacket and a liner to go inside my new zero-rated sleeping bag. I learned vocabulary words like *pile* jacket and *therma*-something long johns as I stuffed them into my pack.

When she put on a video about avalanches, I glared at her. "This is not going to happen," she assured me. "We're just doing everything we can to prepare."

I looked at her sideways. "Maybe I should wear an inflatable bubble suit?"

"But if you tripped," she snorted, "you'd bounce down the mountain."

We laughed, but after she left, fear took another swing. What if you die-e-e?

Instead of freaking out, I stood tall. What if I did? Compared to this world, heaven's looking better by the day.

Wow, death no longer scared me. But when my alarm clock went off at five twenty-five the following Friday morning, the imminent adventure did. Was I up for it? Snowshoeing couldn't be that hard, but maybe I should have taken a spin around the yard first.

Amy picked me up and we drove down to Tito's Discovery café in Hope, Alaska. The town's name didn't seem coincidental.

"Yes, Lord, I *hope* I survive this trip!"

A waiter filled our cups with coffee and placed three menus in front of us, "I recommend tri-berry pancakes." He winked. "A hearty breakfast will start your day."

"I can justify that with our long trek ahead," I said. The others agreed.

"Where are you going?" He collected the menus.

I looked at Amy, and Ruth said, "Caribou Creek Cabin."

A guy at the table behind said, "In this weather? Snow's s'pose to keep comin' all weekend."

Undaunted, well, sort of—Amy and Ruth anyway—we piled into the car after breakfast and inched our way onto the road toward Resurrection Pass. At ten-twenty, a little behind schedule, we stepped out of the car. I took a deep breath. My nose hairs froze. Snow landed on my lashes as I piled on clothes, couldn't see a thing in the whiteout. "Where's the trailhead?"

"Follow me!" Amy led the way, and we began our race against daylight. Once she set the pace, my mind wandered back to church. *I see why people give up on organized religion.*

I think God smiled. Was I onto something?

Lots of people *do church.* They attend meetings and set up programs doing good things like feeding the homeless or taking care of widows. Was that me? Hanging out with the youth group in a rented dunk tank at the Fall Harvest Festival, cold and shivering, hoping the next kid hit the target because the water in the tank was warmer than the air.

Had I ditched God and made church my community center? In all the busyness, maybe I had lost sight of our friendship, trading God for church.

A few hours into our hike, after the snow let up, I lifted my eyes and admired the little red berries in the dark blue and white landscape of snow-covered mountains. Quiet natural beauty. I was reminded of Africa, where I first started spending time with God. I inhaled the cold, fresh air and sighed. Birdcalls reminded me we weren't alone. I stopped for a minute's rest.

Ow! My body ached, probably not just from exercise but ongoing stress. I plunked down on a fallen log and dug through my pocket for chocolate as I re-visited the beginning of my faith walk, starting with forced church attendance and Mom's rules. I'd set those aside until my experience on the boat brought me into this new community. Then what the heck happened?

"You okay?" Ruth's muted voice came from the path below.

Great question. I was okay. And I still wanted God. What would I do without Him? It's just His people. I struggled with some of them. As Ruth came around the corner, I shivered and pasted my worn-out smile back on my face, heaving myself up off the tree. "I am taking a break."

Like a little kid, bundled beyond recognition, I set out on the snowy path once again. I wanted desperately to leave my angst on that log, but it dogged me.

For the last couple of weeks, wherever I turned, at work, on TV, or in books, I kept being reminded of what the speaker had said at the conference after I got off the boat in the Caribbean. "Do you have a personal relationship with Christ?"

I thought I did. Where did I put it?

All day, I deliberated as I put one step in front of the other. Each time I looked up at the next rise and thought I couldn't go on: *come to me all who are tired from carrying heavy loads, and I will give you rest* (Matthew 11:28, GW) encouraged me in more ways than one.

After my experience on the boat, God and I had begun this conversation. It hadn't made sense to invite someone in and leave Him standing there in the living room of my heart, never to talk to Him again. But along the way, I quit making time to hang out.

\* \* \* \* \* \*

Finally, Amy yelled, "The cabin!"

Up ahead, she pointed to a bit of roof sticking out of a snow bank. Her excitement brought me out of my head. At five minutes to four, the sun had set, and I shivered uncontrollably. "Thank God!"

"No kidding," she agreed. "Since we had ditched the tent because we have so much stuff, where would we have slept if we didn't find the cabin?"

I glared at her, clinging tightly to my poles so as not to fall, too tired to challenge her. We cleared the snow and checked for wood. Again, she cheered, "Enough for the night! Let's build a fire and warm up with some *orange blossom nectar* (a.k.a. hot Tang)."

Inside the ten-by-twelve-foot cabin, two shelves up over the sink boasted seven packets of Ramen, five pots and pans, a dishtowel, and a sponge. A saw and an axe leaned casually against the wall like a couple of Texan cowboys ready to lend a hand.

The lantern Amy and Ruth had used the year before was gone. Oh well, we had flashlights.

On the opposite side of the room, two double beds with a single bunk on top faced each other. A single bed hovered over each, and there was a table in between. When the fire gave off enough warmth, we shed our suits, put on warm, dry clothes, and hung the wet ones around the room. Then we boiled water for pasta and topped it with salmon. By six forty-five, we'd cleaned up the dishes, and I was never so ready to crawl into a bed in my life. I had visions of staying there all the next day until but then my weary bones hit that hardwood. "Ow!" Advil made its first appearance, but certainly not its last.

On automatic, I'd placed one foot in front of the other without paying much attention to the pain till now. Huh, it was the same thing I'd been doing spiritually.

The three of us liked to write, so we'd brought samples of our work to share that night. Amy passed me the flashlight and, lying in my sleeping bag, I went first. I'd never read anything I'd written out loud. Sharing an essay, my attempt to put all I'd been through at work on paper, tested me. Amy and I had recently gone to counseling, so emotions and tears didn't surprise us, but Ruth looked at us in a funny way. Then out of the blue, she confided, "I've never told anyone this, but my father molested me from the time I was five until I was fourteen."

Silence filled the room. Neither Amy nor I knew what to say. After a long moment, I took a deep breath and said, "I am so-o-o sorry."

"Don't give me your pity," Ruth snapped. "What the hell? You two talk about abuse like it's coffee talk then I speak up and everyone goes quiet. Just forget I said anything." She grabbed the flashlight and flicked it off.

*Forget she said anything?* I lay back and ached for her more than all the other things put together.

Gathering firewood with Amy outside the cabin the next day, I said, "How do we help Ruth?"

"I don't know." She shook her head.

"I'd like training on how to respond to people." I cleared the snow from a log so Amy could chop it, and then continued, "I've had other experiences like this, and I hate not knowing what to say or hurting someone by accident. I wish Ruth could get therapy, and I hope she doesn't pass on the idea because sharing with us didn't go so well."

I veered off the path in search of kindling and prayed, "God, I'm so grateful to have worked through things with Chance. I hate seeing Ruth struggle, knowing that there's healing available and with help, she could live the rest of her life in a better place."

Then my mind went back to the congregation at church. Who knew what traumas each faced on top of the mess we were currently wading through together? I wondered if that's why I was still there. I love advice columns. I used to run for Mom's new copy of Ladies' Home Journal to read *Can This Marriage Be Saved?* And in college I thought counseling would be too much fun as a job, but it scared me, too, because I didn't have answers.

"You knew all that," I said to God. "And You know exactly what everyone needs! Couldn't I, couldn't *we* counsel together?

The guy at Tito's was right. Snow fell all weekend. After breakfast on Sunday, we cleaned the cabin, piled everything back onto our sore bodies, and hit the trail at the Alaskan sunrise, 10:00 a.m., not as painful as our start.

The *swish-swish* of the snowshoes sliding through freshly fallen snow calmed me. Knowing what to expect made the return easier and so did this new excitement about helping people. How would that work exactly?

The same people who kept asking about a personal relationship with Jesus recommended *quiet times*, spending an hour a day with God. It sounded like another thing to add to my overloaded to-do list, but when I'd first started hanging out with Him, we'd spent lots of time together. I wanted to and never saw it as a duty.

In the alpenglow of the afternoon, the idea took up residence, nesting in my mind like a bird on a birch tree. Not just because I needed to duke this out, but I missed God. I love what He teaches me through the Bible. I need His promptings, His nudges, and His Presence. Not just the wisdom to know what to do or His favor on my life, but Him. And it's not that God can't be found in church, but religion can get icky. I'm so grateful that my relationship with God is not about rules and good deeds.

"Okay, Lord," I smiled as I looked up at the golden sun sparkling on the snow-covered mountains and adjusted my goggles as I admired the hoarfrost coating each branch. "You and I need a do-over! Can we start tomorrow?"

# TIME TO HIT THE RESET BUTTON WITH GOD

R*-nn-t. R-nn-t.* The alarm clock woke me earlier than usual the following morning. *Oh yeah, my new plan; spend time with God. Re-connect.* I moaned as I hit the snooze button. After snowshoeing back the day before, every muscle rebelled—Advil, Advil, need more Advil. I pulled myself up and limped to the medicine cabinet and then to the grocery store. Back home, I hobbled up three flights of stairs, shuffled into my living room, and looked at the clock. No time for God now. I've got to go to work.

Of course, it turned out to be the busiest day ever without even time for lunch.

I dragged myself up those steps again at 6:30 p.m., just in time to host a new prayer group for a friend who'd attempted suicide and asked if I'd do this. I wanted to help people with their problems, right? Ready, set, go.

After, I went straight to bed and then remembered, *Oh yeah, God.* It was just like every other time I started something new with Him—the battle. The reminder that something or someone tries to keep us apart gave me fresh motivation. I turned on the light and sat up.

Rubbing my face, I wondered, how does this quiet time thing work?

In the prayer group, we shared our requests with God, but didn't expect to hear from Him. However, if He and I were going to spend time together, I once again assumed that talking would be part of it, conversing as we did in *Experiencing God,* so I pulled out my journal.

I figured I could start by listening. How was I going to hear anything if I didn't do that?

*Okay, so pull my fingers out of my ears and quit doubting I will hear.* I'd heard God before and I knew *I* wasn't capable of making up all I believed He'd done in my life, the impressions, goosebumps, and tears. I hadn't always credited God. In front of friends, I might have called them *coincidence,* but I believed He'd had a hand in all of them.

Since I'd been asking Him to reveal Himself, I decided to be willing to receive every subtlety that could be Him, to stop batting them away. "So, God," I prayed, "I lay down all my preconceived expectations and performance anxiety. Help me stop trying to control everything and quiet my mind to hear You, nothing but You. Thanks."

Before I finished, I clearly heard in my mind, "I love you." I knew I didn't make that up. It'd been a while since I'd heard God's all-time favorite one-liner that melts my heart every time.

"Sorry," I said, "I'm late."

"I'm just glad you came." I could hear a smile in His voice. "I've missed you."

I blushed, even though I felt no blame. "I've missed You, too."

Just like old friends, we picked up right where we'd left off, talking about work, current relational issues, the usual. As we chatted, I leafed through my Bible and flipped open to no place in particular, or so I thought, and landed on a story in Genesis about Jacob, one of the patriarchs of the Old Testament. I stopped to read it.

Jacob had packed up his family to go meet his brother. Years before, Jacob had run from his parents' home because his twin wanted to kill him. He hadn't been back since. After his family dysfunction and nonstop struggle, Jacob stood at the pinnacle of his life. His imminent future held the realization of his greatest fear—you know, that place where you're finally ready to duke it out with God because, really, what else can you do?

Getting closer, Jacob chickened out, sending his wives and kids ahead; I don't get that part. Why didn't he put them in a safe place?

Anyway, he wanted to talk to God. That's when the real struggle begins. The angel of the Lord showed up. The study notes in my Bible say it was the physical manifestation of God Himself. God, in the form of a man, duked it out with Jacob. Why?

Well, after the weekend I'd just had, I could guess. I think God knows that sometimes we need to wrestle things out. And by that I mean that I was probably doing the *girl version* of what Jacob did. Instead of fighting, don't we tell God exactly what we think about everything, dare to come clean with the most honesty we can muster?

I think Jacob just needed to get real. He needed to go through his cranky bits with God and name them.

And sure enough, near daybreak, Jacob owned his need for God and confessed his decision to depend on Him. I put the book down, went to the bathroom, brushed my teeth, and procrastinated a minute. "I don't know why, God, but I've been trying to do life without You when I know how much better it can be *with* You. I'm sorry."

In the story, the angel tried to get away, but Jacob wouldn't let him. He told him, "You're not going anywhere till you bless me."

"Your name shall no longer be Jacob," the angel said, "but Israel, because you have struggled with God and with men and have overcome" (Genesis 32:28, NIV).

In that culture, names were important not only as monikers, but they described the nature of a person. Jacob came face-to-face with an angel or with God, fought Him, and lived to tell about it, then hobbled away with a new name, a new nature. Transformed, Jacob steps, or maybe limps, into his destiny.

I wanted that.

Again, I turned to my favorite verse, but in a different translation to get even more perspective. "I know the plans I have for you . . . plans for peace, not evil, to give you a future and a hope—*never forget that*" (Jeremiah 29:11, TV). It reminded me of what God had told me in my writing office at Jewel's: "Write in a book all the words I have spoken to you" (Jeremiah 30:2, NIV).

So, in the weeks to come, I spent time with God every night. No matter how late I got home, I'd pick up my Bible, read a little, and say, "What do You think?"

Over and over, God helped me apply His ways to my life. Like this thing with Jacob; it turns out that God doesn't mind a tussle.

After we had hung out, I'd drift off to sleep grinning from ear to ear. God cracks me up, except when He said, "Why don't we meet in the morning instead of at night?"

I groaned. "I'm not a morning person."

"If we di-i-id," He sang, "You could wear that smile all day long." He had a point.

I set my alarm for six-thirty, knowing I'd hit the snooze at least three times, especially when I remembered *I didn't really have to get up*. Quickly, I learned that if I didn't, I'd fall back asleep and be late for work. Time with God can be like going to the gym. I always feel better after I do it, it's just getting there that's often the hard part. God helped by stirring my desire for a hot cup of tea. En route to the couch, I'd put the kettle on and check email. Then I'd land with my Bible, journal, and whatever feelings I had connected to dreams, an email, or a current dilemma. I'd deflect and procrastinate until I could sit still and focus.

Then I'd make a list of things I wanted God's help with and set it aside, needing Him to calm me down first. I'd pick up my Bible and read some devotionals. Often, He continues our conversation using the words I read next. I stop freaking out as He answers me. My daily challenges look different with God. As I take one issue from my list, I spill my guts till I have nothing left to say. Sometimes I sit at a computer searching for the exact words to describe the situation or how I'm feeling, as if God needs clarification. I write and delete until ironically neat paragraphs evolve from the original screaming hot mess, the lyrics of my emotional healing.

When I hang out with God, I gain understanding and make decisions differently with ideas that I know come from Him because in the past I would never have done things that way. With context and understanding only He has, God blows me away with incredible insight and simple solutions, like back in Africa when He said, "Don't jump!"

I got pretty good at owning my bad and forgiving. I never expected those things to feel good. Even apologizing, too. I used to hate that, but now I love to see what God will do next with everything I give Him. Like Jacob, I wrestle until I have an answer. Then I lean back and camp in that seemingly elusive place of peace it took me so long to find.

God doesn't give one-size-fits-all answers. Sometimes He does things one way and sometimes another, depending on who's involved and what they're going through.

Often, I run into a friend who's learning the same lesson as I am but in a totally different way. We sit together and share what we've learned. God's craftsmanship is like sun shining on a crystal hanging in a window. Colors bouncing off each prism, as He once again works all things together for good for those who love Him, just like He promises in Romans 8:28.

He wants not just the best for me, but for the people around me, too. He's amazing!

What I needed to do came down to one phrase, *Abide in God*.

John 15:5 says, "I am the vine; you are the branches. If you remain in me and I in you, you will bear much fruit; apart from me you can do nothing" (TV). To help that sink in, I painted it on my wall. Not my quote room wall, but my bedroom. And all by itself, so it stood out.

Once God and I spent time together, I felt plugged in, connected to His power. He gets the *ick* off me and by the time we finish, I've got my joy back. Because of that, I aim to stay current. When I skip our daily time, well, I can tell and so can the people around me.

Over and over, I realized how badly I needed this relationship with God.

Aside from my decision to make Him my Savior back on the boat, the choice to make Him my Lord, to listen and follow, was the most important thing I have ever learned. He changes me day-by-day, not just in ways I haven't wanted to, but in ways I never thought possible. I sometimes forget following Jesus includes an afterlife. It turns out that I can't imagine not having Him around now.

In the end, I didn't give up organized religion or my friends at church. Instead, I discovered that I needed God more than ever, even in church. Maybe especially in church.

# MASTER OF THE GAME

"Cal thought of us as pawns," Kelly told me on the phone at work. All day, the words replayed in my mind even as I headed home. Crossing the street, I thought, *Ew, he liked to control us.*

I climbed the cement stairs two at a time, thrust my keys into the lock, and pushed open the door. Inside, I dropped my purse on the kitchen counter en route to my bedroom. I grabbed a pillow and struck it as I screamed, "Betrayal sucks! I feel used, deceived, and ma-nip-u-la-ted." I punched the rest of my strength into each syllable.

"He stopped us," I crumbled, "from praying together."

Tears came. I climbed onto the bed, tugged the furry blanket over my head, and curled into the fetal position. Kelly and Hannah both said Cal told them not to trust me, the newbie, trying to straighten out her life. Ten, maybe twenty minutes later, I reached for a Kleenex. As I sat up and caught sight of my reflection, tributaries of mascara mapped my face.

"What do I do now?"

"Let's chat?" God said in that peaceful, calming way.

I got up, grabbed my Bible from the dresser, and headed for the couch. "You like forgiveness, acceptance, and tolerance." I shivered then looked at the ceiling. "Even after this? Jesus burst into the Temple and toppled the tables when He didn't like what the moneychangers were doing. Maybe You could send Him by?"

I smiled then opened the Bible. *Cal, a predator.* Turns out he was not only a predator but a slick manipulator. He took on the role of spiritual leader, willingly and knowingly positioned himself, built trust, then did this?

I sighed as I flipped through the pages: "Our fight is not against people on earth. We are fighting against the rulers and authorities and the powers of this world's darkness. We are fighting against the spiritual powers of evil in the heavenly places" (Ephesians 6:12, ERV).

"So, God, what are You saying? I'm not ready to let Cal off the hook. We're responsible for our actions, right? He may have been used by evil, but what he did was wrong. I guess he could be a predator *and* a pawn."

I didn't like him thinking of us as pawns, but I sure liked calling him one. And the recognition that evil stole from him, too, and that he didn't get off scot-free, all forgiven and everything without any consequences? I liked that more than I wanted to admit.

Matthew 7:15 warned, "Watch out for false prophets" (NET).

"You definitely could have mentioned that before." I shook my head. "So, he was not only predator and pawn but an archetype? You're right. Evil dresses people up like wolves in sheep's clothing so often that it's a cliché. Again, I can't deny Cal's responsibility, but we worshipped him instead of You, didn't we? Then we stood by like day-old chicks in an open field while he took advantage of the power that *we gave him*."

I tucked my legs up under the blanket and opened to 1 Corinthians 5:1.

It talks about a man who slept with his stepmother. How did the church deal with that? Back then, you couldn't just pack up and move when things got messy. People had to stay and deal with the fallout like I had to since I'd bought the condo.

That first morning, the elders had rushed off to their jobs, but since then they'd been doing what elders were supposed to. They had to acknowledge the liaisons and stop them, get counseling for staff members, gather a team to support the women, and install windows in office doors. And that's when they decided no more one-on-one counseling.

Did the elders make mistakes? Of course, they did. Did they struggle to cope and process? I'm sure.

At the front desk of the church, I repeated the story over and over, on the phone and in person, until the horrifying account became rote. "Three women came forward and accused Cal of sexual misconduct. The elders asked him to step down."

"I always wondered why he worked nights," one said.

". . . always working late with Hannah," another said. On and on it went, hindsight painting the picture with uncanny detail. I whined to the volunteer working with me at the front desk. "How did I miss it?"

"It wasn't your job," she assured me. "God brought you into this community to nurture you. We're supposed to be 'innocent as doves' like it says in Matthew 10:16, right? Stuff like this isn't supposed to make sense."

"Good." I reached for the phone as Michelle, the new Christian I worried about most in the midst of it all, passed my desk. I held up my finger motioning for her to wait. She put an unlit cigarette in her mouth and tilted her head toward the door. I nodded then leapt across the entryway when I finished my call, bursting through the door. "Hey, baby! How're you doing?"

"Aren't we supposed to forgive?" She flicked her cigarette. "If we're not going to pardon Cal, I don't think I can come here anymore."

I took a deep breath and looked out at the parking lot. After setting aside heroin and finding new life, I think Michelle understood the grace we're supposed to offer others better than I did. On this emotional rollercoaster, my perspective changed constantly. Caught me by surprise, like at that moment, when I actually missed Cal. *Really?* Yup! Wait. I did not miss him, but his ability to help people. Many had come to the church because of him. Some were mangled by other experiences of organized religion or never having given God a chance in the first place. Many were seekers, like Michelle. She valued what he had to say. He was supernaturally gifted to talk her off ledges. Who'd help her now?

Instead of taking evil and turning it for His glory like God often does, it seemed like the opposite was happening. Now when people needed God most, hundreds blamed Him and jumped ship. There are good pastors, but also there are spiritually abusive ones who stain the reputation of the position. In the wake of this evil, the ripple effect . . . who am I kidding? The *tidal wave* hurled church members in every direction.

Without Cal, I wished God would pick up the slack and send someone in to explain things. But maybe that was the point. Maybe it was time for each of us to turn to God instead of a man?

Some sympathized with Cal, gathered around, and helped him start a new church. I'm not kidding. Do we tolerate denial because our false sense of survival depends on it? Do we offer abuse another chance? Please, no. My internal wrestling match continued with each layer of drama.

Outside the church that day, I stood with Michelle, my arms wrapped about me, shivering off the cold. "Well, yeah, but . . ."

I chewed on this for hours and then ranted at my boyfriend Jim, "It's like this whole thing has turned God's house of prayer into a circus. What happened was so far from the teachings of Jesus that none of this would have been alright with Him. Yes, He pardons, but He doesn't condone. We're called to repentance. Yes, we receive forgiveness when we confess, but we're told to 'go and sin no more' (John 8:11, paraphrase of the Bible), change our behavior."

"What pissed me off," Jim had never said *pissed* before. I sat down and shut up. "was the night I walked into church and caught Cal rubbing your back!"

"*What?* I do *not* remember that."

Ew! Just like I have a peace-meter, I've got an icky-meter. It rang, *Ding! Ding! Ding! Ding!* Why didn't I hear it the night Cal rubbed my back? Shame slithered up my spine.

*Wait, why do I feel shame?*

I carried the thoughts home and sifted through them with God. In a world full of men who don't listen, I felt sucked in by Cal in the same way as Kelly had. I shrugged hard in an attempt to rid the stress from my neck.

I didn't sleep with Cal, but still.

If not for God's grace, where would any of us be? I saw then where I'd been blind, naïve, and innocent in a way that did not feel good. In my initial anger at the women, I hadn't seen my own vulnerability. That we're all susceptible to deception and often afraid to question those in authority.

But if we don't, aren't we partnering in the abuse?

The next day, I went back to work and dug through my files. I found the collection of poems which I had written to Cal requesting his sermon title each week along with his replies. I shredded them then buried them in the trash before I threw myself into the chair.

*Cal supervised Hannah as she counseled our Wounded Heart group.* That meant my history of sex abuse fell into the hands of this pastor who now knew confidential stuff about me. I felt like prey. Deceived on so many levels, I moaned to a friend who'd stopped by my desk. "I wish God would lead me away from this job."

"You and me both." She laughed. "Not happening, is it?"

"No." I guess the good news is, I didn't run. I couldn't imagine leaving with such a lack of resolution, such a need for redemption, and without His direction. Once again, I processed out loud. "So, what's the deal? We need support, right? Especially in the middle of something like this. I guess we can help each other more when we know how it feels, when we go through something like this together."

"How do we justify what we can't understand?" she asked.

"We don't!" Again, God put the words in my mouth that I needed to hear. "Instead, let's surrender. Not in some namby-pamby way, but with all the strength it takes, again and again." I lifted my eyes to the ceiling and smiled, reiterating my new refrain: "I can't wait to see what You're going to do with this!"

# THE SKELETON IN
# MY CLOSET

Six days after receiving the explosive news of our pastor's infidelity, I sat in church on Sunday with a pit in my stomach, watching most of the congregation hear about our pastor's transgression for the first time. As soon as I could, I fled.

I needed to forgive those involved, but how? I got behind the wheel of my Sunbird to duke this out with Fred so I could return to work on Monday in a better frame of mind.

With only four highways in Alaska, I had a limited choice. South, why not? My favorite drive in the world was from Anchorage to the Kenai Peninsula. Just past the De Armoun exit, the highway dips under Rabbit Creek Road and opens into an expanse, a real-life *National Geographic* centerfold. Snow glitters on part of this scene most of the year, but not that day. No sun, no shine, only cloudy and gray.

I chewed on my lip as I thought about my *friends*. Thank God, I hadn't crossed paths with Hannah yet; I couldn't look her in the eye. "You, Lord, You pardon me the way I want to forgive," I blubbered as I stomped on the gas pedal. "I don't know why, but I can't . . ."

Without missing a beat, He said, "You're having a hard time because you haven't forgiven yourself."

"For wha-a-at?" I moaned.

His next words included the one we never spoke aloud, "The abortion."

I lifted my foot from the accelerator and pulled off the highway into the parking lot at Beluga Point. For fifteen years, we'd never talked about *it*, ever. I hadn't even told my best friend. If something triggered me, I'd turn away and put the reminder in my blind spot until now. The unspoken spoken. With a steep cliff at my back and the ocean in front, I gazed at the mountains across the bay, looked for glaciers, and tried to avoid the topic one last time.

As I thought about it, but pretended not to, the skeleton in my closet breathed down my neck. His glowing eyes leered through the crack in the door. Sneering, he rubbed his hands together, reveling in power.

In the past, I'd slammed that door, bolted the lock, and thrown myself against it. I dragged a couch over and jumped on it, ignoring the thought, *What if they find out?* Finally, I'd calm down by repeating, "I'm okay," but a piece of my mind always guarded the door.

I pulled myself back to the present. The weight in my stomach rolled and protruding needles pricked me from inside as I rifled through my purse. *Dammit, where're the Tums?*

This time, I wasn't going to run. I began with what I knew: I get to choose.

All those years ago, I'd escaped the pain by abusing drugs. I slept with men because I thought I had to in order to keep a boyfriend. Then I ended my baby's life when I got pregnant because telling my parents scared me. Selfishly, I didn't want to give up *my* future.

A dark shadow—fear personified—skulked inside my brain. Fear of what?

My parents. High expectations heavily weighted both sides of my family and getting pregnant at seventeen wasn't part of their well-rehearsed plan that included college, a husband, *then* kids.

But fifteen years later, how would they react? What could they do now?

And, Fred, we'd been getting along so well. If this relationship was anything like the ones I'd had with real men, Skeleton could be a deal-breaker. We'd had a few differences, but nothing like this. I cringed just like I did when I was a child waiting in the back hall for Dad to come home and punish me.

Afraid I'd slip up and sleep with someone, I'd steered clear of boyfriends for the first eight years of being a Christian. Dating Jim was a big deal. I thought he'd run when he found out about the skeleton, but he didn't.

The reptile of shame shifted on my back. So used to its weight, I didn't know what it was like to think about this without it. I'm not excusing the behavior. I just hadn't allowed myself to dream about freedom from shame's grip. But I could never tell. Allow my worst fear to share its secret? Nope!

That's what I used to think, but as I stared at the scene before me, watching the snow paint the mountains white, the charcoal drawing of the cloudy day commiserated with me, revealing its own unique beauty. What might God do with the dark shading of my past as we combined it with my present? Finally, at long last, a single tear and then another slid down my cheek as I wept for my unborn child for the first time.

"You did the right thing," people said. I shook my head.

"You did what was best for you and your baby at the time." I disagree.

"You'll get another chance." That did not turn out to be true. She will always be my only child. Bawling again, I turned to God to confirm what I somehow knew, "A girl, right?"

"Yes."

I shuddered and wrapped my arms around myself as a fresh wave of tears washed my face. After long moments, I whispered. "Is she mad at me?"

"No." God smiled. I blushed as I wondered, *How can He smile at me now?*

"She forgives you, loves you." He said.

Long-buried tears streamed from my swollen eyes since I no longer held back. Blowing my nose, I looked from right to left hoping no one saw. Then I asked, "What's her name?"

"You're her mother. You tell Me."

Another unexpected convulsion of pain erupted from deep within. How could I still merit that privilege? I stopped her from living. Now, I got to name her?

Another long silence ensued until my soul hushed as my thoughts stopped racing. Ashley Dawn, of course. The name I chose at seventeen. I didn't have to think about it. I named her long ago.

"I forgave you when you first asked," God said, "for this and everything else, but you've never let yourself off the hook."

How do I do that? "I forgive myself for aborting Ashley Dawn. Is that all?" It seemed too easy. Like there should be more to it. Penance, *major* penance.

We sat for hours. Each labored thought wearied me, sucking my energy until I fell asleep. Late in the afternoon, I woke, still sitting at Beluga Point with my head leaning against the cold car window. I shivered, rubbing my tear-stained face and puffy eyes before starting the car to warm up and head home. I decided not to pussyfoot around anymore.

What the heck? Jesus paid for my shame. But I'd hung onto it. I'd kept it, not doing anyone any good, least of all me. Sure, part of that was cultural. My grief wasn't just sorrow or conviction. I berated myself because of how I thought God would respond, or more likely because of how the church people around me would respond. Once again, mixed feelings weighed heavily in my stomach like a ball of rubber bands, stretched and tightly wound around the others, melding into something I couldn't name.

I didn't have to hold back anymore. God already knew what I did. He forgave me. If someone wanted to give me crap about it or leave, they might as well go now. I was ready. I didn't want my relationships built on pretense anymore. "Lord, let's talk to my parents and take this skeleton down once and for all!"

Like a release of white doves in memory of my child, the effects of the afternoon birthed freedom in my heart. Relief flooded my body.

After the intensity, I surprised myself with a giggle.

"Well?" God said.

"Well, what?"

"You know, the whole reason you came out here."

With everything exposed in church, I'd wanted to forgive the women involved. "That's easy now. I totally forgive them."

I had no idea that when I couldn't forgive myself, it was impossible to pardon another. Afterwards, it was simple.

# FORGIVEN AND SET FREE

T hree days later, I sat at my desk working on the weekly eight-page bulletin for the church. My co-worker brought me a flyer from the local Crisis Pregnancy Center (CPC) advertising a class based on a book called *Forgiven and Set Free*. As I skimmed the ad, my face flushed. Even after Beluga Point, I yielded to shame once again, buried the piece of paper in the stack on my desk, and casually talked to my co-worker as if nothing bothered me.

When she left, I shuffled through the pile and found the ad, my personal invitation to more freedom. The time had come to take another step. I called my co-worker back into my office and told her my story, ending it with my new refrain: "I can't wait to see what God does with this!"

That afternoon, I called CPC and added my name to the list for their next class. The daytime group had already started. Since I was the only person who signed up for the evening class, they postponed it. A surge of disappointment took me by surprise, but the desire to move as fast as possible, my modus operandi, didn't.

Maybe waiting was part of the healing?

I thought about Christina, a new friend who'd recently confided that she, too, had had an abortion. In the middle of her story, she said, "I don't know why I'm telling you this? I haven't told anyone, not even my fiancé."

Maybe God had her tell me so I'd invite her to the class? I picked up the phone. She agreed. A teacher turned up and CPC called me with a start date. The workbook we used, *Forgiven and Set Free*, walked us through the same exact things God took me through at Beluga Point. I love how He does that, warns me of things, or prepares me. He knows how much that helps me.

"What did you lose when you had the abortion?" the curriculum asked.

"I'd never thought of it as a loss. I only remembered relief. I guess I forgot my baby was a person."

The teacher reached for my hand. "Why don't you ask God?"

The following week I had a list. As I sat with God, He reminded me of three friends who each had a daughter. One at a time, their relationships with their daughters glowed as if highlighted, their little girls some of the most precious gifts they'd ever received.

I'd sent mine back, along with her dance recitals, proms, wedding, and more than I could imagine. I missed out on her first smile, tooth, walk, and the first time she called me "Mama."

I suffered a loss too great to comprehend.

In this group, I continued the healing that had begun at Beluga Point, bringing more and more restoration than I'd ever understood I needed.

Do I think God places sin in a hierarchy, like abortion being a *super sin*? I would say definitely not. But I order what I do wrong, and I never thought anything I did before this was officially sin. Tripping on acid, I knew I'd conceived. I did a home pregnancy test to confirm and called the abortion clinic right away. "Check with a doctor," the receptionist said. "Then book an appointment six weeks out."

*Six weeks?* The wait was painful. I suppose it offered me a chance to change my mind. I wish I had. On the first day possible, I terminated my pregnancy.

Of course, now I sentimentalize all my baby's firsts and ignore how hard caring for a child on my own would have been. Would I have made mistakes? No doubt!

As I listened to Christina's woe, I put my arm around her. We mourned our lost babies together. As I listened to her grieve, I ached for her in ways I hadn't for myself. My friend's presence helped me to recognize my dead zones. Owning the losses revealed more places where I needed to grieve. Only then could I experience the emotion I hadn't and work through another layer, acknowledging the grief and feeling the pain.

After the class, I flew home to Boston to spend time with family.

My cousin shares her daughters with me. In light of recent healing, I paid careful attention to them. Without knowing what I'd been going through, my cousin said, "I wish you had a child. I hate for you to miss this experience. There's nothing like it."

Eight and ten years old, her girls phoned me. "We, um, have a fèis, an Irish step-dancing competition, on Saturday. Ple-e-ease come?"

"I wouldn't miss it!" I hung up the phone. Wow, this would be the first item on my list of *things lost*. That's not a coincidence!

Because I lived so far away, the few events I attended held magnified importance. As I stood in the crowd waiting for the music to begin, I watched the girls in their ringlet wigs and bright, embroidered dresses, peek through the curtain and wave at me from backstage.

A lump rose in my throat.

On the way home to pack for my return to Alaska, I remembered my sister's plea. "Before you leave, can we go for a walk?" The request grew heavy with importance. I drove to her house.

We grabbed umbrellas and set out in the summer rain as we used to when she brought up the reason she'd asked me to come. She knew about my abortion and all I'd been through and said, "I wondered what it's like for you to see me with a baby when you don't have one. I've tried not to get overly excited in front of you."

"Catherine!" I put my umbrella down and crawled under hers. As I reached to link arms, I received another layer of healing. My tears fell with the rain, "You give this baby all the love you have, and I'll give her mine, too!"

# INNER HEALING[9]

B ack in Alaska, I took a class with my new friend, Kath. If I'd stereotyped her, I'd have guessed she was in the National Honor Society and in choir or orchestra in high school. Back then, we never would've hung out. I was too busy skipping school and getting high.

Without God, we wouldn't have been friends. But with Him, we found a depth in relationship that shocked me. She and I both wanted as much healing as possible and kept running into each other in the same classes. So finally, we joined forces.

After an inner healing training, a few of us went down the hall to find a room to *practice*. Of course, prayer is prayer and God shows up; nothing's practice for Him.

One woman, I'll call her Sue, wanted healing after having had an abortion. That theme seemed to be going around. Kath led the session. Even though she's sensitive, she's bold, confident, and trusts God to show up and heal. She sees things in others they may not see in themselves and shares honestly. I confess I'm not always ready to hear what she has to say, but afterwards, I'm grateful for her words. I know she cares and speaks from a place of love, so that makes a big difference.

As we prayed for Sue, I offered quiet prayer support.

We closed our eyes and Kath said, "Tell us what you remember."

"I went to the abortion clinic on Lake Otis."

As she spoke, I pictured what she described, ascended the stairs in my mind, and entered a generic-looking waiting room.

At the same time, an internal urgency wanted to hurry me along. What was it?

Kath took her time. "What went through your mind?"

I shook my head from side to side in an effort to dislodge the thoughts of my own experience and dug through my purse for Tums. I set the roll on my lap and ate one after another as my leg jumped up and down.

"After they called your name," Kath said, "what happened?"

* * * * * *

I hadn't really thought about my own experience since the day it happened. A nurse escorted me down the hall for a brief "counseling" appointment, nothing more than a compulsory ten-minute slot to satisfy governmental qualifications for the clinic, no doubt. I sat with four others, awaiting our "procedure" in white hospital gowns wide open in the back.

I shivered, but not because I was cold.

Looking around the room, I blushed. Everyone else sat with their moms or their men. My mom didn't know. Tony said he loved me then he got on a plane and moved out of state. He rejected me, as I was doing by aborting our child. But that morning, I didn't see that part. At seventeen, I saw a problem I needed to solve.

What about the others? What led them here? The older couple, was he abusive? Or maybe she got raped? I wished we could go have a cigarette together, share stories.

"As long as everyone's ready," the counselor smiled brightly, "we can return to the waiting room." Oh yeah, ready, that's me. I wrapped my johnny more tightly. Back down the hall, I smiled weakly at my friend who'd journeyed into Boston with me, prepared to spend the day.

* * * * *

"It's time." Kath brought me back to the present. "Tell me what happened."

In my mind, I followed Sue down the hall into the operating room. As I came around the corner, I fully expected to see her on the table, but instead, *I* lay there. *My* memory traded places with her description.

Gasping for air, I opened my eyes then closed them again tightly as I prayed, "Lord, I'm here for *her*!" and tried to return to my version of her memory. As if trying to resume a dream, I couldn't.

"It's okay." God attempted to ease my panic.

"Look around the room," Kath said. "See if you see or sense Jesus."

*No!* I hyperventilated as quietly as possible. It wasn't that Jesus wasn't there. I knew exactly where He was, over my left shoulder, but I didn't want to look at Him, not now. I twisted my head and put Him in my blind spot. I breathed as if I were giving birth.

Weren't the others aware of my struggle? I opened my eyes to peek. They had their eyes closed. That's when Kath said, "What do you smell?"

I jerked back from the instant body memory, rubbing alcohol. I held my breath and shook my head.

"What'd you hear?"

No! No, please? In my mind, I heard the sound of a vacuum, like a dentist's drill, causing me to stiffen and sit up straight. I squeezed my eyes shut and my stomach pitched.

"And see?" she continued.

The doctor had his head and shoulders between my legs. The nurse next to me asked nonchalantly as if we were having tea, "So, you're going to college?"

I tried to respond, but at the same time the liar impersonating my own inner voice whispered inside, "I had no other choice." I believed him as I lay on that table at the abortion clinic, wondering the name of the drug that made me feel so good, too good while doing the worst thing I'd ever done.

Then over and over, the liar repeated his next line, "Oh well, nothing I can do about it now."

"When you're ready," Kath said, "Look at Jesus."

I froze.

"Can you see Him?"

I could if I wanted. I inched my head back, then forward, stealing a quick glance, then turning away until I had the nerve to stop and look. Expecting His wrath, my whole countenance shifted as I watched tears stream down His anguished face. He had one arm behind my neck and the other alongside the left-hand side of my body. I could feel His touch.

At the same time, He held me. It's hard to explain because it's impossible in the natural, but I also saw His outstretched arms hanging on the cross.

I'd heard Scriptures quoted in church about how Jesus paid for my sins on the cross, but I never thought I did anything *bad enough* that required that. Well, except this.

Now He personalized His atonement for me. Never again would I question.

Up close and personal, Jesus loved on me at the same time He paid for my bad choices, even for this and for everything I've ever done or will do.

I caught my breath and cried with Him.

At the moment I ended my baby's life, Jesus embraced me with a heart of sorrow for *my* loss. And on that cross, He paid for my choice, dying for me in love, not in anger. For the first time, I got it, really got it. The revelation strengthened my understanding with spiritual rebar.

I needed Jesus' sacrifice to pay for my sins so I could be made right with God.

# TRUTH DOES SET US FREE!

*is-s-s.* The furnace clicked on in the empty church building. I flinched in surprise as I prayer-walked the dimly lit halls. Barely awake, I'd found a way to keep my promise to God to hang out with Him in the morning *and* get exercise at the same time, but I still wasn't a morning person.

"Knowing I adore you," He teased, "doesn't put you in a better mood?"

I rolled my eyes as I crossed the gym when He said, "Wait a minute."

I stood in front of the lone chair in the whole room. I sat. Then He whispered, not audibly, but inside. "Kneel down." I did. Resting my elbows on the chair, I folded my hands and noticed my shadow swaying back and forth, ever so slightly.

Finally cracking a smile, I caved. "Are You rocking me?"

He sang me the words to an old song. And I had to agree. I had never been loved that way before because God loves us as no one else can.

Because I'd found comfort in the motion, I'd rocked my way through childhood. As I leaned on that chair, watching my shadow, a tear rolled down my cheek. Memories and realizations came fast, as if I, once again, sat in the old brown recliner. Daddy's chair.

My sister and I would *call it* when we took a bathroom break or when we ran to get a snack. "I get Daddy's chair when I get back, *black, white, black, white.*"

*R-r-rick Rak, R-r-rick, Rak,* the rickety song of the chair almost distracted me from painful thoughts, but this time I wouldn't let it. It was time to face the music of my emotion, time to hear the song I'd tried so long to suppress.

"Why do you rock all the time?" Mom had asked.

I shrugged. "It feels good." My negative emotions hovered in my core. I complained about them often. "My stomach hurts."

*R-r-rick Rak, R-r-rick, Rak.* When I rocked, I didn't feel it. So, I rocked in Daddy's chair, in bed, any place I sat on, and or even when I stood. I didn't know any other way to deal with my emotion of all the normal stuff of life, like trying to please my parents.

Over and over, I'd crawl into my fantasy world and rewrite the events of the day, making myself a hero. Recently I'd recognized this as a form of self-comfort and protection. I justified the defense mechanism as a good thing. Sure, the *survival skill* built self-esteem but in a misleading way.

When God said, "Let's go to the nursery," I stood from the chair in the gym, went to the small quiet room, and sank into one of the glider rockers. I put my feet on the footstool and closed my eyes. All week long, I'd been asking. "God, what's the lie I believed when I aborted Ashley Dawn?"

There in that room, where babies are rocked every week, He said, "'I have no other choice.' That's what you believed."

I twitched. "You're right. I didn't see it as a lie, but I could have given her up for adoption or kept her."

"But since you believed a lie, you acted on it as if it were truth."

"I did." A wave of peace washed away my angst. God knows the way my beliefs, like threads, tied my thinking into knots. With this one-liner, I felt a release inside, as if a cord was cut, breaking me free from bondage that had held me captive. He and I went back in time and re-wrote my stories with truths instead of lies.

Lies lose their power when you stop believing them.

Each time I went into a memory with God, I'd hear and see things I hadn't before. Since Jesus has always been with me, I'd search for Him to see what He was doing. With one of His looks or words, I'd understand the situation differently. As I replaced the lies with truths, I changed my behavior.

In this way, God gave me the skill set I had prayed for and altered my path. As I learned and grew, I made different decisions. And that *rocked*, pun intended.

Truth set me free while pain taught me.

Offense helped me see the people I needed to forgive. Confident and bold, anger barked like a dog, often stating the obvious. "Someone's at the door. Are you going to answer it?"

"Yes, I am! I'm not hiding anymore. Just because anger is louder doesn't make him more important than anyone else." Sadness gave me permission to cry and joy danced with me every time I remembered God and I were good. He and I had taken down the walls between us.

It wasn't time that healed my wounds. It was God.

In order to get better, I revisited long-repressed memories and addressed what I'd refused to before. I pulled out hidden pain from internal pockets where it had festered and gotten infected, where it had leaked. I sat with all the layers of emotion and allowed them expression. All that I'd run from took minutes to feel. The pain of the past healed with attention.

It turns out that every time I agreed with a lie, consciously or unconsciously, I got ripped off. That understanding drove me to seek them out and help friends who wanted to do the same. After working all day at church, I set up appointments at my condo at night.

Could all our pain be traced to lies?

# MY BOYFRIEND'S SECRET

"What do you think Jim's secret is?" I needled my friend, Michelle, as we prepared dinner in her kitchen. "He just got back from visiting a *friend* in North Carolina. Do you think she's more than that? The strange thing is, he brought me lingerie."

"Why's a naughty nighty weird?" Michelle, also new in her faith, looked at me.

"Well, the Bible says we're not supposed to have sex till we're married."

"Where?" She handed me her copy.

"In a lot of places." I leafed through. "1 Cor. 7, 2 Cor. 12, Heb. 13, Gal. 5. Apparently, the Greek word *porneia* which is often translated as *sexual immorality* includes not only fornication, sex before marriage, but other things, too."[10]

"Okay, okay." She held up her hand with a laugh. "I believe you."

"I could do a sermon on this." I closed the book and paced the living room of her doublewide trailer. "I want to do God's will, so I've been searching for a loophole."

"Are you really going to wait?" She pulled salmon from her freezer to throw on the grill.

"I am planning to wait." When I lived with my ex, I knew God didn't want us sleeping together. All that sex we had outside marriage, I never really, I don't know, liked it. I felt guilty. Now that I've committed to God, I need to back my faith up with action. A clean conscience rocks. It might even be worth not doing what it took to get it dirty.

"I don't think I could do that." She took dishes from the cabinet. "I'm glad I'm married."

"I get it! But to get married, I've got to date. I didn't think I could without sleeping with someone. Instead of screwing up, I quit dating for eight years. Jim's my first Christian boyfriend and he's never pressured me for sex. In relationships in the past, lingerie made sense. But now, with both of us trying to hold back, why would he give me a teddy?"

"Wait! He never pressured you for sex; do you think he's gay?"

"No. I wondered in the beginning, but my good friend who has lots of gay friends, said, 'If he's going to church, I don't think so.' And if he likes men, why come to a church singles' group and date women?"

Even as I said the words, I thought about a night a few weeks back. Jim and I rolled around on the floor in my condo, making out. When we separated, I saw the outline of an erection then an expression on his face. What was it, like a sense of achievement?

*Aha, I can get hard for a woman.* Crap! I didn't say anything to Michelle.

On the drive home, my stomach churned. I rounded the corner, and up in the sky I saw three tall stick figures, not with my eyes, but in my mind. That had never happened before. And at the time, I'd never heard the term *open vision*, but since then others have described experiences like this and that's what they've called them.

I don't know how, but I knew they were angels. Before I had a second to question, a clear and instant understanding came; the issue between you and Jim is homosexuality.

*No-o-o!*

A moment before I'd have fought that with everything I had, but not because I was in denial. I hadn't chosen to wear blinders and ignore the truth. It's just that, what? I believed a lie again.

*Crap!* I'd sensed it, but I wanted to believe my old roommate because I wanted a boyfriend and I liked Jim. After my conversation with her, I totally ignored the twitchy bits inside. Maybe God was showing me from the beginning and told me plain as day.

I flicked through my recollections trying to make sense of things. I landed on the expression on Jim's face the night I found out about my pastor's sexual transgressions.

Jim had asked, "Why do *you* feel betrayed?"

"Are you kidding? His actions, like a disease, affected everything. The way he spent time, the way he counseled, and the way he encouraged. Why aren't *you* upset? Your pastor taught you one way to live but didn't follow it; doesn't that make you mad?"

"Ah." Jim's eyes brightened then he furled his eyebrows.

Now, the eyebrows made sense. At the time, I thought, *What goes through that boy's head?* But he was doing the same thing, living a double life that betrayed me as well.

Over and over, I said the word: *homosexual.* Burying my face in my hands, unable to wrap my brain around what was going on, I felt like such a fool. Why was Jim dating me, then?

The next day at work, everyone kept asking. "Are you okay?"

I shook my head. "It's not my story to tell."

Cindy stepped into my office and closed the door. "Go home. Take the day off."

I ambled across the street like a zombie and sat on the floor in front of the mirrored closet in my bedroom. "God, what am I supposed to do?"

The answer came immediately, "Love him."

"Are you kidding me?" I squirmed. Staring at my reflection, I rolled on my back and stamped my feet. "Are you freakin' kidding me?"

"No, the answer is always love."

I did love Jim. And this didn't stop me. You can't just turn love off, right? Obviously, we had a giant lack of authenticity, but we had an unspoken agreement to marry. He'd said, "I've picked out names for our kids."

"Seriously, when were you going to tell me this?" I railed at him, reliving every moment in my mind, not knowing which hurt more, the lack of honesty, or knowing I couldn't compete with a man.

Was he born gay or choosing a man over me? Was he rejecting me or using me as a cover?

When I finally peeled myself off the floor, I picked up the phone, put it down, picked it up again, held my breath, and dialed his number. "I, um, can you stop by on your way to work?"

I needed to talk. I just didn't know what to say.

All afternoon, I practiced. "Jim, I've got to talk to you about something." Ugh, that sounded like Mom, always putting me on the defensive. I didn't want to do that.

"Jim, can I ask you a question?" Nope, that was spineless. Suck it up, girl, and stand up to him.

"There's someone else in this relationship." I finally said as he shook his head. "And it's not another woman." I'd hoped the angels were wrong, but I could tell by his flinch they weren't.

"Homosexuality, right?" I pressed, needing to nail this down.

He nodded then looked at his watch. "I've got to go. I'll call you tomorrow."

He didn't.

But three days later, we had our longest chat ever. With the wall I-didn't-even-know-was-there down, we spoke openly for the first time.

Three times, he asked, "Do you want to double-date with a friend Friday night?"

*Seriously?* The first two times he asked, I changed the subject. I wasn't about to get duped again, but I was curious, so I finally asked, "What friend?"

"My hair stylist." He waited as I tried not to laugh. So stereotypical, I thought but kept my mouth shut. Then I couldn't help myself, "I'll go." I wanted to see what was going on, but choosing the truthfulness we'd so recently discovered, I put a stake in the ground.

"Just to be clear, this isn't a date. We're no longer boyfriend and girlfriend, but I'm here for you. I can be your friend, but knowing this, I can't be your partner."

"God told me I could trust you," he said, and we hung up.

Receiver in hand, I sat there thinking. The Truman Show came to mind. In that movie, Truman was the only one who didn't know he starred in a reality show. The people in his life were characters, acting. Writers scripted his life.

*Was God doing that to me?* The hair on the back of my neck stood as I thought about Christof, the character who played the director. He'd formed a corporation to adopt Truman as a baby and controlled everything from who had access to Truman to when a love interest was introduced, and even when he wrote her off the show. By ordering the turn of a few knobs, Christof had Truman's father killed in a fake storm at sea that scared Truman from ever trying to leave the island, the set where the show took place.

Weirdly enough, I'd turned to Christ, the Author of my life, on a boat in a storm. Instead of causing the sea to rage, He'd calmed it. Set me free to choose life. My wild God invited me into amazing experiences, all the while protecting and empowering me with the boldness I needed to follow His lead into the desires He gave me.

So similar, Truman's life with Christof and mine with God, yet they were so different.

Truman's bondage and my freedom revealed the opposing motivation in the hearts of those behind us. Christof used the popular star to make a fortune while God worked on my behalf. Christof wrote the love of Truman's life out of the show. God, looking out for me, brought Jim's secret into the light, tried to tell me in the beginning when I didn't want to know, and then stopped me in my tracks before it went any further. God's love always offered more freedom with more truth.

\* \* \* \* \* \*

On Friday, Jim and I drove up a long driveway off of O'Malley Road into a landscaped garden of a yard filled with cages of exotic birds. Peacocks ran free. I forget the hairdresser's name, but he met us out front, a handsome man in a black muscle shirt tucked into tight jeans. Lagerfeld cologne wafted past as I shook his extended hand. Jim made the introduction, but I was in my head. *Where had I seen him before?* He was picking up his kids from Sunday school.

"Let's go inside." He opened the beveled glass door. "I'm keeping an eye on a roast."

A lavish spread of hors d'oeuvres welcomed us in his kitchen. And with a familiar flourish, he cracked open a beer and handed it to Jim . . . who didn't drink. *Huh?*

Grateful for the beers he offered me and the anesthetizing buzz that came with them, I fell back into the partying world for the night with ease, sitting back to watch the show. Eventually, a girl showed up. The guy's girlfriend? I don't think so. Who was this charade for anyway, me? And was I reading too much into this or not enough?

After the last week, I couldn't help but take out my crayons and color everything in.

After dinner, Jim drove me home. I hadn't had more than the occasional beer in a while, so my head spun as I crawled into bed with too many unanswered questions. On the ride home, I hadn't known where to start. Now I reached for the phone and dialed Jim's number. It'd been an hour since he'd dropped me off, plenty of time to get home, but the phone rang and rang.

*Ah, the real party.*

Can I punch hindsight in the face? Everything so obvious now, how hadn't I seen it coming?

I hadn't wanted to.

"Love him." God had said, not *out him*. So, what did love look like?

As a result of all I'd learned, I'd done something new. I'd confronted Jim and cried the tears I felt after being betrayed, as well as for the ten years I'd stayed away from men and the possibility of not meeting another in time to have a family.

Grieving sucked, but it felt so much better than adding to the sack of un-dealt with emotion I'd been carrying around. I didn't want to haul any of this into my future.

That week, God picked me up and carried me as I wept. In the form of raindrops, His tears mingled with mine and fell to the ground. On Friday, He set me back down. Like a child, yearning for more of her parent's embrace, I reached up toward Him. He stayed close but didn't pick me back up. Instead, He cared for me through the words of friends. "Our eyes are the windows to our soul." An ex-boyfriend emailed completely out of the blue, not knowing what was going on in my life. "Maybe God is washing your windows with tears so you can see more clearly?"

Maybe. I painted his words on my quote room wall.

# FOR ONCE, I DIDN'T
# WANT TO RUN

"Rick's coming!" Kim told me the next morning at work. "It's a total God thing." She and I had an unlikely friendship. Without having God in common, we wouldn't have been friends. Why? Well, we're just so different. But as we became prayer partners, we got close. We looked for ways to surprise each other, like when she painted my office hot pink or when I kidnapped her in her pajamas for a birthday breakfast.

"Great!" I said. "That's what I need right now, another man in my life. Who's Rick?"

"You'll love him! He's a crazy biker with a wild past, a missionary in Africa. He quit his job, sold his stuff, and planned to come back and open a school of ministry, but then the sponsoring church decided to wait a year.

Rick and his wife prayed, 'Lord, we thought you said Alaska.'

Sensing peace, they continued packing. An hour later, *our* elder board called and offered him the interim position to replace Cal for that exact time period. Cool, huh?"

The following Thursday, a short, stocky guy with a big smile carried a guitar into a staff meeting. *Rick?* What did he think we were going to do, sing? This wasn't Africa.

We sang. And without members of the congregation tapping me on the shoulder as they do during a service, handing me their latest bulletin announcement, I closed my eyes and really worshipped for the first time ever: "O-o-open the e-e-eyes of my heart, Lo-o-o-ord."

Tension slipped from every part of my body as we serenaded God until He answered our prayer. Boy did He. Jam-packed with peace, alert, aware, and ever-so-present, I lay back on the couch, limp, as if transported to another dimension. A piece of me floated above the room, filled with His presence, like a balloon in the Thanksgiving Day parade.

So, *this* is worship? It's almost like smoking a joint.

Loving God like that changed me. Never again would I roll my eyes when Rick showed up with his guitar. In fact, I couldn't wait for him to hook me up again.

Two months later, Rick stopped by my office to talk to me about Kelly, my *Experiencing God* co-leader who, you know, *with Cal*. Since our class had ended, I'd considered backing away from our friendship because I hated what happened, the duplicity, and did not want to be a part of that.

Wrestling again, I thought about God. He'd have me carry on and forgive some more. "Do unto others," and all that (Matthew 7:12, paraphrase of the Bible).

I took a deep breath and let it out hard.

If I hadn't talked to God, that would have been my default. I would pull myself together and, oh yeah, love. But recently I'd heard someone say, "People use that Bible to make it say anything they want."

*Ew*, really?

Sure enough, proof texting is when a person pulls a Scripture out of context and applies it however they choose. I didn't want to do that, so I asked God to show me what He wanted.

As I waited, I read, "A time is coming and has now come when the true worshipers will worship the Father in the Spirit and in truth, for they are the kind of worshipers the Father seeks" (John 4:23, NIV).

Yup, when I study the *logos* word, the Bible, with the *rhema* word, the Holy Spirit, God explains things. He might say, "It's like that," and bring a circumstance to mind. Then He doesn't have to repeat a whole story. I get the comparison and recognize the nuances that apply to both.

But in this thing with Kelly, He didn't do that.

He showed me something new. 1 Corinthians 5:9-11 said: "I told you not to associate with people who indulge in sexual sin. But I wasn't talking about unbelievers . . . You would have to leave this world to avoid people like that. I meant that you are not to associate with anyone who claims to be a believer yet indulges . . . Don't even eat with such people" (NLT).

*Could that be right?* "Wait, God, don't answer that! I'm not ready."

As frustrated as I was with Kelly, I didn't put friendships down easily. My questions weren't rhetorical. I needed a minute, so I took a walk, watched a movie, then went to bed before resuming that conversation.

I trusted God with small things at first. I did what I thought He said and watched what happened. By now, after hanging out with Him for eight years, I had a lot of God stories. But I wrestled on occasion, like now.

I pictured Kelly and me staying friends, and I found that I had no peace. If I stepped away, I found peace.

"Are you sure, God? Because this doesn't feel like love; maybe tough love or brutal love." Again, I struggled between peace and no peace. So, I backed away even though it hurt. God knew my heart, what I did, and why. If I was making a mistake, I trusted Him to correct me.

That's when Rick came into my office. "God's all about restoration with Kelly."

"I'd say *yes*, but God said: 'with her do not even eat.' Talk to me, Rick."

He flushed as he backed out of my office. "You do what God tells you to do."

As our new pastor, Rick validated my relationship with God without speaking for Him. In the situation with Cal, I'd exchanged my relationship with God for one with a human. After all of that, I needed Rick's kind of support and the confirmation that he believed it was God I was hearing, even though I was half-hoping he'd tell me to stay friends with Kelly.

I wasn't trying to be catty. I was just figuring out my walk with God. I liked the peace I felt when I followed His suggestions, and I didn't want to live without it anymore.

\* \* \* \* \*

All too quickly Rick's time with us ended, and the new call-it-like-he-saw-it pastor stood in my office, holding my aquarium full of sea monkeys to the light. Then he bent down and examined the previous year's financial reports on my bookshelf and leaned in closely to peer at the various notes on my desk, all the while keeping an eye on me. "Why are *you* the bookkeeper?"

"What do you mean?" I grabbed the sides of my desk, clenching and releasing my jaw.

"You're not operating in your gift cluster!"

*My what?* I held my gaze. Just before Rick left, he'd warned, "Pastors often start over with new staff." Was that about to happen?

That night, I admitted, *This guy's right. I don't have what it takes for this job.* I'm a people person. *Why am I stuck in an office crunching numbers?* I was there because after everything went down, people quit. When the church offered me this position, I took it in order to keep a job. It didn't occur to me to say no. For eighteen months, I'd tried, but those piles of paper made me swear.

But if this wasn't my place, I didn't want to end up *placeless.* The urgency of that epiphany drove me to the phone to call my new boss, the financial director. Good thing I glanced at the clock. It was eleven. I set the receiver in its cradle and chewed my nails down to the quick.

Early the next morning, I waited for Kim in a classroom. We'd never met before work, but God knew I needed to and set it up. Kim took one look at my disheveled hair and gave me a hug, "What's wrong?"

"You know how hard I work," I started to cry. "I hate year-end. I can never balance the books, and I give you such a hard time when you help; I suck at this!" I took the Kleenex she offered and blew my nose. "But this is all I have. No husband, no kids."

As a single person, Kim understood. "To top it off," I put my head in my hands and sobbed, "Spot died."

"Who?" Kim put her arm around me.

"My flippin' bird. I can't even keep a parakeet alive."

Kim tried not to laugh. Then it was her turn. I don't remember what she said until, "By the end of February, you'll know what to do."

Those words caught on something deep inside. She doesn't remember saying them and blushes when I remind her. She had never prophesied before, but I knew she was right. By the end of February, I'd know what to do!

I grabbed onto that life preserver before going down for the count. It was early November. Only one, two, three months away. I could do that. For a minute, I got a grip, crept to my office, and started working. Then the financial director strode by, briefcase in hand. He called out his usual, "Morning!" did a double take, and backtracked into my office. "What's wrong?"

"God moves us around, right?" I wiped my eyes. "I don't want to be in someone else's place."

"What do you mean?" He sat.

I filled him in.

"We won't fire you!" He assured me. "If this isn't where God has for you, we'll pray and see what He does have and help you transition."

I smiled weakly, but after he left, an old familiar temptation taunted, "Want to run?"

"No," I shook my head. "I don't. I want God's will." I couldn't wait to spend time with Him and see what He had to say. And sure enough, that night, God said one of the coolest things ever. "If you could do *anything*, what would it be?"

"I would buy a hippie van, drive around the country, and do volunteer work." I perked up as a video clip played in my head. In San Francisco, I had planted a garden for an elderly woman, a powerful prayer warrior who prayed for my friends.

"I'd love that, Fred!" I hadn't called Him that in a while, my term of endearment, easier than "Holy Spirit." As He and I brainstormed, I shared with a friend who said, "I could finance projects and buy seeds for that lady's garden."

I jumped up and down, made lists, and found a van while part of me chewed on my lower lip. I wondered how I'd pay for everything.

That's when I recognized a familiar cycle in my life: first, a wish. I daydream as I go about my daily routine while not yet packing to leave everyone behind or transition into a new space with all its unknowns. The dream, not yet real, keeps me from grieving the losses while it also offers excitement and possibilities of things to come. The best of both worlds.

As I step into the dream good-byes hurt. A world full of strangers become my reality until some turn into friends. It's a process. When I used to do it on my own, without God, I could count on a miserable first month in a new location. Now though, even when I don't have anyone else, I have Him. And that's more than okay.

While all this was going on, I'd started working with our new shepherding pastor, a lover of all people if there ever was one. Kids who didn't even know him ran up and hugged his legs. He would grab them and swing them in the air, laughing more than they did.

With connections around the state, he couldn't go anywhere without running into a friend. Not only did he know the person, he knew their story. That's what happens when you sit with someone in the hospital, a jail cell, or alongside the road waiting for a tow truck. He'd counseled and prayed from one end of the state to the other. And lately, he'd been asking me to join him in his office when he met with women because of that new rule: *no men counseling women alone.*

As I prepared to head down the hall and join him for a session, my boss stopped by. I said, "I'll get the bookkeeping done, even if I have to stay late."

He looked at me like I'd lost it. "You like helping with the counseling?"

"Love it!" I closed my filing drawer and buzzed the front desk to let them know where I'd be.

Then that Friday, at the end of February, I passed my boss on my way out. He called from inside his office, "Got a sec?"

I stepped inside.

"On Monday," he said, "you'll begin working in the shepherding ministry building teams to pray, counsel, and help people with practical matters."

"No way!" I leapt in the air as my hippie dream came true, and I didn't even have to move.

# WHAT IF GOD IS GIVING ME A CHOICE?

I loved every second of the four years I worked in Community Care, praying for people, organizing volunteers to hold preemies in the hospital, and finding mechanics to work on cars for single moms. But most of all, I loved lay counseling. It gave me an avenue for sharing the healing I'd received with others who needed it. Anytime anyone asked, "What do you do for a job?" I'd say, "I can't believe I get paid to do what I do."

But now, the next new pastor stood in the doorway of my office, "You love counseling, so why don't you go get a degree?"

*Go?* Instead of preening as he stroked my ego or focusing on the wisp of desire in his suggestion, I shuffled papers as if too busy to talk. He didn't usually pay much attention to me, certainly not in such a flattering way.

"Dan Allender's a friend of mine," he went on.

*Hey, I know that name!* Oh yeah, he's the guy who wrote *The Wounded Heart*, the book we'd used in Hannah's class for women who'd been sexually abused. My heart leapt while I continued filing as if Tom's words had no effect.

"Dan is president of a seminary that offers training in counseling."

*What?* Okay, usually I knew the God nudges, but this combination of encouragement and excitement, coupled with what felt like a backhanded compliment, confused me. I needed to talk to God.

I excused myself and headed for the ladies' room. Inside, I paced. "Now that my fear of commitment is gone, You want me to leave? What about my condo?"

That night I invited five friends over to pray. Friends who spend time with God, hear, and see. Friends who drop everything and gather at the last minute. In my living room, we sat in a circle around the dining room table chatting with expectation, the air electric. One woman prayed with her hands held high, "I see a careening bus. God wants you to get off before it gets into an accident."

A shiver ran up my spine. She didn't know about the bus crash in Africa, but God did. And He knew the effect her words would have on me.

Before I could linger, another spoke, "What do *you* want?"

"I'm not sure. If I stay, but lose my job, what will I do?" This particular decision-making cycle freaked me out because I hadn't initiated it. But if I'd never left Africa and come here, I'd have missed all these friendships. Did I have to go in order to grow?

Something twitched inside. Dang it, I'd promised God to stop taking polls and ask *Him* my questions. Why hadn't I? Was it out of habit or fear of what I'd hear? If He said, "Go?" I'd have to, I couldn't say no to God now. The ladies left, all but the one who stared at me from the living room floor. "What if God is giving you a choice?"

"I've made so many bad ones. I know it's ironic, but after my rebellion against people telling me what to do, I'd want His direction." I sat down across from her. "When He speaks, I can hear it. Well, when I'm ready. A person can say the same thing, but when they do, there's always a motive. Not with God."

She looked at me with a knowing smile. "Are you ready to hear?"

I took a deep breath and glanced around my living room garden at the white picket fence, the teakettle watering can with daisies coming out the top, and the waterfall. Then I looked back into the eyes of this friend who'd become very special. A tear slid down my cheek as I nodded.

Kneeling on the floor with our eyes closed, we prayed, "Lord, what do You think?"

Immediately, I saw a vision. "The two of us are standing at the front desk of the seminary. Over the receptionist's head, it says, 'Mars Hill Graduate School!' "

I opened my eyes and bit my lower lip but knew-that-I-knew-that-I-knew I had my answer.

"When I brought you the picture of us this afternoon, God said it was a going-away present," she confirmed. "I would have told you, but you needed to hear it for yourself."

I nodded again. Then we hugged and cried before she left, and I went to bed.

That night, I dreamt about a cartoon family of eagles. Feathers flew as one of the adult birds chased an eaglet around a nest attempting to head-butt him out into the world. It might have been funny if I hadn't imagined myself as that baby bird scrambling to get out of the way. The dream woke me. "God," I said, "what are You trying to tell me?"

"It's time to fly."

"I don't know how," I confessed.

"I'll give you flying lessons," He promised.

When the alarm went off in the morning, I jumped out of bed, which was not my normal. "Woo hoo! I've wanted a counseling degree forever. How did I forget? And if I can study under Dan Allender, yes, please!"

But by the time I reached the kitchen, hesitation set in. Leave Alaska and my friends? *No-o-o!* But each time there was hesitation, I remembered the vision, and my desire increased.

Time was short. That weekend, I packed. In a box of important papers, I found a list of goals I'd written ten years before. Number one: Get a master's degree in counseling by the year 2002. If I started now, I'd graduate in 2003. It would be a year after my goal, but really close to an ambition I'd forgotten about.

Digging further into the box, I pulled out a newsletter from the University of Houston. As a student, I had crossed the campus en route to accounting from psychology when *I should major in counseling* traipsed through my mind. But then that other thought came. *That would be too much fun.* That should have been my clue to go for it.

An old letter from my tent mate in Africa read, "Would you consider counseling people? You'd be good at it." I smiled as the papers from my past concurred with God's direction and my decision to follow Him into the future.

And each time I told someone, "I'm moving to Seattle," he or she solved another piece of my puzzle. "I have frequent flyer miles. Go look at the school." Or "I'm having a garage sale. If you come up with at least one item, I can honestly call it *multi-family* and I'll do all the work."

Even the pastor pushing me out of the nest said he would email the seminary to see if they had a part-time job, but then God said something weird: "Don't work."

*What?* I'd worked since I was fourteen. How would I pay my rent?

As I filled out my application for school at the dining room table Sunday after church, the phone rang. I picked up. Mom said, "Are you getting excited?" I smiled, glad to be on the same page with her. Still working on our relationship, I'd never expected us to get this far.

Finally, I got it, *She loves me.* Struggling with depression and everything I slung at her, she was human and probably wanted to say "F U" at times, but that's not her way. She did it with her actions instead. Does that mean she didn't do her best? I don't think so. Maybe we all need to say F U every now and then, especially when we're missing the skills to do anything else.

"Hang on," she said, "your Dad wants to talk to you." Well, miracles never cease.

"Hi, Dad, I know you always wanted me to be an accountant."

"What do you mean? I'm an engineer. Accountants and engineers are like cats and mice in the business world."

"Dad, don't you remember? You made me take those aptitude tests in high school. The final analysis said: 'Elizabeth should be an accountant.' You approved the idea and herded me in that direction. That's why I always end up in bookkeeping jobs."

"I thought that's what you wanted, so I supported your decision."

*Another lie?* Ugh! "Well, I want to be a counselor."

"Then I want to pay for your expenses. All I ever wanted is for you to have meaningful employment that you enjoy."

I was speechless. That's how I'd pay my rent! Then it occurred to me, "Is that what you meant by wanting me to make a difference in the world?"

"Of course!"

*Of course?* Why the heck hadn't I clarified this before?

After all my effort to gain Dad's approval, I got it. Not because I pursued his recommendation, but because I stood up for what was important to me. Well, knock me over with a freaking feather. Then I realized, if I hadn't worked so hard for his pat on the back, I'd have settled for less instead of chasing destiny. Who knows what I'd be doing?

In Dad, I had searched for something I never could find in a human being; I'd looked for God. And Dad could never be my god. I guess some people worship a person, but Dad would never live up to my expectations.

Ha! And all this time, I thought it was about me living up to his.

\* \* \* \* \* \*

On July 3, 2001, I pulled onto the Glenn Highway one last time. With the long road ahead and plenty of time to think, I shook my head in disbelief as glimpses of my past connected like dots of importance.

Outside Wasilla, veering toward Glennallen, I thought about how God had asked me to save ten thousand dollars a year when I moved to Alaska. Initially, I did, but after I quit Service with a Smile and bought the condo, it didn't seem possible until that afternoon when I picked up a check for nearly $50,000 from the sale of the condo.

Through the accelerated equity plan, an increase in the housing market, and God being God, my bank account had soared to eighty thousand dollars almost to the flippin' penny. Ten thousand for each of the eight years I'd lived there after working fewer hours with less pay.

Then I thought about the speaker at the conference after the boat. Boy, was she right. Just like the other people who kept telling me I needed a relationship with Christ. I almost missed out because I thought if I was a Christian that life would be boring, and I'd have no cool friends.

It all sounded so "no thank you!" to me, but God did something through my friends at church. He introduced me to my Prayer Mama whose art is in the Smithsonian and my ex-hero-in-addict friend, Michelle. I came to know Melody who no longer has lupus but has her castle now in heaven. And Gus who makes me smile every time I think of her. And Kim who brings tears to my eyes. Each made a difference. Without our connection in Christ, I would never have met them.

The church I'd been tempted to blame for the betrayal of a few had given me so much. God had specifically asked me to take that job *and* buy the condo. Now I saw why.

On the plane ride home from Africa, I'd carried a few belongings inside a dirty backpack, bedraggled and broken. Now, eleven years later, I couldn't see out of the back window, my car so filled with treasure. My body was no longer broken but was healed physically, spiritually, and emotionally as I set out on a mission from God. My pockets were full of money as I went on my way, being just about as unlikely a representative of His as any.

And Truth . . . I wished I could sit with my grandmotherly seatmate again and share this next segment of my story. On top of the world, on a desolate highway in the land of the midnight sun, in an '87 Sunbird without cell coverage, I wept. They were happy tears because I'd found what she had known I was looking for, even though I hadn't believed her. It was God and all the things that came with Him like purpose, peace, healing, freedom, acceptance, and love. Real love.

I'd looked for all that in Dad, in guys, and in friends. In drugs, alcohol, and adventure. And now, in this amazing relationship with Jesus, I understood what Truth meant. I couldn't have found this in anyone else but God. He hooked me up with an incredible community and job. He set me free from lies, filled my bank account, and reminded me of my dreams.

A smile on my face, I ventured on purpose, no longer in fear. Hope morphed into expectation because even though I didn't know what lay ahead, I knew who rode with me.

# CONFRONTATION WITH
# THE EX-PASTOR, CAL

Seventeen years after working at the church in Alaska, the one
where the pastor left because of sexual harassment, I returned
to Anchorage for a visit. It never occurred to me to go see him
because I didn't plan to give what he did any more attention by
writing about it. Also, I didn't want to relive it as I didn't see the
need. But memoirs, like kidnappers demanding ransom, stipulate
their requirements and leave you little choice. If I wanted to share
the cool stuff God did, I had to show what He'd redeemed, so . . .

A few days after I landed, my friend Kath stopped by to see
me at Kim's house. "I've got a weird idea," I said. "Do you want
to visit Cal's church?"

She perched on the couch then bit her lip. "Why?"

"That's what God said!" I leaned back in the rocking chair
opposite. "I don't know. I woke up with this odd desire, and I
can't shake it."

So, there we were at ten-fifteen the following Sunday on our
way. I sipped my coffee and asked, "What do we say?"

"This is your deal!" She laughed. "I'm just along for the ride."

I'd hoped to blend in with the crowd and have a chance to
scope Cal out from afar before encountering him, but as we drove
into the parking lot, I counted five cars and pulled a face. Oh yes,

it was dip-netting season in Alaska. Most people would be out fishing.

Kath reminded me, "We don't have to go in."

Sometimes that's what I need, a reminder that I get to choose. "Let's do it."

Inside the sanctuary, we picked two chairs in the middle and sat a third of the way back from the lectern where Cal would stand. That's when his familiar voice reverberated from the back of the room. I shivered as I turned. There he stood in a suit and tie as usual. His brown hair was still parted in the middle, thinning a little. His face had aged. He looked directly into the eyes of the woman with which he spoke, spread his legs wide, dug deeply into his pockets, chatted easily, then turned and caught my gaze. I twitched.

"I thought that was you." He ambled over. "Why have you come?"

"To spy on you." Kath cloaked a half-truth in a joke.

"If I could take everything back," he said, pushing his glasses up his nose then crossing his arms, "I would, but I don't understand why people are still so upset by something that happened such a long time ago."

*Bzzzt!* I hadn't understood before that moment, but there it was—the reason I'd wanted to come. I'd hoped to see sorrow and recognition of the harm he'd caused. Instead, wasn't this evidence of its lack?

"You hurt them," Kath said. "Deeply."

Later that afternoon, back at Kim's, I called my prayer group leader. "What was I thinking, going to see him?"

"You responded exactly how you were supposed to," she picked up as if there hadn't been a super long gap in our interaction, "to a God-given desire."

"You're right!" I wrinkled my nose. "That wasn't *my* plan."

"Three's are important to God. Whenever something happens in the Bible that many times, God's making a point. You told me God had *three* people ask why you wanted to go to Cal's church. In that way, He prepared you for the question Cal asked you three times, 'Why have you come?' "

My hand flew to my mouth. I'd forgotten how powerful our chats could be. She saw things so clearly that I missed. As I thought about that, she pressed on.

"God doesn't want you hanging onto a lack of unforgiveness and all the bitterness that comes with it . . . besides, you are writing your story. You need to share your why's."

Yes, I did. What were they?

The following morning, as I sat in Kim's kitchen with my first cup of tea, I turned on the computer to check Facebook. I clicked "you have a message" without any thought, then leapt from the chair, spilling tea on myself when I came face-to-face with Cal once again. His picture, anyway, and his emboldened name and question: "Still wondering why you came?"

"Are you flippin' kidding me?" I screamed into the kitchen as I held my burnt hand under cold running water.

"Okay, God, I admit it. I haven't forgiven him. Is that what You want? When everything happened, I was so far down the line I didn't even consider going to talk to him. What do You want me to do now?" Then I ostriched, like I do when I'm not ready to hear what God has to say.

When I got my counseling degree after I left Alaska, I learned to name things and to clarify situations causing me angst. I couldn't deny this invitation to put words to unresolved pain. I went to the bedroom and pulled out my journal, brought it to the couch, and sat down.

As a church employee, I'd hoped Cal's departure wouldn't bring the congregation down. Because of that, and without even realizing it, I'd fought to keep the system we had in place, minus Cal. In doing so, I denied the immensity of the situation and downplayed what went on. I didn't call what Cal did *abuse*, but *affairs* because of the willingness I perceived in the women. I didn't understand the violence of power then.

"Lord, help me name my truth to the best of my ability, as clearly as I can today."

My face muscles tightened as I crafted my ideal response to Cal with words I needed to say, even if I only ended up sharing them with God. Then I put my journal away and took a day to pray. If I was going to do this, I wanted clean motives and friends to help me see things I might not. I didn't want to get manipulated, wanted to do exactly and only what God directed, and wanted to get the healing He had for me without harming anyone, even Cal.

As mad as I was now, I didn't want to, I don't know, waste a sin on him.

After a few conversations with friends, I went back to the computer and threw up on the page. Another thing I learned in school was to sit in the pain, to feel it. So, I sat with anger, hurt, and betrayal. I let them speak. I listened to what each had to say. As I did, some of my emotion dissipated. I prayed and revised. As my thoughts simmered down to their essence, revising taught me the nuggets I needed to share.

"Why did I come? It's like Kath said, I trusted you. You let me down. Now I feel sheepish around you, like I need a witness. That's why she's included in our correspondence, I question your motivation and your discernment. What once felt ideal for a pastor now seems predatorial. As my spiritual leader, you pursued me, invited me into your office, asked questions, and listened carefully. More intently than any man ever had. As a new believer, I valued your opinions. I appreciated your attention, and I wanted your approval. The interaction felt appropriate until the truth came out. Then I wondered, were you grooming me, too?"

"No," he said when I finally shared with him on Facebook.

But I disagree. What he was doing with me may not have been about sex, but it certainly was about power, and that's abuse, too.

Our Facebook correspondence continued for months after I left Alaska. I couldn't hurry the process even though I wanted to. I needed to let it take the time it took, let my thoughts and emotions bubble up when they did.

When I looked back on our history, it seemed Cal manipulated me into coming on fulltime at the church and through weekly writing assignments. As the supervisor to my counselor, he was privy to confidential information about my sexual past. One by one, my answers to Cal's "why's" put words to my beliefs and brought healing, all the way down to the humdinger at the bottom of the pile.

"What happened sucked because I introduced you to family and friends as a good spiritual leader. I trusted you with the people I cared about most. They came to church looking for God, the only one who could help in the way they needed, and I thought you were the perfect person for them to talk to until I found out what you were doing."

There it was, my other bzzzt. I clenched my teeth and rocked as I struggled to focus. "What bugged me most was the effect you had on Michelle."

The day before I visited Cal's new church, I'd had lunch with her, her daughter, and her grandbabies who were now three generations away from God.

Two months later, as I worked on this chapter, I got up from the computer and climbed on the bed for more fetal-position time. After a while, God said, "Do you want to chat?"

"Not really," I mumbled as I hugged my pillow. "I get that Michelle has her own walk, but I want to blame Cal. Without what he did . . . "

"The experience could have drawn her closer to Me," God said, "like it did you."

"But it didn't. The thing that scares me is exactly the thing I needed, or I don't think I ever would have yielded my life to You. It's free will. I needed to know I had choice. With it, I wanted You, but here we are again. What if my friends miss spending eternity with You in heaven because they choose not to?"

"You can't blame Cal for that."

"Crap!" I reached for the dog, grateful for his cry to get on the bed. No one else wanted to snuggle me when I got that messy. Exhausted and drained, I couldn't scare up any more emotion. Realizing I'd let go of my grudge, I peeled myself off the bed, made a giant bowl of popcorn, and stuffed my face.

The next day, I sifted my words with God until I had peace to hit *send*.

Not long after, Cal's reply nearly caused me to hit the ground. "I'm sorry."

*Wow.* His acknowledgment felt better than I'd expected. *But was he for real?*

Before my mind followed that rabbit down a hole, I said, "Lord, I can't see his heart, but You can. I'm going to leave that between you two. I'd rather have the freedom that comes with his apology than waffle about what's in his head."

* * * * *

Of course, all this took a minute. Okay, more like seventeen years.

After forgiving him and being heard, I could now hear what Cal had to say. And the care I had for him and his family returned, not to the point of pre-ordeal or where I wanted to crawl back into relationship, but to where I'd hoped they'd gotten the help they needed.

The freedom of forgiveness does that. It softens my heart. After doing what God asks, I've never once said, "I wish I didn't do that."

No longer afraid of conversation with Cal, but without putting my guard down, I breathed a sigh of relief and wrote one last note. "I needed to speak and process. Thank you for listening and responding."

I couldn't make sense of everything, but I could keep following God, forgiving people, and receiving the healing that came from it.

Again, "God is able to orchestrate everything to work toward something good *and beautiful* when we love Him and accept His invitation to live according to His plan" (Romans 2:28, paraphrase of the Bible). I don't know why, but it still surprises me when He does that for me.

And my friends. On the day I had lunch with Michelle and her family, her daughter said, "I've been doing memory work with people. Going back into their pasts to look for the lies they believed and the actions they took because of them."

"I used to do that all the time when I lived here!" I picked up a cookie from the plate in the middle of the table. "Since I believe Jesus is always with us, I'd ask where He was and if there was any truth He wanted to reveal."

"That's weird," she said. "I don't ask where Jesus is, but twice, He's shown up!"

# NO LONGER WOUNDED HEARTS: MY CHAT WITH HANNAH

Without fearing confrontation, but still careful, I cared more. That's where forgiveness takes me. Of course, controversy riles me up. Conflicts trigger as they reach deep inside my stories and yank on my lack of healing. But it felt so good to have grace, to purge the anger, and forgive.

With God, I learned that forgiveness doesn't always make sense, but it always feels better.

So, I did it again. I called Hannah, my ex-co-worker and counselor, one of the women exposed in the scandal with Cal, and asked if we could talk. After what happened, I hadn't wanted to continue our friendship, but God had kept us close, crossing our paths often.

With Cal, I hadn't cared about *his* story until I dealt with my anger.

But with Hannah, it was different. She'd apologized right after everything happened. Since I'd forgiven her, I didn't have bitterness and resentment. We'd moved on. So, I asked her to write this chapter with me as I listened to her side of the story again.

After so many years, I was in more of a there-but-for-the-grace-of-God-go-I place . . .

On a cold, rainy afternoon in October, I picked up the phone and dialed her number. As usual, we jumped right in deep. "I haven't talked since your father's memorial. How're you doing?"

"You know he molested me when I was ten. Drunk. I confronted him the day after, then when I was eighteen, and again at twenty-eight. He cried and apologized, but we always had a distant relationship. At the funeral, I honored him, but I'm still dealing with my emotions."

The effects of abuse framed our conversation, maybe even our friendship.

"We've come a long way," I sighed. "One look at the news and I'm reminded that we aren't the only ones who've dealt with sex abuse. That's why I'm sharing more than just what happened to me. Because maybe someone needs to recognize that they're going through something similar and see how they can stop the violence, turn the rudder of that ship and get help for all involved. Whoever will receive it. It's tough because in church, we're not supposed to talk about people, least of all the pastor. So, how do we alert others who're sitting under these leaders?"

"If our stories can help others," Hannah agreed, "let's share them."

"Yes! So, remind me how you and Cal got involved?"

"After I gave my first husband an ultimatum, 'Get counseling or I'll leave,' we set up an appointment with Cal. At twenty-one, I'd moved to Alaska for my husband's job as a heavy-equipment operator. He didn't want me to work, but I got lonely in the apartment all day. After five years, I found out he'd cheated on me. In counseling, Cal met my emotional needs and believed in me. I divorced my husband and came on staff at church as a counselor.

"Soon after, Cal kissed me. I knew the interaction was wrong, but his support felt good.

"Recently divorced, I was conflicted. He could tell and asked if I wanted to back out of our relationship. I didn't because of the companionship, and I loved my work as a therapist, but I prayed God would end the liaison between us. I was too weak to walk away.

"When his involvement with another woman came out, I confessed my own. God answered my prayer, but the process wasn't easy.

"Right after the scandal broke, I didn't want to live. I'd never felt that way before. It was scary. A dear friend flew to Alaska to stay with me. Her support, prayer, and companionship amidst the pain, sorrow, and guilt was a gift. God showed me, in the scope of eternity, this was a bump in the road. His words gave me the powerful hope I needed to live."

"I'm sorry." I didn't know what to say. I'd never heard that part of the story. "I can't imagine what it was like for you to be disciplined, for months on end, in front of the congregation as the church attempted to restore you *biblically?* You stayed and faced everyone and apologized ad nauseam. You're so brave!"

"I didn't feel brave." She laughed. "During therapy, my counselor advised me to write a letter to my clients and approach those I knew one-on-one. What a huge mountain, telling everyone, 'I'm sorry for my choices, I hope you can forgive me.' "

"You infur-r-riated me."

"I remember," she said.

As I heard her voice shift, I pictured her familiar smile on the other end of the phone and said, "You invited all of us, your counselees, together as a group. As I came down the hall at church, I spotted you up ahead. It was the first time I'd seen you since.

Even then, you appeared composed, unruffled. You always look like you have it together."

"I definitely don't." She laughed again. "And you used to keep everything hidden. You wanted to heal, but it was like pulling teeth to get you to talk."

Now it was my turn to laugh. "And here we sit discussing our pasts and the emotions that came with them so that I can write a book. Now, that's God! I remember something else you said back then that really bugged me." I didn't want to leave one stone unturned. "You said you saw the relationship with Cal as a compartment of your life that didn't have anything to do with our relationship."

"Yes," she agreed.

"For me, your illicit relationship with him contaminated everything, like a disease. As my co-worker, you received special treatment from *the boss*. As my counselor, you had permission to share confidential information with him about me. And within our church family, you were intimate with our spiritual dad. Yes, he abused his position of authority, but that didn't stop me from being mad at you, too. The spiritual incest, I couldn't get past that."

"I'm sorry." Hannah reiterated. And then for a minute, neither of us spoke.

"People reacted differently," she went on. "Some wouldn't respond. Others looked at me with hatred. Cal's and my relationship were about emotional intimacy more than it was physical, but that didn't matter. I was guilty.

"A guest preacher talked about hidden sins at church the other day. God spoke to my heart right in the middle of the sermon, as He often does, and reminded me how my father sinned against me. But I was no better than he was, because the way I met my needs was wrong, too. As a young woman who wasn't healed from my father's harm, I had no inner strength to stand up and say *no*. My lack of healing caused me to be a victim but also to commit sin. We all do something to get our own needs met."

"If it doesn't include God," I said, "it's always a departure from His best for us."

Back then, forgiving Hannah seemed impossible until I spent time with God. Under His direction, I forgave myself for the abortion. Then pardoning her became easy. Both then and now, Hannah's and my willingness to walk through painful places together strengthens our friendship.

# A CONVERSATION WITH
# THE HOTTIE WHO'S NOW
# MARRIED TO A MAN

I was on a roll, and I couldn't stop there. Jim was next, the hot guy I'd dated from the church singles' group who preferred men. After all these years, the betrayal I felt when I thought about *us* still hurt.

As I'd worked at naming the tangled ball of emotion inside, I singled out one thread at a time, starting with fire-engine-red *resentment* at his dishonesty, another deception in the midst of the new Christian circle I trusted. Then royal blue flooded my broken heart; the breakup hurt after falling in love and expecting to marry and slide in under forty with a couple of kids. *Really, really hurt.* Electric-orange *frustration* reminded me that Jim wasn't attracted to me in the way I thought. Maybe couldn't be. I pulled out the gray strand of grief and realized I'd yearned for him while he silently lusted after other men. I felt duped. But with my own fear of intimacy, well, maybe he wasn't the only one incapable of the relationship I'd hoped for.

As I waited for him inside Panera Restaurant on Cape Cod where he now not so coincidentally lived a few miles from Mom, I wiped sweaty palms on my jeans. *Would I recognize him?*

No more long hair but with a little gray, he came through the door. With minimal eye contact, he laughed at everything I said as we stepped up to the cash register to order. I fumbled with my wallet while he paid the bill for both of us, then we made our way to a booth. Sat down. I took a long sip of coffee, stalling, before I said, "I'm writing a memoir and working on a chapter about us. Can I ask you a few questions?"

"Sure." He smiled, looked at me, then away, his teeth still whiter than white.

"If you're attracted to men, why did you come to a church singles' group?"

"For a social life," he answered without pause. "I grew up in church. It's familiar. Everyone thinks they're supposed to be perfect, so they hide imperfections. I knew I wouldn't be the only one presenting a façade."

My mouth fell open. *Everyone's posing?* Ugh! Never thought of it that way. How sad, and yet, I'd been doing the same thing. No one had known about my abortion or my drug use. We all want acceptance.

If people knew who we really were, would they still be our friends?

"When you and I broke up," he said, "I considered another relationship with a woman, but knew I'd eventually cheat on her and get divorced again. I tried to stay monogamous. Using pornography, I could hold off a long time."

I took a quick look around, wondering if anyone was listening.

"I didn't cheat on you," he said.

"Not with the hairdresser?"

"No!" he said proudly. "I didn't hook up with anyone until after we ended."

*I didn't cheat on you* lingered in my mind as if it came with *Did you expect more?*

And "cheating . . ." The word triggered me because of past experience, previous boyfriends with other women. That was hard, but for me, way easier to deal with than this. Why didn't Jim tell me he was attracted to men? Because he knew it'd be a deal-breaker.

"After we broke up, I came out to my parents." He sipped his drink. "Until then, I survived without really living. Never let me feel."

*Yup!* I'd just learned how to feel when I met Jim. It's like we'd had an unspoken rule between us to help each other avoid it. As if hiding things ever spared anyone pain, especially since it eventually came out. Yeah, came out.

"Were you always drawn to guys?"

"Ever since pre-school. I didn't know what *gay* meant until someone called me *queer boy*."

I winced. "I knew it wasn't good," he continued. "Afraid of being found out, I held back and didn't get close to anyone."

My smile faded. How lonely. I remembered how he'd admired my friendships. For the first time, I understood why and how important a social life was to him after such isolation. Yearning for connection, he'd hidden. How can you bond when you live like that?

As I thought, I missed some of what he said.

Something about *us*. It'd been a long time since I'd thought of us as *we*. I looked down at his left hand and noticed a wedding band when they called my name over the loudspeaker. The food ready, Jim bounced up to grab it.

Quickly, while I was alone, I turned to God and asked Him, "Married to a man or a woman?"

"Man." I heard God say as Jim came around the corner with a tray.

Surprised even still, I said to God. "You could have warned me. What does my face look like?"

Must have been okay because Jim picked up where he'd left off. But, of course, he wouldn't ask questions if he noticed a funny look on my face. That was part of our deal. Don't ask, don't tell.

But then again, here I was asking. And he was telling.

"I moved here from LA after I broke up with a guy. I realized I wanted love in my life. I didn't want to be lonely. By choosing a male partner, I was just making a different choice, like picking vanilla over chocolate."

My eyebrows shot up, never having heard it explained that way.

"Once I gave up trying to be straight, I felt less puny."

*Less puny?* Diminished, I guess. Okay, I get that.

"Relieved I could be myself, I called the guy back. *And you know I never call.* We got married."

"Wow." Not knowing what to say, I took a bite, a big bite, and chewed slowly. After a swallow and a long swig of coffee, I still didn't know what to say, so I changed the subject. "When do you want me to show you what I write?"

"After you've published. It's your story. Tell it how you need to."

He caught me off guard. Perceiving his words as incredible trust, I choked. *That's not how anyone else answered that question.* "You want an alias?" I asked.

"No." He laughed. "Use my real name, and I'll get you a flash drive with our pictures on it."

I wiped a tear from my eye. His grace gave me empathy for him. Again, I'd needed to deal with my own emotion before I could enter his story and love him better. I wanted to have compassion for Jim and for what he'd been through.

At the time, God specifically told me to *love him*. I wish I'd done a better job.

Before I left town, we met again. A month later, he moved back to Los Angeles with his husband. If we hadn't gotten together when we did, it wouldn't have been face-to-face. We could have talked on the phone, but that wouldn't have been the same. I smiled, realizing God's hand in the timing.

Then I looked back at my ball of emotion and noticed a change. Because of the healing conversations and the compassion I now had, the strand of grief glittered. No longer gray, but silver, it reminded me of the way God always brings light into my darkness.

# NOW THAT'S WHAT I
# CALL REDEMPTION

In 2009, thirty years after *the* date with Alex and eight years after I left Alaska, I opened Facebook at an internet café in Africa where I worked as a missionary. I found a message from him. While others in my Wounded Heart class had confronted their offenders, I hadn't.

I wrote back, "I didn't give you my virginity that night."

Alex and I weren't young lovers who fell into passion. Awe-struck by the status of his band, I put him on a pedestal and didn't know how to say *no* to his sexual advances. As a college student full of hormones, maybe that's what he was looking for? Alcohol and drugs decreased my inhibitions, and well, we've heard the story before, right? Too many times. A man takes advantage, exploits a woman, and objectifies her then says, "It was consensual!"

*Really?* If we could go back in time and talk to the women, offer them an out, we'd find lots of what's been defined as *consensual* wasn't. Sex is a powerful drive and these stories are about so much more than people doing the wild thing.

At fifteen, I craved belonging, acceptance, and love. What happened with Alex and the promiscuity afterwards was about being wanted. I acted on my beliefs so that once I believed *It didn't matter how many men* and *If I wanted a boyfriend, I had to have sex,* I followed a trail of lies that cost me dearly. When I finally told my high-school friends, too many of them shared the name of the guy who did the same to them. And emotional numbing, workaholism, indecisiveness, and risky behavior—thrill seeking that looked cool but came with ongoing digestive issues—are all symptoms of post-traumatic stress syndrome.

In college, another man grabbed me, a worker on the property where I lived. I got away. The president of the campus stuck up for me and contacted the guy's boss who drove miles to ask, "Do you want me to fire him?"

"No," I shook my head. I didn't want him to lose his job, but would he stalk me when no one was around?

"What are you doing?" an acquaintance accused. "You got away. Leave it."

There it is, the shameful stigma and unspoken warning always attached to abuse in one way or another. *Keep your mouth shut!* Suck it up, right?

Before I let her comment take root, I remembered her story. For years, her husband molested her daughter, and she said nothing. *Nothing!* We all come from our stories and make mistakes, but parents are supposed to offer their children a safe space to grow with as much protection as possible, right?

When there's incest by a father, the damage is done by a person who represents God as Father. Don't you know it's much harder for someone to trust God after that? I bet He hates that.

And I forget this mom's excuse, but of course, there's shame, her own story, and way more narrative behind the comment. But you can see what a perspective like hers does to keep victims in cycles that continue.

Society sanctions this stuff, and two wrongs—or three or four or five—don't make a right.

It's not okay, and it's still happening all over the place. If we don't do what we can, we endorse it, right? So, go ahead, call me a snitch. But let's take a hammer to this culture of conformity. Name what happened as clearly as possible and help each other so we can all walk in freedom and healing. Not just the girls, but the guys, too.

Did that make you twitch? It did me the first time I considered it, because I'd blamed men for years, but they need help as much as women.

And I'm mad enough at evil to want healing for them, too.

Facing the truth takes guts, but the other side of conflict can be redemptive. I wouldn't recommend reconnection in every situation, but when it's safe, it rocks. Even though I'd forgiven Alex years before, it felt good to hear him say, "I'm sorry I hurt you."

With the universal need to make sense of things, I pressed on, searching for meaning. I couldn't undo my past, but I could own my story. In my quest for love, I'd looked for someone to define me and found yet another person who didn't truly see me. Without a grip on myself, knowing who I was and what I longed for, I gave my power away. No wonder knowing and being known, real intimacy within safe and healthy relationships, has become so important to me. Both with God and with people.

God wants to meet our needs, answer our questions, and help us find the destiny He wrote for us before the beginning of time.

He *is* love, the antithesis of shame. He's the Healer. And He knows the words we need to hear to heal our deepest wounds. He worked through my greatest failings. He didn't tell me to accept things that were wrong but helped me forgive them.

That gave me the desire to mentor, because we all want support, right?

I needed others to help me. People who genuinely cared for me, not in some narcissistic way, but with love. The real thing instead of a warped version. If I'd had that in the beginning, my ripple effect would have been different.

Now, I partner to protect women. When I sense something's about to happen to one of the girls I mentor, I speak up in order to help write a different ending.

# THE LAST TIME I SAW TONY

Back home in Boston visiting family and friends, I kept getting nudged from God, *talk to Tony*. I'd heard God say that before, but Tony and I didn't often run into each other. And when we did, we waved briefly or spoke only a few words.

What was I supposed to do, call him at home? I didn't think his wife would like that.

As I thought about it, God said, "Don't leave town until you do, okay?"

I knew I was supposed to share my faith, but Tony would think I was whacked.

The next morning, on my way to exercise class, I saw him landscaping a neighbor's yard. Each of us, wearing earphones, looked up and nodded. I kept walking, still waffling with God in my head.

In the center of town, a quarter of a mile away, God said, "You think I want you to tell him that I'm real."

I stopped. "That's right. What do You think?"

"I want you to tell him I love him."

I could have turned around and done what He said right then, but I continued on to Zumba class. An hour later, headed home, after I'd forgotten all about Tony, God started again, "Will you tell him?"

"Who?"

That's when God gave me *the look*.

"I don't know . . ."

"Promise you'll tell him?" Back and forth we went until, how can I explain this? God knew what was happening, knew I wouldn't want to miss this, and knew I needed His help.

In a perfect world, I aim to do His will all the time. But sometimes, and I don't even know why, I waver.

Then it's like the Holy Spirit caught me by the scruff, intercepted my flesh, and spoke straight to my spirit. As I argued, "yes" came out of my mouth. Instantaneously, Tony called my name from the gas station across the street. We'd never done anything together since we broke up, but that day, as he headed into the convenience store, he called out, "Want an iced coffee?"

I looked up at the sky, at God, and nodded before answering, "Yes," then crossed the street to join him. Tony and I made chitchat as we doctored our drinks, stood in line to pay, and walked outside. Then he turned toward his truck and said, "Have a nice day."

"Wait," I said. "You're going to think I'm nuts, but, well, God wants me to tell you He loves you. Really, really loves you."

Without missing a beat, Tony said, "I took my girls to church. I want to go more often."

"We have a lot of old friends going to church now." And without trying to squish the message in that I thought I was supposed to share, without thinking, really, I said, "God's real, you know."

"I know God's re-e-eal," Tony said as if I was accusing him of being stupid.

I smiled, realizing that God was confirming our earlier conversation, the one clarifying the message.

Tony and I said good-bye and started to part ways when he turned and yelled my name again. I looked back. Stopped in the parking lot fifty feet away, with all earnestness and heart he said, "I'm sorry!"

His apology carried a boatload of application. Two small words that covered everything from being late to dinner to leaving me pregnant. And after twenty-five years, I received them for every wisp of possibility there was a reason for them.

And I hope my reply of "Me, too," as small as it was, felt the same to him. Because when we used to fight, he'd say, "Can't I be right *one* time?"

I cringe as I write this. My response was always the same. "You've got to be right to be right."

Of course, there were times when he was spot on, and I was dead wrong. So, I hope my response carried the understanding of my own admission that I had plenty to apologize for, because I never saw him again.

Six months later, Tony was gone.

I didn't attend his funeral because I was out of town, but I heard hundreds of people showed up. I heard he'd lived a good life as a local business owner, had a wife and children who adored him, and friends who appreciated his heart and generosity.

As high-school sweethearts, Tony and I weren't good for one another. We enabled each other's bad behavior, but somewhere between the events of our past and the life he whittled out as a loving husband and father, Tony achieved some wholeness and a community who loved him. The goodness of life.

As I grieved, I told a friend, "It would freak me out if I saw his ghost."

"If he had the opportunity," she laughed, "you'd definitely be on the list of those he'd visit."

Instead, as I walked the beach that week, I found twelve whole sand dollars. Unbelievable, when I'd only ever found one at a time before that. It felt like a gift from Tony. They reminded me of the fun we had and the Legend of the Sand Dollar that I still have somewhere.

# ALL THAT TO SAY . . .

I spent a good chunk of my life desperately trying to satisfy the longings of the bottomless pit inside. You know the longings I'm talking about. *I must have the next essential oil to complete my life*, or, *I must have that man.*

Then I realized I had a God-sized hole. Ever heard of that? That we each have an empty cavern within that only God can fill. I used to think that sounded stupid until, well, I'd tried everything else. When God said, "I love you," He wrecked me in a good way.

I couldn't not give Him a chance.

When I did, I learned I'm not a misfit. I'm a free spirit!

My spirit may not be a dove, but more like that of a seagull, and that's not a bad thing. It could be that is what He planned all along as He made me brave and independent yet at the same time meant-to-depend on Him. Contrary to popular belief, God is our biggest cheerleader.

He's not mad at you. He loves you, and He's the only one that will never leave you. But you get to pick if you want a relationship.

I believe existence is meant to be a love story. We seek to be filled because we're never complete in ourselves. He's the only thing that fills the emptiness inside. I'd been trying to name my quest for years without understanding that God's the only thing that could.

When I gave Him a chance, I got what I believe He has for everyone, a unique and personal adventure that not only includes God but the destiny He wrote on each of our hearts. It doesn't come without challenge, because, well, a story without tension would be boring.

If we could ask Cinderella, she'd tell us that living out a fairy-tale is harder than watching one on TV. But the thrill? We'd never get that from an armchair.

It turns out happiness does come in relationship with the right guy.

I found my Prince Charming in Jesus, my very own freedom fighter, supernatural life coach, and Prince of Peace. He comes through every time, saves me because He can't not. That's His nature. And I've peeked ahead to the end of the story. The Bible says He's coming back to get us, riding on a white horse; no wonder that makes my heart skip a beat.

Whenever I speak to a group, I always ask, "God, what is it You want me to say?" Over and over, and as if for the first time, He says, "Make sure . . ."

I lean in, curious, totally forgetting the last twenty times. "Make sure of what?"

"Make sure you tell them," He pauses for effect, "that I love them."

# AUTHOR'S NOTE

As with any memoir, this account is written to the best of my remembrance. A few particulars are blurred to protect the privacy of another, but each person is real, even if he or she preferred an alias. Timelines have been condensed and quotation marks indicate where similar conversations occurred. Everything's true to the story's essence even when I couldn't remember exact detail.

And each Bible passage is marked with the specific translation. The versions basically say the same thing, but like a thesaurus, sometimes one pegs the meaning better than another. Rather than stick to one, I like to use them all.

For God, I used male pronouns because I got to know Jesus as male and God as father. It just made sense. And the capital "h" felt like a sign of respect, a small way I could honor God. Compared to all He's done for me, it seems so tiny, but I love to give back to Him.

And the profanity, you have no idea how much I have wrestled with God about leaving it in or taking it out. It's honest, but I know it'll cause a problem for some. If that's you, I'm sorry. But as I stand before God, I don't have the peace to take it out. He loves people who swear, and sometimes we need to be reminded of that.

# ENDNOTES

1. R. Gerlings, *Hey, Diddle, Diddle and Other Best-Loved Rhymes* (Windmill Books, 2009), p. 32.
2. Words by Clare H. Woolston, and music by George F Root, *Jesus Loves the Little Children*. https://library.timelesstruths. org/music/Jesus_Loves_the_Little_Children/ (accessed October 22, 2018), public domain.
3. Elisabeth Kübler-Ross and David Kessler, *On Grief and Grieving: Finding the Meaning of Grief Through the Five Stages of Loss*. (New York; Toronto: Scribner, 2005).
4. https://adultchildren.org/literature/laundry-list/ (Accessed October 22, 2018).
5. Margery Williams, *The Velveteen Rabbit*. (New York, NY: George H. Doran Company, 1922).
6. https://upjoke.com/marooned-jokes (Accessed December 13, 2018).
7. Dr. Dan B. Allender, *The Wounded Heart: Hope for Adult Victims of Childhood Sexual Abuse*, (Colorado Springs, CO: NavPress, 1990).
8. Dr. Henry Cloud, and Dr. John Townsend, *Boundaries: When to Say Yes, How to Say No to Take Control of Your Life*, (Grand Rapids, MI: Zondervan, 1992).
9. I am not a licensed doctor or therapist but my desire for anyone wanting to try inner healing is that they find someone who's experienced to work with, at least in the

beginning. I know I'm asking you to do as I say and not as I did, but it's because I care. And I've been so blessed by having someone alongside, listening with me.

10. *Strong's Exhaustive Concordance: New American Standard Bible.* Updated ed. La Habra: (Lockman Foundation, 1995). http://www.biblestudytools.com/concordances/strongs-exhaustive-concordance/ (Accessed October 22, 2019).

# BIBLIOGRAPHY

Allender, Dr. Dan B, *The Wounded Heart: Hope for Adult Victims of Childhood Sexual Abuse.* Colorado Springs, CO: NavPress, 1990.

Cloud, Dr. Henry and Townsend, Dr. John, *Boundaries: When to Say Yes, How to Say No to Take Control of Your Life.* Grand Rapids, MI: Zondervan, 1992.

Gerlings, R., *Hey, Diddle, Diddle and Other Best-Loved Rhymes.* New York, NY: Windmill Books, 2009.

Kübler-Ross, Elisabeth and Kessler, David, *On Grief and Grieving: Finding the Meaning of Grief Through the Five Stages of Loss.* New York; Toronto: Scribner, 2005.

Williams, Margery, *The Velveteen Rabbit.* New York, NY: George H. Doran Company, 1922.

# ABOUT THE AUTHOR

While working as a missionary in Palestine and Mozambique, Elizabeth Bristol found purpose for her wanderlust. She loved feeding people, hitchhiking through the West Bank, and spending a night each week on top of the Mount of Temptation fasting and praying. She loved the miracles and healings she saw on a regular basis even though she often wondered, *Will I live through this?*

She'd always thought hanging out with God would be boring and she'd have no cool friends. What a big lie that turned out to be. She's driven across the country 48 times often arriving at "just the right time" to process a road-killed moose or throw on a hoop skirt and dance the Virginia Reel at a Civil War reenactment. She's spoken to all kinds of groups and worked as a camp counselor where she created a virtual mission trip for kids. Come check out her photo album at www.elizabethbbristol.com/maryme/photos/ to see pictures of the stories in this book and join her spiritual adventure team.

Made in the USA
Middletown, DE
02 September 2020